COMMUNICATION, CULTURAL AND MEDIA STUDIES

Communication, Cultural and Media Studies: The Key Concepts is an indispensible guide for anyone studying this fast-paced and fascinating field. The fourth edition of this classic text continues to provide an up-to-date, multi-disciplinary introduction to the most important terms in the study of communication, culture and media, exploring their origins, what they are used for and why they provoke discussion.

This new edition includes:

- over 200 entries ranging from audience to modernity, and narrative to visual culture
- 50 new entries covering the latest trends and developments such as hacker, network theory and the knowledge economy
- a fully updated bibliography with 400 items and suggestions for further reading throughout the text
- revisions and updates to every entry.

John Hartley AM is Research Director of the ARC Centre of Excellence for Creative Industries and Innovation, and Distinguished Professor of Queensland University of Technology, Australia. He is author of many books and articles on television, journalism, cultural studies and the creative industries. Recent books include *The Uses of Digital Literacy* (2009), *Television Truths* (2007), *Creative Industries* (ed., 2005), and *A Short History of Cultural Studies* (2008).

ALSO AVAILABLE FROM ROUTLEDGE

COMMUNICATION, CULTURAL AND MEDIA STUDIES

The Key Concepts

Fourth Edition

John Hartley

Routledge
Taylor & Francis Group

LONDON AND NEW YORK

Fourth edition published 2011
by Routledge
2 Park Square, Milton Park, Abingdon, Oxon, OX14 4RN

Simultaneously published in the USA and Canada
by Routledge
711 Third Avenue, New York, NY 10017

Routledge is an imprint of the Taylor & Francis Group, an informa business

First edition published by Methuen 1983
Third edition published by Routledge 2002

British Library Cataloguing in Publication Data
A catalogue record for this book is available from the British Library

Library of Congress Cataloging in Publication Data
Hartley, John, 1948–
Communication, cultural and media studies: the key concepts / by
John Hartley.—4th ed.
p. cm.—(Routledge key guides)
Includes bibliographical references and index.
1. Communication. 2. Mass media. 3. Communication and culture. I. Title.
P90.H334642 2011
302.2—dc22   2010051288

ISBN: 978-0-415-55075-8 (hbk)
ISBN: 978-0-415-56323-9 (pbk)
ISBN: 978-0-203-81428-4 (ebk)

Typeset in Bembo by
Book Now Ltd, London

MIX
Paper from
responsible sources
FSC
www.fsc.org   FSC® C004839

Printed and bound in Great Britain by
TJ International Ltd, Padstow, Cornwall

CONTENTS

PREFACE TO THE
FOURTH EDITION

The fourth edition sees *Communication, Cultural and Media Studies: The Key Concepts* revised and updated from A to Z. Some *concepts* survive from earlier versions, but every *entry* has been revised, and there are 50 new entries. These include those that relate to interactive media and the knowledge-based economy, as well as to developing fields of study. As ever, the guiding principle has been to offer clear explanations of key concepts, showing where they came from, what they're used for, and why they provoke discussion or disagreement in the field. The extensive bibliography has been fully updated. It contains over 400 items, with many suggestions for further reading.

This is the latest edition of a bestselling book, first published as *Key Concepts in Communication Studies* (with multiple authors) in 1983. The second enlarged and revised edition was published in 1994 as *Key Concepts in Communication and Cultural Studies*. It was brought under my single authorship for the third edition in 2002, as *Communication, Cultural and Media Studies: The Key Concepts*. The book has remained in print and in demand throughout that time. It has also been translated into Chinese, Spanish, Portuguese, Korean and Bahasa Malaysian. Now here it is again, maintaining the tradition of producing a new edition for each decade, under the title of *Communication, Cultural and Media Studies: The Key Concepts*, fourth edition.

INTRODUCTION

Communication, cultural and media studies are relatively young by academic standards. They grew out of the period in the 1960s and 1970s when higher education began to take modern communication, culture and media seriously. They began to be seen as a central component of contemporary human experience; a major and expanding economic sector; and as a fascinating arena for the creative imagination. Who would not be interested in a field that promised to answer questions like: 'how does sense-making *work?*' and 'how do *I* make sense?' alongside the more immediate one of 'how do I *get* work?' in an industry that so evidently combines – and sometimes confronts – both cultural and economic values.

This early period was also the time when universities in the United Kingdom, Europe, Australia and elsewhere began to open their doors to people whose families, like mine, had never sent a daughter or son to university before. Since then, new technologies and globalised markets have had a major impact, not only on communication, culture and media themselves, but also on higher education. The combination – new ideas, new objects of study, new students, new countries – has made this field dynamic, interesting to work in, and also controversial.

Communication, media and cultural studies have been character-ised by fast-moving and innovative research work; by the attempt to say new things in new ways. At the same time, they have borrowed widely from a variety of established academic disciplines and discourses, as well as from 'ordinary language' and commonsense concepts. As a result, there is often an uneasy period of disorientation for the newcomer, until they get their bearings. The book is therefore designed not only for commencing and continuing undergraduates, but also for newcomers to the field of study from other disciplinary domains, including postgraduates, teachers and faculty from an increasingly multi-disciplinary research environment. That it has been used in this way over the years is attested by the number of citations it has received as an original research source in its own right. That is an unusual record for a reference work, but perhaps not so surprising in a changing field, where this book and its predecessors have played a shaping role since the early days.

The book is not a dictionary – it does not claim to treat concepts 'definitively'. Instead it is a critical history of ideas. The entries are not destinations but starting points for further intellectual and practical work. It is designed to put together in an accessible form some of the most important concepts that you will encounter, and to show some of the ways in which these concepts have been (or might be) used. A review of the previous edition stated its purpose better than I could: It is certainly *meant* to be 'accessible and highly readable, and notable for both clarity and a tone that comes across as helpful and to the point' (Clover, 2003: 13).

What follows is a field guide. As one who has toiled in this field since its boundaries were first marked out, I hope you find the work as rewarding and fruitful as I have, not least because those boundaries have been expanding and changing ever since. Some of my own ideas have evolved over the years, so new explanations and new concepts have come to the fore, and traces of a changing conceptual history will be evident in some entries. It may be that getting to know a new area of study is best done by the usual method: crashing about in the dark and bumping into things. So it certainly was for me when I started trying to find my own way around in the early days. So it still is, really, given the speed and scale of change in all of these domains. Always there's something new to discover, and people keep moving the furniture around when you're not looking. I thought at the time that a guide would be handy, and still do. Here it is.

John Hartley AM
Brisbane 2011

ACKNOWLEDGEMENTS

John Hartley is the recipient of an Australian Research Council Federation Fellowship (project number FF0561981), and acknowledges the ARC's support of the research on which this book is based.

Thanks to Dr Deborah Thomas for research assistance in the preparation of this edition.

Most thanks, as ever, to Tina Horton, without whom it would not have come to this.

LIST OF KEY CONCEPTS

Aberrant decoding
Access
Actuality
Aesthetics
Affect
Analogue
Anti-globalisation
Art–science interface
Articulation
Audience
Author/ship
Bardic function
Bias
Binary opposition
Biopower
Biotechnology
Branding
Bricolage
Broadcasting
Celebrity
Censorship
Citizen
Class
Cluster
Code
Communication
Commutation test
Complexity
Connectivity
Connotation
Consensus
Consumption/production

Content analysis
Content industries
Context
Conventions
Convergence
Conversation analysis
Copyright
Creative destruction
Creative industries
Cultural capital
Cultural citizenship
Cultural science
Cultural studies
Culture
Culture jamming
Culture wars
Customisation
Cyberculture
Cyberdemocracy
Cybernetics
Cyborg
Deconstruction
Deixis
Democratainment
Denotation
Deregulation
Diachronic
Dialect
Dialogic
Diaspora
Diegesis (diegetic), hyperdiegesis
Difference, différance

Digital
Digital/analogue distribution
Digital divide
Digital literacy
Discourse
Diversity
DIY culture
Edutainment
Effects
Entertainment
Ethnic, ethnicity
Ethnography
Evolution
Ex-nomination
Fans, fandom, fanship
Flow
Framing
Frankfurt School
Frequency (of communication/ media)
Games (computer/video)
Gatekeeper
Gender
Genre
Globalisation
Hacker, hacktivism, hackability
Hegemony
Identification
Identity politics
Ideological state apparatuses
Ideology
Image
Impartiality
Independence
Individual
Individualism (methodological)
Information society/economy
Infotainment
Infrastructure
Innovation
Intellectual property
Interaction design

Interactivity
Internationalisation
Interpellation
Intertextuality
Journalism
Kinesics
Knowledge
Knowledge economy
Labour, precarious labour
Language
Language, functions of
Langue
Lifestyle
Literacy
Localisation
Mass communication
Mass society, mass society theory
Meaning
Media policy
Mediasphere
Medium, media
Metaphor
Methodology, method
Metonym
Mode of address
Modern, modernity, modernism
Multi-accentuality
Multiculturalism
Multimedia
Myth
Narrative
Nation
Naturalising
Naturalism
Nature
Network society
Network theory
New economy
New media
News, news values
Noise
Objectivity

Orality
Ordinary (culture)
Orientalism
Panopticon
Paradigm
Paradigm shift
Parole
Participant observation
Performance, performativity
Phatic communication
Phonemic/phonetic
Phonology
Platforms (media)
Plebiscite
Plenty, philosophy of
Political economy
Polysemy/polysemic
Popular, popular culture
Pornography
Postcolonial, postcolonialism
Postmodern, postmodernism
Power
Pragmatics
Production, producer
Propaganda
Proxemics
Public
Public service broadcasting
Public sphere
Queer theory
Race
Readership, reading public
Realism
Reality TV

Rearviewmirrorism
Redaction
Redundancy
Referent
Regulation
Representation
Rhetoric
Semantics
Semiosphere
Semiotics, semiology
Sign
Signification
Stars, stardom
Stereotype
Structuralism
Style
Subculture
Subjectivity
Symbol
Synchronic
Syntagm
Technological determinism
Text
Textual system
User
User-created content, user-
    generated content
Violence
Virtual communities
Virtuality
Visual culture
VSR
Whiteness (studies)
X, Y, Z (generations)

Note: Words in **bold type** in the entries are cross-references to other entries in this book.

COMMUNICATION, CULTURAL AND MEDIA STUDIES

The Key Concepts

ABERRANT DECODING

A concept from Umberto Eco, identifying a mismatch or asymmetry of **meaning** between sender (encoder) and receiver (decoder) of any message, from ancient art to contemporary media. Eco himself used the term in a 'semiotic inquiry into the television message', first published in 1965 in Italian, a pioneering attempt to apply **semiotics** to mass communication (Eco, 1972). He suggested that 'aberrant decoding' was an accident in pre-industrial societies, an exception from the expectation by speakers and artists that their own communities would normally 'get' what they were on about.

There are four classes of exception to this rule:

- people who didn't know the language (what meanings did the Greeks, and then everyone till Jean-François Champollion who first deciphered them, ascribe to Egyptian hieroglyphics?);
- people from future generations (what meanings did medieval Christians ascribe to Greek and Roman art?);
- people from different belief systems (what meanings do modern tourists ascribe to the stained glass windows of cathedrals like Chartres or the terracotta warriors of Xi'an?);
- people from different cultures (what meanings do settlers ascribe to Aboriginal art?).

But, and this is the importance of the concept, Eco argued that contemporary media like television are communicative codes in which aberrant decoding is the norm, not the exception. TV communicators know a priori that their code is not shared by all the receivers. Eco therefore proposed that research into television requires three phases:

- *semiotic analysis* of television 'messages' to establish what **codes** were used by the transmitting organisation and producers, and what references audiences were expected to have in order to decode them;
- *field research* into 'how the messages, previously analysed, have in fact been received in selected sample situations';
- *comparative analysis* to determine the extent to which the two sets of results tally.

Eco speculated: 'We could discover that the community of the users has such freedom in decoding as to make the influencing power of the organization much weaker than one could have thought. Or just the opposite' (1972: 107). This research agenda has proved remarkably stable. Its combination of textual (semiotic) and audience (sociological) analysis designed to assess the ideological power of media and the room for manoeuvre of audiences, remains to this day at the core of academic media research.

Eco's article was translated (by Paola Splendore) and published in the Birmingham Centre for Contemporary Cultural Studies' journal *Working Papers in Cultural Studies* in 1972. It was thereby directly influential on Stuart Hall's 'encoding/decoding' thesis and much subsequent work by media researchers at the CCCS, for instance Charlotte Brunsdon and David Morley, Ian Connell and Lydia Curti, and thence made its way into the mainstream of media studies.

ACCESS

The use of external **actuality** sources by broadcasters. 'Accessing' is the practice of including verbal quotations and film/tape interviews or statements (in news/current affairs coverage) which originate from people or groups not directly employed by the media organisation itself. It is what broadcasters do to 'access' public opinion and actuality footage. 'Access' on the other hand is what community, activist and other associations seek when they call for a democratised **media-sphere**.

Accessing is a serious matter in broadcasting organisations, because scarcity of airtime means that it has to be heavily rationed, which is why for such organisations it is a political issue. In post-broadcast (online) media, access does not need to be rationed and is therefore less of an issue, at least for users with 'access' to a computer terminal. Problems remain in *how* to access the popular voice online. Professional media commentators have proven hostile to the blogosphere precisely because participation is free and access is open. Meanwhile, online versions of traditional news outlets encourage access by offering comment facilities and sometimes allowing room for consumer co-created stories or pictures. But they also restrict access by moderating comments and treating the whole user interface as a part of marketing and brand-profiling rather than newsgathering or knowledge creation.

Demands for broadcast access are based on a *reflection theory* of the media – that is, that the media *ought* to reflect the plurality of different groups, politics or lifestyles that can be identified outside the media in social life. Many groups argue that their access to television is blocked and that as a result they are unable to establish their point of view in the public mind. The assumption often is that the blockage is caused by a more or less deliberate conspiracy by the media to exclude them. Even when access is achieved, 'minority groups' are often disappointed with the coverage they get. As commercial and industrial organisations with an extensive division of labour and an occupational ideology of professionalism, broadcasters won't let you simply appear on television or radio and state your case or tell your story. Despite the media's centrality to public life and to citizenship, there is no *right* of access. Whether you get on air depends on the professionals' assessment of your talent, newsworthiness or representative status, and what you say is mediated through their professional codes and production processes.

The professional mediation of accessed voices extends to the mediated text. Even when you have your say on television, you won't speak for yourself. What you say becomes what television says, and television discourse has its own peculiarities. Thus, when a newsreader quotes or an interviewer questions you, your utterance becomes a discursive element that is subordinate to the narrative flow and visual codes of the item as a whole. Its meaning is not self-contained, and certainly not under the direct control of the speaker, but depends on what is said and seen before and afterwards. You become, in effect, one actor in a drama, and even if you're lucky enough to be playing the lead it is still the case that what you say is significant only in the context of what all the others say, and of what the dialogue as a whole is about. Further, one aspect of your role is entirely at odds with your own purposes. For simply by accessing you, the institutional discourse is able to claim authenticity and credibility for itself. You become the means through which the *legitimacy* of media representations can be established – whatever it is that you actually say. There is a 'conflict of interest' between professional media discourses and the demands for access that various groups express.

The way this has been handled in practice takes two forms. First, news and current affairs subscribe to the principle of **impartiality**, thereby ensuring that a (narrow and 'balanced') range of voices is accessed on any one topic. Second, specialist *access programming* has been established on many networks, especially among **public service broadcasters** (PSBs). In these off-peak slots media professionals may relinquish editorial control of the programme content, but retain control of the production process. These well-intentioned practices have unforeseen consequences. Impartiality legitimates the mainstream bipartisan form of politics at the expense of various single-issue groups (e.g. environmental campaigns), identity-based groups, radical and community groups that tend to end up having to make do with the marginal access slots or no access at all. For such groups, the very fact of 'winning' access results in representations that seem 'naturally' to confirm their marginal status. This is why many of them have migrated to the internet.

On the net, access changes in nature. It is less a problem of the mix and multiplicity of voices within a national context; more a question of the legal framework for 'open access' for users (in rich nations), or a question of access to the net at all (among poor populations especially in developing or emergent countries).

In relation to 'open access', legal scholars like Lawrence Lessig, Yochai Benkler and Jonathan Zittrain have argued convincingly for the need for open access to and use of online networks, seeking to overcome the closed-system thinking of proprietary brands, which favours strict and prior enforcement of **intellectual property** rights (**copyright**) in relation to all online material, a stance that drastically limits the knowledge-sharing 'commons' that the net might otherwise foster. Lessig's Creative Commons initiative is a practical attempt to reconcile users' rights and those of copyright-holders.

In relation to access by the world's poor, various initiatives have been made to extend the wonders of the internet to the 'have nots'. One prominent example was the idea put forward by MIT Media Lab's Nicholas Negroponte in 2007, which turned into an organisation called One Laptop Per Child (OLPC), whose mission is:

> To create educational opportunities for the world's poorest children by ensuring each child has a rugged, low-cost, low-power, connected laptop with content and software designed for collaborative, joyful, self-empowered learning . . . . With access to these tools, children become connected to each other, to the world and to a brighter future.
>
> (laptop.org/en/vision/index.shtml)

While such efforts are to be applauded, actual patterns of usage suggest that the technology of choice for developing countries and emergent technologies may not be the computer, at least for the time being, but the mobile (cell) phone. This has given billions of **users** access to previously unimagined levels of connectivity and content, including access, for instance, to healthcare:

> 'There are 2.2 billion mobile phones in the developing world, 305 million computers but only 11 million hospital beds,' said Terry Kramer, strategy director at British operator Vodafone at

the *Mobile World Congress* [February 2009]. That's why Vodafone, along with the United Nations and the Rockefeller Foundation's *mHealth Alliance*, have banded together to advance the use of mobile phones to better aid those in need of healthcare in the developing world.

(www.readwriteweb.com/archives/mobile_phones_to_
serve_as_doctors_in_developing_countries.php)

Further reading: Hartley (1982, 1992a); Lessig (2004); Benkler (2006); Zittrain (2008)

ACTUALITY

Professional term for film/tape/digital footage used in news and current affairs broadcasts, which records events as they happen. Contrasted with studio presentation (talking heads) and with archive (stock) footage.

In **semiotic** analysis, actuality is seen as a key device in producing ideological closure, by anchoring the *preferred reading* on the apparently unarguable 'facts' of the event-as-filmed. Actuality is presented as self-evident, in a naturalistic/realist mode of **representation**; the production processes are rarely shown, so that viewers are encouraged to make sense of the footage in terms of the event, and not of the way it is represented. However, actuality rarely appears on the screen without an accompanying commentary – and considerable professional skill is expended on contextualising it for the 'benefit' of viewers. Actuality is thereby a device for **naturalising** meaning (it proposes the cultural as natural).

This is why there is such a high premium on actuality footage in news shows, resulting in the sometimes undignified antics of ill-briefed news anchors who leave the studio to be helicoptered into some disaster area in order to combine the *authenticity* of 'being there' (the eyewitness) with **affect** (viewers' emotional **identification** with a trusted or admired celebrity) that will (they hope) be parlayed into ratings for that station's coverage.

Further reading: Hartley (1999)

AESTHETICS

A term from the philosophy of art, aesthetics refers to the contemplation of beauty. It goes back to Aristotle, who distinguished aesthetic beauty from logical truth. The wider use of the term was popularised in the nineteenth century, following John Ruskin's influential writings on the **political economy** of art, as a means of separating art from craft, artist from artisan – oil painter from house painter. In this tradition, aesthetics provided a paradigm for talking about texts as art, and art as humanising civility, not mere decoration. The theory of aesthetics understood its practice as objective. The properties of artworks were read as expressions of universal values, open to the same interpretation by all who were free. The theory relied on the assumption that aesthetic criteria lay within the work itself, negating the need to consider issues of **context** and the means of production.

The aesthetic movement in art and literature ('art for art's sake') certainly *sought* universal values or truths in certain kinds of expression, but what they *found* proved to be a remarkably robust distinction – lasting to this day despite rejection from various quarters – between 'the New' (avant-garde art; contemporary, experimental or 'original' expression) vs 'the repeated' (popular, mediated, 'mass' or commercial expression) (Barthes, 1975; Adorno, 2004). This is a characteristically **modernist** position on aesthetics, placing great emphasis on the artist/producer (supply side) and little on the user/consumer (demand side), so it is habitually suspicious of market as opposed to aesthetic 'values' (although many modernist artists enjoyed the success the market conferred). Instead, modernist aesthetics favours 'difficulty' in interpretation (the consumer has to work hard), because if an artist is trying to say new things in new ways then it is quite likely that they won't be understood by mainstream contemporaries.

As a result, the modernist aesthetic is at once the harbinger of new meanings for a given culture or period and the subversion of what it currently holds most sacred. And because non-experts cannot understand what the modern artist is 'trying to say', modernist aesthetics begat a whole new occupation – the critic – who could decide which outsider-artist was a genius and which a charlatan, and interpret the meanings not readily discerned in their work for the wider public. Some of these critics themselves became world-famous and influential, from Ruskin himself to Robert Hughes (art critic of *Time*). As a result of the popularisation of the modernist aesthetic, the invidious distinction between 'the New' and 'the repeated' can now be found at all levels of **popular culture** itself, for instance to create evaluative taste distinctions between musicians – contempt for 'the repeated' has become one of the most repeated types of aesthetic judgement you can find; a cliché of mass culture.

Aesthetic judgements in Marxist theory are considered a form of

ideology (as in 'bourgeois aesthetics'). Whilst this is certainly a valid point, attempts by, for example, Marxists, feminists and queer theorists to subvert aesthetic hierarchies have arguably continued the tradition, simply expanding the category (Buck-Morss, 1990). Attempting to replace 'universal' assumptions about taste with **subcultural** categories creates many splinter aesthetic theories that, although speaking on behalf of smaller groups, continue to imply a set of common beliefs around notions of truth, beauty and art.

The term aesthetic gained some currency in **semiotic** analysis, especially in the notion of an 'aesthetic code', in which the production of meaning is not the aim but the starting point of a given message. This corresponds closely with the linguist Roman Jakobson's notion of the 'poetic function' in language (Hébert, 2006). It prioritises the signifier over the signified, and seeks to exploit rather than confirm the limits and constraints of the form, **genre** or **convention** within which it operates. Hence aesthetic codes put a premium on innovation, entropy, experimentation with the raw materials of **signification** (words, colours, composition, sequence), and evoke pleasurable responses for that reason. Semiotics goes beyond idealist aesthetics in its attempt to find a value-free and culturally specific description of aesthetic codes, and thence to find such codes operating in discourses or media not usually associated with the category 'art': advertising copy, political slogans, graffiti, and the output of consumer and entertainment media.

This kind of aesthetics can be taught as a technical skill for producers and designers (Zettl, 2010). More ambitiously, the mature writings of some astute observers can build and argue for an entirely new approach to the aesthetics of a given medium of cultural form – Sean Cubitt's *The Cinema Effect* (2005) is a good example. Of course, **new media** have prompted new interest in the aesthetics of the digital era (e.g. Sutton *et al.*, 2007).

See also: **Art–science interface**, **Language, functions of**, **Modern**, **Realism**, **Style**

Further reading: Barrell (1986); Eagleton (1990)

AFFECT

Not to be confused with *effect* (as in media **effects**), affect, used as a noun, is a term from psychology that focuses on the evaluative (good/bad; feeling/emotion/desire) side of communication rather than on its cognitive, rational or reflective aspects. Brennan (2004: 5) defines it as 'the physiological shift accompanying judgement'.

It is based in interpersonal relationships (as distinct from individual identity), where communication expresses human values and status-based interaction rather than simply conveying morally or emotionally neutral information.

Immersed as everyone is in mediated and technologically enabled communication, affect has migrated from face-to-face communication into the world of mediated **representation**. Here it applies not only to the obvious affective emotions evoked by or projected onto morally evaluated fictional characters (heroes, villains, victims, objects of desire), but those we experience in relation to abstract values (freedom; family; underdog; un/fair play) and even bits of kit (mobile phones, automobiles, clothing accessories). Thus affect has become an important criterion in persuasive communication, including political campaigning and commercial marketing, where it is mobilised not only in product promotion but also in the deep substrate of product design: why do small cars seem to smile?

Further reading: Ahmed (2004)

ANALOGUE

Analogue information works by resemblance, as opposed to **digital** information, which works by fixed code, especially the zeros and ones of computer code. Thus, a painting or photograph is analogue, while video discs, computer displays and digital 'photography' (images made of pixels) are digital. Analogue visual images may display infinite gradation of tone, colour, hue, line, grain, etc., whereas digital images break down such variation into standard blocks of information.

It is possible to identify the late twentieth century as an *era* that was passing from analogue to digital. **Broadcasting, mass communication**, cinema, illustrated newspapers and magazines, and the recorded music industry were based largely on analogue media technologies. In film, analogue cameras and tape recorders gather the action, and reproduction (screening) is also done via photographic film and optical soundtracks. One important feature of such kit is that it is generally expensive, cumbersome, and requires skilled operation, thereby restricting the production base to professional crews and well-capitalised companies. New **interactive** media, on the other hand, are entirely digital, including cameras, sound recording and playback devices, etc., all the way through the production chain from image- and sound-gathering to eventual consumer/user download and inter- action. In this world, the cost of gear and of the production process has radically reduced, so that in theory – and occasionally in practice – individuals can produce and distribute full-length movies or publish photos, text or music using 'amateur' or consumer-level digital equip- ment.

The digital era differs from the analogue one in the newfound productivity of consumer experience. Ordinary people can now make and publish digital content (for instance on YouTube, Facebook, Flickr or other social network sites) as 'producers', thereby blurring the analogue-era or industrial 'division of labour' between expert professional producers and amateur or passive consumers (*see* **user- created content**).

Analogue artforms retain a nostalgic aura of authenticity both artistic and legal. A 'metaphysics of presence' (*see* **difference**) made artists feel better about analogue images that you could actually see in their mate- rial form, on film, canvas or paper, unlike entirely **virtual** digital images.

Although paintings were faked, and photos doctored, throughout the analogue era, digital images could be manipulated more readily than analogues, i.e. cheaply, using commercially available software, without needing professional skills. A consequence of this is that greater sophistication is required of readers and users. The naive (analogue) idea that photos depict or record unarguably some actually existing scene is a matter for scepticism, not least because increasingly users have the digital means to manipulate, improve, subvert and embellish information for themselves. But on the flip side, it is still the case that one of the triumphs of digital art is to make the result *look like* analogue, so that extensive press coverage is given to advances that allow a digitally animated movie/games heroine to look like a real woman (even though she's, say, blue), or a hairy monster to look truly hairy. This is the phenomenon that Marshall McLuhan called '**rear- viewmirrorism**', when a new medium copies its predecessor; digital is out-analoguing analogue, for the time being.

On the consumer side, in the shift from analogue to digital forms even larceny has transformed, from (e.g.) stealing books or magazines from retailers to (e.g.) downloading and sharing music or picture files (*see* **intellectual property**).

See also: **Art–science interface, Digital/analogue distribution**

ANTI-GLOBALISATION

A euphemism for anti-capitalism; the anti-globalisation protest movement gained visibility as the Cold-War antinomies of 'capitalism' vs 'socialism' lost force in the 1990s. Now it is **'globalisation'** vs 'anti-globalisation', the latter being a loose and unstructured coalition of workerist, environmental, **postcolonial** and alternative lifestyle activists whose main activities (of interest to the media, at any rate) seem to be to dog world leaders, economic forums and regional summits with noisy mass protests and radical street theatre.

Resistance to globalisation has manifested in a number of forms, out of disparate and sometimes conflicting interests. Early anti-globalisation sentiments focused on the loss of jobs for workers in industrially advanced societies as corporations increasingly sought to outsource product manufacturing to countries where labour was less expensive and industrial laws lax or non-existent. This concern waned, however, and it became apparent that forces other than globalisation were largely responsible for unemployment (Castells, 2000).

A new group of activists took up the anti-globalisation banner, this time out of concern for workers and communities experiencing economic inequality and political disenfranchisement as a result of globalisation. Much of this movement's initial attention was focused on the 'sweatshop' issue that gained prominence in the mid-1990s, singling out the Nike brand as hypocritical in its marketing strategies (which promoted freedom and agency) while it countenanced what were seen as exploitative manufacturing practices in developing (post-colonial) countries.

The movement escalated in 1995 around a separate issue when Ken Saro-Wiwa, a Nigerian writer and environmental leader, was imprisoned by the Nigerian military government for leading a campaign against Royal Dutch Shell's oil-drilling in the Niger delta. Saro-Wiwa and eight other Ogoni activists were executed by the military later that year (Klein, 2000: 331). In this case, as in others featuring global brands, unethical alliances between multinational corporations and oppressive regimes were seen to be a central negative consequence of globalisation.

Such protests, designed to expose specific practices, later joined together in a general campaign through a series of large demonstrations. Gathering outside the conventions of the world's political and business leaders in Seattle (1999), and since then regularly around the world, groups including anti-capitalists, environmentalists, anarchists and human rights campaigners brought the anti-globalisation movement to the global (media) stage.

The 'anti-globalisation' tag is misleading; possibly even a straight contradiction of the activists' desire for global fair play. If there is a key demand it is to see the establishment of international laws, democratically organised institutions capable of regulating global capital, and for international solutions, sourced from 'bottom-up' organisations, to rectify inequalities in the labour market. The aim is not so much to stop globalisation as to find equitable solutions for a globalised society. Naomi Klein, a champion of the movement, has pointed out: 'the triumph of economic globalisation has inspired a wave of techno-savvy investigative activists who are as globally minded as the corporations they track' (Klein, 2000: 327). Indymedia (www.indymedia.org) was an early instance of network of global resistance, a collectively run web-based media outlet that spawned local sites and centres throughout the world.

A separate wave of anti-globalisation sentiment manifests as a conservative scepticism about the rapid increase and hybridity in cultural choice, brought about by forces described as globalisation. *Localism* is upheld as possessing authenticity and 'natural' community in these discourses; and face-to-face relations are privileged over mediated communication. The prescription underpinning this stream of anti-globalisation thinking is a return to smaller, geographically centred communities; the 'slow food' movement is relevant here, connecting such concerns to the related phenomenon of 'fair trade' in commodities (notably coffee). Some critics have seen the revival of the local as a nostalgic yearning for an analogue past that overlooks the benefits of an extended and diverse cultural field.

Meanwhile, as the economy and culture have become ever more globalised, politics has narrowed somewhat, to focus more on local issues (again, often associated with environmental problems) than on previously more general aims such as class solidarity, identity-emancipation, or 'free enterprise' affiliations. This is especially true the field of citizen-initiated politics at the hyper-local level, where single-issue activism can be just as important as old-style party loyalty. This development is in part an expression of popular frustration with globalisation, where the scale of systems and remote decision-making radically restrict people's ability to make a personal difference on the ground. Perhaps this is why anger is vented against multinational brands such as McDonald's, which has attracted widespread anti-globalisation protest, including by French farmer and anti GM-food activist José Bové, whose part in the 'dismantling' of a McDonald's franchise in 1999 was a foundational event in the anti-globalisation movement. After ten further years of international activism, Bové was elected to the European Parliament in 2009 on an ecology ticket.

See also: **Culture jamming, Globalisation**

Further reading: Eschle and Maiguashca (2005); Held and McGrew (2007)

ART–SCIENCE INTERFACE

Despite the doubts of **modernist** critics, for whom art trumped 'civilisation', modernity (the period) was characterised by the ascendancy of useful over fine arts; technology over old master. Engineering vied with artistic movements to define the age. This applied equally to spectacular, *fatal* constructions such as bridges and skyscrapers, airships and ocean liners, and to mundane, *banal* machines like trains, planes, automobiles and kitchenware. Indeed, engineering (steel-frame buildings) combined with an artistic movement (art-deco) to build the icon of modernity itself, namely New York City – a true art–science interface.

However, following a book by novelist C. P. Snow, it became widely accepted that contemporary societies had fractured into 'two cultures', one based on science, the other on the arts and humanities (but see Edgerton, 2005 for a contrary view). Recently, interest in the art–science interface has revived in the wake of biotechnology, but the fact is that the entire modern era – from the Renaissance and Reformation in Early Modern Europe – *is* an art–science interface. In particular, modern communications media combine technology with artistic and **aesthetic** content. Such media include publishing, photography, cinema, radio, recorded music, television, computer software, games and the internet. Like architecture and engineering, but in forms that compete directly with more traditional arts, such media cannot exist without scientific inventions, but would find no public without their artistic content.

Popular aesthetics – what people in general as opposed to philosophers have liked – was always an art–science interface. The idea that truth could be revealed by technological means, rather than by a Kantian artistic genius that was always in the end ideological or manipulative, was inherent in the popularity of aestheticisations of science itself, whether via Jules Verne, photos from outer space, wildlife documentaries on TV, or the entire dinosaur industry (Mitchell, 1998).

The human condition (previously the domain of literature, painting and the pursuit of 'beauty'), became a province of science. Beauty was found in truth, not fictional imaginings.

On the other hand, some popularisations of scientific advance have displayed nostalgic sentimentality about the human condition amounting to serious bad faith. A paradigm example of this is the Steven Spielberg movie *ET: The Extra-Terrestrial*. This fable used the latest scientific cinematic equipment to propose a world where technology (in the form of government agencies on the lookout for ET) was the enemy of the values embodied in the human child (conquering all with a heart and sentiment). The movie used science to condemn it; and like so much popular culture praised the individual while glorying in high-tech cinema effects.

Cultural theorists such as Donna Haraway (1990) explored the human–science–technology interface in work on the **cyborg**. The art–science interface has extended the challenge from architecture, engineering and media to riskier territory, notably that of **biotechnology**. Cultivated, organic, self-reproducing objects have been produced for non-utilitarian purposes, e.g. skin-graft technology applied to artistic ends. But the biosciences didn't really need to commission specialist artists. Sometimes they appeared to be enacting the darker nightmares of modern art entirely by themselves, for instance via the widely circulated photograph of a rodent with a human ear grafted on its back in a ghoulish reminder of Daliesque surrealism. Other bioscientific advances, such as cloning, seemed to be vying successfully with science fiction fears of genetic manipulation.

See also: **Aesthetics**

Further reading: Kagan (2009); Wilson (2002)

ARTICULATION

In cultural studies, articulation doesn't carry its familiar sense of 'uttering clearly'. It is used in the sense you may recognise from 'articulated vehicle', where articulation denotes the joining of two things together. In cultural studies, what may be articulated are not two components of a vehicle but large-scale social forces (especially modes of production), in a particular configuration or formation at a particular time, called a conjuncture, to produce the structural determinants of any given practice, text or event. Just as an articulated vehicle has a prime mover and a trailer, where the prime mover, though smaller and lighter, determines the movement of the trailer (it provides motive force *to* the trailer, so articulation describes not simply a combination of forces but a hierarchical relationship between them). Forces aren't simply joined or jointed, they are 'structured in dominance'.

The term comes from Marxist analysis, where it refers to the articulation of different 'modes of production'. The economic and social relations of a society during a given epoch will display an articulation of different modes of production – capitalist, feudal and even communal, all at once – but one of these modes is *structured in dominance* over the others or 'overdetermines' them. It obliges them to adapt to its needs or integrates them to the mechanisms of its reproduction. Hence the feudal monarchy survives into the capitalist epoch, but is adapted to its purposes; or an industry like publishing retains feudal relations between author and publisher within the overall capitalist mode of production of books; or a social institution like the family allows for communal modes of production to be exploited by a capitalist economy. These are classic articulations.

The term has been extended in use to include articulations of other social forces. You might read, for instance, of the articulation of race and class in an analysis of **subcultural** music; or of the articulation of **gender** and **nation** in an analysis of sport. The term peppers the writings of analysts who are connected with British cultural studies. Elsewhere it has been used to account for certain problems in cultural anthropology, especially the specific forms of, say, Asian or preconquest American modes of production within a Marxist (i.e. Eurocentric and modernist) framework of analysis.

See also: **Ideological state apparatuses, Interpellation**

Further reading: Barker (2008)

AUDIENCE

Originating as a collective noun for those within earshot, who can 'audit' a dramatic performance or hear the words of a monarch or pope, the term audience is now used to describe a large number of individually unidentifiable and mutually anonymous people, usually united by their participation in media use. Given the varying demographics of this group, not to mention variations between nations, the concept itself is a means by which such an essentially unknowable group can be imagined. Naming an audience as such usually also involves homogenising it, ascribing to it certain characteristics, needs, desires and concerns, especially those that a producer-organisation is setting out to meet. Thus the audience can be imagined as an agent in its own right. This 'knowing' audience is a *construction*; a discursive abstraction not a natural phenomenon. Beyond the live event where audience members are co-present, it is impossible for 'the' media audience to act in concert, and therefore an audience *as such* cannot want, know, believe, like or oppose anything.

This construction serves the interests of three 'producer' groups:

- media organisations;
- media researchers (including polling agencies and academic critics);
- regulatory (governmental) bodies.

Audiences enable *media organisations* to sell advertising or to fulfil their public and statutory obligations, whether for television, radio, magazines or the press. It is important to know the size, quality (demographic composition) and characteristics of audiences for this purpose – these data relate directly to revenue. This accounts for the continual measurement of viewers, listeners, readers, and users. For media organisations, the concept of audience allows the exchange of information and entertainment to become commodified.

For *media researchers*, audiences may be studied as a 'whole' if the purpose is to generate general sociological data, as for example in the work of Pierre Bourdieu on taste distinctions in French culture. But very large-scale statistical techniques are nowadays beyond the reach of most academic researchers, and are found only among commercial audience research and polling organisations (Morrison, 1998), although the situation is different for online 'audiences' (social networks), which can be tracked through computer activity (e.g. clickstream).

In media and cultural studies, researchers have turned to the study of selected groups, identities, or constituencies among the overall audience, often in very small samples. They may also make such selections according to their own research and political priorities rather than following any naturalistic sub-grouping within an audience, assuming that agreement could be reached on how such groupings might be identified. What is of interest is not the self-understanding of the audience as a collective 'knowing subject', because such a thing cannot exist, but answers to questions generated by the research agenda. In particular, early audience research was conducted by social scientists interested in social problems such as **violent** behaviour and the possibility that media 'exposure' might affect that behaviour for the worse (*see* **effects**). Such concerns still motivate quantitative audience research in the '**mass communication**' tradition. More recently, qualitative 'media ethnography' has concentrated on the way that social variables such as **class** (Morley, 1980), **gender** (Ang, 1985), age (Buckingham, 2000), family circumstance (Morley, 1986), ethnicity (Gillespie, 1995), **fanship** (Jenkins, 1992, 2006b; Hills, 2002), etc., cause audiences to interact variously with media texts.

Meanwhile, commercial agencies prosper by commodifying the audience research process itself, such that current TV ratings, for instance, are proprietary not public knowledge, and of high value to the ratings agency. Similarly, political polling is part of a competitive commercial environment and fully integrated into daily news routines. Marketing agencies of all kinds employ their own techniques – many of them trade secrets – to produce psychographic descriptions of audience preferences, attitudes, and the like. Market prominence can follow if an ad agency is successful in sticking its analytical dipstick in the right bit of the zeitgeist at the right moment to profile an audience or to identify what it 'wants'.

For *regulatory bodies*, media audiences (unlike those for 'cultural pursuits' like live theatre) are routinely equated with the public at large. The audience is also the consumer, in need of protection (by one part of government), as well as commercial exploitation (promoted by other government departments). The audience is also the citizenry or public (voters; taxpayers), and so subject to political, moral, welfare or educational policies. **Regulators** therefore occupy a *governmental* position in relation to audiences (*see* **power**). Legislation may be restrictive (censorship, pornography), or enabling (freedom of speech). It may be conducted at the highest level of international policy (Rupert Murdoch deals with Prime Ministers and Presidents), or by usherette (enforcing age restrictions in cinemas). But in all of this, audiences do not *self-regulate* in any organised way.

The audience does not constitute itself; it does not 'know' itself; it does not govern itself. All this is done by institutional bodies – media organisation, research and government agencies. Hence the audience is the 'imagined community' (Anderson, 1991) that enables those institutions to operate.

The views of the audience enter the **semiotic** or **diegetic** space of the media in the form of **accessed** letters pages, talkback radio, or online comment. Model audiences (i.e. semiotic representations of the act or experience of being an audience) are included in entertainment formats, as game-show participants, studio audiences and laugh tracks, where they act as a kind of guide to appropriate or desired response – enjoyment, laughter, applause, euphoria . . . and occasional shoe-throwing.

Notably absent from the formal process of gaining knowledge about audiences are 'consumer' groups – audience sections representing themselves. Individual people rarely self-identify as mass audiences, and are but thinly represented directly by their own organisations, which are normally single-issue associations devoted to moral entrepreneurship, from 'cleaning up' TV's apparent propensity for sex, violence and bad language (Hartley, 1992a: 105) to child protection activists seeking to stop perceived media exploitation of minors. Occasional online petitions swirl through cyberspace when a favoured show is suddenly cancelled, but this simply shows how powerless audiences themselves are in pursuing their own collective interest within the current institutional framework of the media.

Nevertheless, a strong tradition within media research has been the study of the 'active audience'. This goes back to early media sociology, where people's *use* of the mass media was first studied under the banner of 'uses and gratifications' (e.g. the work of Elihu Katz). The 'active audience' was also prominent in early semiotic studies of television (e.g. Fiske and Hartley, 1978), on the grounds that 'decoding' media messages is itself a creative and productive process, albeit one that is undertaken on the couch. Later, fan studies demonstrated that the audience is active in a continuing engagement with favoured shows, forms (e.g. manga) or fictional characters going well beyond the act of consumption itself, and resulting in further textual productivity through inter-fan engagement and tribute productions. Finally, the 'active audience' became an economic reality with the success of the internet, which allowed the once contradictory idea of the 'productive consumer' to move to centre stage, with **user-generated** and **user-created content** marking the cutting edge of innovation in the creative industries. Here, the 'active audience' at last achieved its own 'mass medium' in the form of YouTube (Burgess and Green, 2009).

See also: **Discourse, Effects, Fandom, Meaning, Public**

Further reading: Ang (1996); Hartley (1992b); Hill (2005); Ott and Mack (2010)

AUTHOR/SHIP

A commonsense term that accounts for meaning by ascribing its *source* to a creative individual. Meaning is seen as a creation or expression of individual genius or experience, which is transferred to the brain of the reader. Such a model of communication implies that an author's intentions govern and warrant what a text means, and that those meanings are a form of private property, belonging to the author (even though the text itself, in the form of a book or download, may belong to the reader). The activity of reading is reduced to that of a passive receiver and paying customer, more or less finely tuned to pick up the already-finished meanings sent down the channel by the author.

This commonsense approach to authorship has its origins in medieval religious reading, when the 'author' of a sacred text like the Bible was thought to be divine, so there was nothing for readers to do but work out the *authorial intentions* from the clues in the text, and then obey them. The idea that readers might 'make' meanings for themselves was literally heresy, for which the consequences could be fatal.

Authors and their intentions have become controversial in modern, secular textual criticism, because this approach takes the obvious fact that texts are written or scripted by a human agent (or agents) and uses it to underpin the highly ideological theory of meaning outlined above. Since the same theory also underpins **copyright** law (Deazley, 2004), it is therefore of enormous economic importance.

But authorship is not as straightforward as that. An author is not in *every instance* 'one who writes'. Only some writers and writings count for the purposes of authorship.

- Authorship is not even coterminous with published writing – bloggers are rarely accorded that status on the basis of blog entries alone. Some highly expert writing is deliberately presented without author credits – the Wikipedia for instance.
- Journalism has traditionally been separated from authorship, on the grounds that journalism is writing for payment, where authorship is writing in the service of truth.
- Private, ephemeral and imagination or functional writings usually don't count as authored; postcards, shopping lists, school exercises, notes in the margins of books, telephone messages and even 'creative writing' – most things that most people actually write.
- In the published domain the same applies. It would be hard to find an 'author' for labels, advertisements, news, posters, street and shop signs, graffiti, junk mail, technical instructions, and **phatic** exchanges online – perhaps most of the public reading matter we encounter from day to day, even though much of it is created by expert professionals.

- Other creative works circulate orally and aurally – stories, jokes, songs, parody, spoof and send-ups. These too escape the traditional definition of authorship.
- The concept of authorship is very hard to sustain in the media (despite the undoubted importance of the scriptwriter), given the input of so many people in the production process, and the possibility of producing media shows without scripts (certain documentaries and live-action sequences). In the context of format shows – *Big Brother*, the *Idol* franchise – the author function is barely recognisable (the format is owned by production companies like Endemol or Celador). Contemporary TV favours the producer, now often called the 'showrunner', as the most creative agent; while in film many regard the director as the imaginative 'auteur' of the work as a whole (see below). But neither producer nor director is an author; according them this status is a **rearviewmirrorist** throwback to provide a disruptive new mode of textual productivity with a cloak of authority, derived from the model discussed above.

Authorship is a creation of literary culture and the marketplace. That is, it is one of the great markers of 'high' as opposed to 'popular' culture, and it is invoked to ascribe not just meaning but value – aesthetic or moral as well as monetary – to works and authors identified by literary criticism (and marketing managers) as 'significant'. Once an author's name has been established, then potentially any writing under that name counts as authored – even down to shopping lists, if any were to turn up that had been penned by, say, Shakespeare.

Authorship is, then, a social system imposed on the domain of writing; it is not the act or trade of writing for publication. It is a system for producing hierarchies within that domain. Authors are a product of a social division of labour, and authorship is an ideological notion that functions to privilege not only certain kinds of writing and writers, but also, more importantly, certain ways of thinking about the meaning of texts and of valuing them in the marketplace.

The ideology of authorship locates the source of literary quality not in aspects of writing itself – the exploitation of genre, convention, rhetoric, intertextuality, and so on – but in the bodies of writers. Creativity, inspiration, experience, the ability to 'express' thought, emotion and truth: these personal attributes are supposed to emanate from a free-floating individual consciousness which is assumed to the source of meaning, with writing merely a transparent medium through which the great thoughts can flow to the reader's equally free-floating consciousness.

That ideology of authorship leads, for example, to the fruitless search for 'what Shakespeare *really* meant' – an impossible quest which leads inexorably to the imposition of authoritarian meanings on a given work by a critic who seeks to establish *one* reading as the only or *true* reading. In other words, any appeal to 'the author's intentions' is coercive – it seeks to impose ideological closure on a text, to minimise its **polysemic** potential. It's dishonest (or self-deluding) too, imputing to the author meanings which are necessarily the creation of the critic. 'Intentionalist' criticism is reduced to second-guessing an author who's conveniently absent, often dead, so it's impossible to verify what his or her intentions were.

Moreover, an author's intentions do not use up the meaning of a text. Even if the author can be interrogated, as, for example, in an interview, what results from this process is not a direct account of his or her intentions, but merely *another text*. Authors always work within the domain of writing, which is an autonomous domain with its own history, modes of production, genres, conventions and established practices. Writers are to a large extent at the mercy of the discursive resources available to them, and creativity comes not from abstract 'genius' but from an ability to exploit these resources, often with completely unforeseen consequences. Once written, a text takes on a life of its own, and what it means depends on the conditions of its circulation and the uses to which it is put in different places and times. Its meanings are always plural, and always exceed what the writer thought was going on, intentionally or otherwise.

However, so established has the concept of authorship become that it has achieved a kind of **hegemony**. It seems to represent a pathological desire for an ultimate origin, a god or 'intelligent designer' who will finally limit the infinite potentiality of **meaning**.

The desire for a singular origin for meaning has proved strong enough to infiltrate areas of culture once regarded as too lowbrow to warrant authors, especially cinema, where the 'auteur' approach seeks to account for certain films by conferring author-status on their director. Naturally, 'auteur' directors are credited with 'significance', which may be traced across a number of films, and their 'genius' is seen as an individual 'vision'. However, the source of meaning in cinema is notoriously hard to pin down, that is to say, there is no one source, even at the point of production, let alone once a film is released into the cultural sphere at large. But 'auteur' theory fixes upon just one person to represent the creative input of the whole cast and crew – often hundreds of people working on and off for months or even years, all of whom may change for that director's next project.

And in the history of cinema it has never been clear who out of all these people should be treated authorially. The screenwriter has never enjoyed this status (Maras, 2009; Corrigan, 1998). It seems in cinema, as in literature itself, that authorship is more a way of organising marketing strategies, and conferring value on intellectual property, than a way of accounting for meaning.

The general reader or viewer approaches authors not as persons at all but *textually*; either solely by engagement with a text (imagined interlocutor), or additionally by knowledge gained *intertextually* about the author (up to and including **fanship**). The author is 'implied' in the writing itself. Hence, for readers, authors are not persons but an ensemble of rhetorical and narrative ploys, dedicated to hooking and drawing them into the writing. Throughout any discursive text or fictional story there are devices which 'guide' the reader as to its preferred reading and direction. Such devices may also be more intrusive or coercive; an authorial introduction telling readers how to read what follows, or a cover blurb which seeks to sell the writing on the basis of the author's name, institutional clout or biographical credibility. Here, the marketing aspect of authorship is clear.

See also: **Meaning, Subjectivity, Text**

Further reading: Gerstner and Staiger (2003); Gray (2006)

BARDIC FUNCTION

A comparative concept, proposing a similarity between the social function of television and that of the bardic order in traditional Celtic societies. The concept was suggested by Fiske and Hartley (1978) to emphasise the active and productive signifying work of television. The idea is that like the original bards in medieval Celtic societies, the media are a distinct and identifiable social institution, whose role is to mediate between the rulers and patrons who license and pay them, and the society at large, whose doings and sayings they render into a specialised **rhetorical** language which they then play back to the society. The concept seemed necessary to supersede previous conceptualisations of the media, which had concentrated on the way they were/are supposed to reflect their society. The notion of the bardic function goes beyond this, first in its insistence on their role as manipulators of language, and then in its emphasis on the way they take their mediating role as an active one, simply reproducing neither the opinions of their owners, nor the 'experience' of their viewers. Instead, the 'bardic' media take up signifying raw materials from the societies they represent, and rework them into characteristic forms which appear as 'authentic' and 'true to life' not because they are but because of the professional prestige of the bard and the familiarity and pleasure we have learnt to associate with bardic offerings.

One implication of this notion is that, once established, bardic television can play an important role in dealing with social conflict and cultural change. Dealing as it does in signification – representations and myths – the ideological work it performs is largely a matter of rendering the unfamiliar into the already known, or into 'common sense'. It will strive to make sense of both conflict and change according to these familiar strategies. Hence bardic television is a conservative or *socio-central* force for its 'home' culture. It uses metaphor to render new and unfamiliar occurrences into familiar forms and meanings. It uses binary oppositions to represent oppositional or marginal groups as deviant or 'foreign'. As a result, it strives to encompass all social and cultural action within a consensual framework. Where it fails, as it must, to 'claw back' any group or occurrence into a consensual and familiar form, its only option is to represent them as literally outlandish and senseless. Bardic television, then, not only makes sense of the world, but also marks out the limits of sense, and offers us everything beyond that limit as nonsense.

Since the emergence of post-broadcast digital media and the burgeoning productivity of ordinary consumers, who can now publish their own media productions without channelling them through centralised agencies like TV stations, it has proven necessary to return to the bardic function, in order to account for *distributed* as well as centralised sense-making. Hartley (2009a, 2009b) has proposed that initiatives like digital storytelling, where non-professionals tell their own stories using audio-visual technologies, and mass distribution sites like YouTube, Flickr and the like, represent an extension of the bardic function to whole populations, where potentially *everyone* is a bard: not only can they sing or tell a story, but they can communicate with others by such means. This suggests that the bardic function may migrate to the internet as a self-organising system with myriad points of production and use, taking on the characteristics of a social network rather than a centralised agency.

This being so, the question arises of how to improve and extend creative performance among myriad ordinary users. Here, the Celtic bardic order can join forces with contemporary entertainment formats, using traditional Eisteddfod competitions for instance to identify the best amateurs in a given discipline, combining that 'folk' apparatus with the contemporary *Idol* format where the actual process of improvement and selection becomes part of reality entertainment. By such means, the showbiz attractions of media can be combined with the 'bottom-up' aspects of orally transmitted culture and the global distribution capacity of online social networks, to develop distributed competence in bardic performance – song and story not only for all but by all; self-taught and self-organised. Experiments are already taking place, one such being the proliferation of 'Complaints Choirs' (www.complaintschoir.org) on YouTube and around the world, after an initial idea by Finnish artists Tellervo Kalleinen and Oliver Kochta-Kalleinen in 2005.

Further reading: Turner (2003); Williams (1981)

BIAS

Bias is a commonsense term in news discourse, using a metaphor from the game of lawn bowls, indicating that a story has deviated from a 'true' line because some inbuilt characteristic (the bias in the bowling ball) drags it off to one side or the other – to the Left, or the Right. This is an apt metaphor for political news, which is perhaps why suspicion of it is so widespread.

There is a tradition of vigorous media critique based on the rhetoric of bias. In the USA this is associated with writers like Bob McChesney (2008); in the United Kingdom it arose with the work of the Glasgow Media Group (1982). Both of these phenomena should be regarded as part of the political process itself, rather than belonging to the framework of explanation. The charge of bias is itself a political intervention.

The problem with it as a concept is that it conforms to a reflection theory of the media, presuming that something external to the process of representation and media production (like a fact) can be gathered and conveyed to the audience without change. Instead of this ultimately futile ideal, it would be better for all concerned to recognise that all stories conform to the mechanisms of their own telling; indeed they are literally the *product* of discursive, semiotic, narrative and production processes themselves. They do not pre-exist the production process even though events do occur independently of their observation or narration, because there are infinite ways in which an event can be represented.

This is not to say that partisan individuals and organisations, and politically motivated media, do not seek to 'sway' audiences – of course they do, as they have from Thucydides to William Randolph Hearst to Fox News. The issue is rather that there can be no such thing as objective reporting in the strict sense, even though that ideal has motivated American journalism since the nineteenth century (Schudson, 2001). What is possible is the determination to tell the truth using the means at hand, and to admit that the means themselves are material and determinate (not to mention accident-prone).

Further, the charge of bias presumes a 'passive' audience who can be led by the nose in this direction or that. This ignores the wide scepticism that audiences routinely display towards both media organisations and the political or partisan players on whom they report. 'Bias' is assumed from the start, and people learn how to 'decode' partisan reporting without necessarily falling for the preferred 'line'. Learning how to recognise and allow for the intentionality of others (including the intent to deceive or distort) is a universal attribute of language-learning, picked up by children in their first decade of life. This 'anthropological' scepticism seems to have intensified in relation to people's encounters with mediated rhetoric of all kinds over the years, including news. So much so that the 2008 Presidential election in the USA was defined not by straight news coverage (CNN, network news) but by commentary on it, both by ideological warriors (Fox News) and by send-up and satire (John Stewart's *Daily Show* and Stephen Colbert's *Colbert Report*), and also by the coming of age of online websites, including Sen. Obama's own. The 'leaning' one way or another of each outlet is part of its attraction, allowing viewers and visitors either to identify with the bias in a deliberate act of partisan-ship, or to compensate for it because 'where it is coming from' is known in advance.

See also: **Content analysis, Ideology, News, Objectivity**

BINARY OPPOSITION

The generation of meaning out of two-term (binary) systems; and the *analytic* use of binary contrasts to analyse texts and other cultural phenomena. This was done first in structural anthropology and then **structuralism** more generally. In contemporary life, it may be that the most important binary is the opposition between zero and one, since that is the basis of computer language and digital technologies. But in culture, binaries also operate as a kind of thinking machine, taking the 'analogue' continuity of actuality and dividing it up in order to be able to apprehend it.

Basic propositions are as follows.

(1) *Meaning is generated by opposition.* This is a tenet of Saussurian linguistics, which holds that signs or words mean what they do only in opposition to others. Their most precise characteristic is in being what the others are not. The *binary* opposition is the most extreme form of significant difference. In a binary system, there are only two signs or words. Thus, in the opposition LAND : SEA the terms are mutually exclusive, and yet together they form a complete system – the earth's surface. Similarly, the opposition CHILD : ADULT is a binary system. The terms are mutually exclusive, but taken together they include everyone on earth (everyone is either child or adult). Of course, everyone can be understood by means of other binaries as well, as for instance in the binary US : THEM – everyone is either in or not in 'our nation'.

Such binaries are a feature of CULTURE not NATURE – that being an *analytic* binary much used in structuralism to distinguish language, symbols and ideology from 'natural causes' (without necessarily tying to suggest that culture and language are not natural). Binaries are the product of signifying systems, and function to structure our perceptions of the natural and social world into order and meaning. You may find binaries underlying the stories of newspaper and television news, where they separate out, for example, the parties involved in a conflict or dispute, and render them into meaningful oppositions, which often appear to be caused by natural differences.

(2) *Ambiguities are produced by binary logic and are an offence to it.* Consider the binaries mentioned above:

LAND : SEA
CHILD : ADULT
US : THEM

These stark oppositions actively suppress ambiguities or overlaps between the opposed categories. In between land and sea is an *ambiguous category*, the beach – sometimes land, sometimes sea. It is *both* one and the other (sea at high tide; land at low tide), and *neither* one nor the other. Similarly, in between child and adult there is another ambiguous category: youth. And in between us and them there are deviants, dissidents, and so on.

The area of overlap shown in Figure 1 is, according to binary logic, impossible. It is literally a scandalous category that ought not to exist.

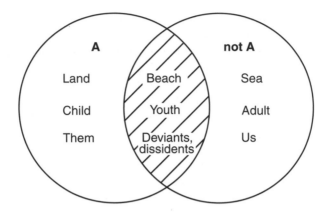

Figure 1 Overlap between opposed categories.

In anthropological terms, the ambiguous boundary between two recognised categories is where taboo can be expected. That is, any activity or state that does not fit the binary opposition will be subjected to repression or ritual. For example, as the anthropologist Edmund Leach (1976, 1982) suggests, the married and single states are binarily opposed. They are normal, time-bound, central to experience and secular. But the transition from one state to the other (getting married or divorced) is a *rite of passage* between categories. It is abnormal, out of time (the 'moment of a lifetime'), at the edge of experience and, in anthropological terms, *sacred*. The structural ambiguity of youth is one reason why it is treated in the media as a scandalous category – it too is a rite of passage and is subjected to both repression and ritual.

News often structures the world into binarily opposed categories (Us : THEM). But it then faces the problem of dealing with people and events that don't fit neatly into the categories. The structural ambiguity of home-grown oppositional groups and people offends the consensual category of 'us', but cannot always be identified with foreigners or 'THEM'. In such cases, they are often represented as folk-devils, or as sick, deviant or mad – they are tabooed.

(3) *Binary oppositions are structurally related to one another.* Binaries function to *order* meanings, and you may find *transformations* of one underlying binary running through a story. For instance, the binary

Masculine : Feminine may be transformed within a story into a number of other terms:

MASCULINE : FEMININE
OUTDOORS : INDOORS
PUBLIC : PRIVATE
SOCIAL : PERSONAL
PRODUCTION : CONSUMPTION
MEN : WOMEN

First, masculinity and femininity are proposed as opposites and mutually exclusive. This immediately constructs an ambiguous or 'scandalous' category of overlap that will be tabooed (e.g. trans-gender phenomena including transsexuality and transvestism). Then, the binaries can be read downwards as well as across, which proposes, for instance, that men (outside; public) are to women (inside; private) as production is to consumption, or:

MEN : WOMEN :: PRODUCTION : CONSUMPTION

This logic 'finds' that production is a masculine domain and consumption a feminine one. As you can see, this feature of binaries is highly productive of ideological meanings – there's nothing natural (causal) about them, but the *logic* of the binary is hard to escape, and large-scale social or institutional practices are then organised around such distinctions.

The ideological productivity of binaries is further enhanced by the assignation of POSITIVE : NEGATIVE *values* to opposed terms. This is guilt by association. For instance, Hartley and Lumby (2002) analysed a number of instances where the events of September 11, 2001 were used by conservative commentators to bring the idea of 'absolute evil' back into public discourse. These activists included Christian prelates and literary critics. They associated 9/11 with developments within Western culture of which they disapproved, including postmodernism and relativism, on the grounds that these had been undermining belief in (absolute) truth and reality. So they invoked Osama bin Laden ('evil') to damn the postmodernists:

ABSOLUTE : RELATIVE
TRUTH : POSTMODERNISM
POSITIVE : NEGATIVE
GOOD : EVIL

Identifying binary opposition is a useful in the analysis of texts and discourses, but these are dynamic and situated objects, so as with any structuralist approach it is important to remember that such structures of opposition are not stable, given, or natural, but produced, achieved with creative (and ideological) effort, and very much open to contestation.

See also: **Bardic function, Orientalism**

Further reading: O'Shaughnessy and Stadler (2009)

BIOPOWER

A concept from Michel Foucault (1978, 1984, 2003), referring to the management and administration of populations by means of the regulation and control of both individual bodies and whole populations of bodies. Biopower in the modern era is the government of life, rather than fear of death, which was the feudal or monarchical form (where sovereignty was exercised on pain of death). Thus it is centred on discourses of reproduction (birth; morbidity; death), health, including the institutionalisation of medicine, 'big pharma' and hygeine, and increasingly on genetics (genomics, **biotechnology**).

According to Rabinow and Rose (2006), the concept of biopower includes:

- *truth discourses* that produce knowledge about the 'vital character of living human beings';
- *strategies for intervention* in the name of life and health, applied to nations or some other large-scale collective, including race;
- *modes of subjectification* 'through which individuals are brought to work on themselves, under certain forms of authority, in relation truth discourses, by means of practices of the self, in the name of their own life or health, that of their family or some other collectivity, or indeed in the name of the life or health of the population as a whole' (Rabinow and Rose, 2006: 197).

As elsewhere, Foucault conceives of **power** as a productive force, not simply a repressive one. Thus, from the nineteenth century onwards, discourses of biopower have sought to maximise the efficacy and efficiency of the body, both individual and collective, as much as to regulate it. These are the two poles of what he called 'governmentality' – productive and regulatory force. Thus public health and personal fitness are both part of the regime of biopower, as might also be eugenics or genocide.

Biopower and the concomitant concept of biopolitics have assumed greater prominence in the era of bioscience and genomics, at the scale of populations; while at the scale of individuals the rise of gym culture, make-over shows on TV, and a general 'ethic' of self-management via diet, exercise, and healthy choices are all symptoms of biopower. Similarly, biopolitics may operate at the 'macro' level of populations, including racial politics; global mental health initiatives; transgenetics and the like; or at the 'micro' level in the politics of drinking bottled water (Hawkins, 2009). Overall, as Rabinow and Rose (2006: 205) point out, 'race, health, genealogy, reproduction and knowledge are intertwined, continually recombining and transforming one another'. They certainly should have included the productive role of media in this process.

See also: **Power**

BIOTECHNOLOGY

The use of biological molecules, cells and processes by firms and research organisations for application in the pharmaceutical, medical, agricultural and environmental fields, together with the business, regulatory and societal context for such applications. Biotechnology also includes applied immunology, regenerative medicine, genetic therapy and molecular engineering, including *nanotechnology*. This new field is at the chemistry/biology interface, focusing on structures between one nanometre (i.e. a billionth of a metre) and one hundred nanometres in size, from which life-building structures from molecules to proteins, etc., are made – and may therefore be engineered. Bio- and nanotechnology bring closer the possibility of 'organic' computers, self-built consumer goods, and a much fuzzier line between human and machine.

Biotechnology has been hailed as a successor to the telecommunications and computer revolutions, especially in terms of its potential for return on the investment of 'patient capital' (unlike the boom and bust economy of the dot-coms). By the year 2006, there were nearly 1500 biotech firms in the USA alone, with a market capitalisation of $360 billion and direct revenues of $58.8 billion, employing over 180,000 people (figures from www.bio.org).

Its importance to the field of communication is that it is an industry based on '**code**' – notably the human genome. This field has transformed the concept of 'decoding' from one associated with linguistic (cultural) or social information to one based in the physical and life sciences. Biotechnological developments in relation to DNA diagnostics or genetic modification, for instance, have implications for society and culture, as well as for science and business. DNA testing has already had an impact on family law because (for the first time in human history) paternity is no longer 'hearsay'; this in turn will influence familial relations and structures more widely. Biotechnological developments in agriculture, and the 'decoding' of the human genome, have radical implications for the relationship between nature and culture, and where that line is thought to be drawn.

Further reading: Shiva (2005); Thacker (2005)

BRANDING

Branding has become one of the most important concepts in what may be called the 'economics of attention' (Lanham, 2006). Where once advertising concentrated on *targetting* the desired consumer, by the 1980s it had turned its attention to *branding* the product and then, more recently producer. Thus it became vital to associate corporations – and their mediated or semiotic representation – with values, ideally reaching all the way from boardroom strategy to the 'mood' of the logo. Whole companies can be organised around the concept of branding, for instance LVMH (Louis Vuitton Moët Hennessy), which owns multiple global luxury brands in fashion, alcohol, perfume, watches and jewellery. This is what that company has said about the value of its brands:

> The power of the companies' brands is part of LVMH's heritage. It took years and even decades to build their image. They are an asset that is both priceless and irreplaceable. Therefore, Group companies exercise stringent control over every minute detail of their brands' image. In each of the elements of their communications with the public (announcements, speeches, messages, etc.), it is the brand that speaks. Each message must do right by the brand. In this area as well, there is absolutely no room for compromise.
> (www.lvmh.com/groupe/pg_missions.asp?rub=2&srub=1)

That is why the company logo is important in branding, to the mock outrage of the tabloids when they see millions spent by organisations ranging from Pepsi to the BBC on revamping logos.

Companies increasingly use 'celebrity branding' to give themselves a face, personality and character, and celebrities themselves are ranked by agencies for clients who want a trustworthy or trendsetting 'face'. Once captured for corporate use, branding can be applied to other entities, from people to nations. There is a thriving industry for DIY 'brand yourself' enthusiasts, showing how to present your CV, website, and living persona to competitive advantage. Simon Anholt (2007) has developed the idea of 'national branding'. A good example of this was the 2008 campaign launched by Tourism Australia, at a cost of $40m across 22 countries, which linked Australia as a tourist destination with Baz Luhrmann's blockbuster film *Australia* (starring Nicole Kidman, Hugh Jackman, David Gulpilil and Indigenous child-actor Brandon Walters). The idea was not only to piggy-back on the hoped-for success of a $130m Hollywood film, but also to 'brand' Australia itself with the transformations experienced by the fictional characters (especially Kidman's) in the course of the plot. Despite the star power and the budget, however, neither the film nor the 'national branding' campaign were judged a success. National branding has a negative side too. Later, Anholt compared Australia's national reputation to that of a 'dumb blonde' – people overseas regard it as 'attractive but shallow and unintelligent', and as 'decorative, but not very useful' (Harrison, 2010).

Further reading: Anholt (2007); Ardvisson (2006)

BRICOLAGE

A term borrowed from the structural anthropologist Claude Lévi-Strauss, to describe a mode of cultural assemblage at an opposite pole to *engineering*. Where engineering requires pre-planning, submission to various laws of physics, and the organisation of materials and resources prior to the act of assembly, bricolage refers to the creation of objects with materials to hand, re-using existing artefacts, and incorporating bits and pieces. Lévi-Strauss used the term to denote the creative practices of traditional societies using magical rather than scientific thought systems. However, bricolage enjoyed a vogue and gained wide currency in the 1970s and 1980s when applied to various aspects of Western culture. These included avant-garde artistic productions, using collage, pastiche, found objects, and installations that re-assembled the detritus of everyday consumerism. They also included aspects of everyday life itself, especially those taken to be evidence of **postmodernism** (Hebdige, 1988: 195).

Western consumer society was taken to be a society of bricoleurs; for instance in youth subcultures. These became notorious for the appropriation of icons originating in the parent or straight culture, and the improvisation of new meanings, often directly and provocatively subversive of those communicated by the same items in mainstream settings. The hyper-neat zoot suit of the mods in the 1960s was an early example of this trend. Mods took the respectable business suit and turned its 'meaning' almost into its own opposite by reassembling its buttons (too many at the cuff), collars (removed altogether), line (too straight), cut (exaggerated tightness, slits), material (too shiny-modern, mohair-nylon), colour (too electric). The garb of the gentleman and businessman was made rude, confronting, and sartori-ally desirable among disaffected but affluent youth. Bricolage was made 'spectacular' in the 1970s by punk, under the influence of Vivian Westwood, Malcolm McLaren and others in the fashion/music inter-face such as Zandra Rhodes. Punk took bricolage seriously, and put ubiquitous 'profane' items such as the safety pin, Union Jack, garbage bags, and swastikas to highly charged new 'sacred' or ritualised purposes (Hebdige, 1979).

Architecture also used bricolage as it went through a postmodern phase. Buildings began to quote bits and pieces from incommensurate styles, mixing classical with vernacular, modernist with suburban, shopping mall with public institution, and delighting in materials and colours that made banks look like beachfront hotels, and museums look like unfinished kit-houses (from different kits). Much of this was in reaction to the over-engineered precision and non-human scale of 'international style' modernist towers. Bricolage was seen as active criticism, much in the manner of jazz, which took existing tunes and improvised, syncopated and reassembled them till they were the oppo-site of what they had been. Borrowing, mixture, hybridity, even plagiarism – all 'despised' practices in high modernist science and knowledge systems – became the bricoleur's trademark, and postmod-ernism's signature line.

Bricolage has entered the digital age in the form of 'remix culture'. Here the idea of creating something new using materials to hand encountered the problem of intellectual property rights, which see bricolage as piracy and seek to forbid or monetise exactly that practice (Lessig, 2008).

BROADCASTING

Jostein Gripsrud (1998) writes that the original use of the word 'broadcasting' was as an agricultural term, to describe the sowing or scattering of seeds broadly, by hand, in wide circles. This image of distributing widely and efficiently from a central point, as far as the reach will allow, is also present within the term's technological meaning, as a distribution method for radio and television. Broadcasting is over-the-air transmission, whereby signals (analogue waves or digital data) are emitted from a central transmitter in the AM, VHF/FM and UHF bands. The power of the transmitter determines how far that signal will reach; and it is usually free to the receiver, thereby distinguishing *broadcast* TV from *subscription* TV (such as cable) or *IPTV* (TV over the internet).

Implicit within broadcasting is the idea of distribution from the centre to the periphery. The centralised one-to-many structure of broadcast television locates it as essentially a *modern industrial* system. In turn, this has given rise to analysis of broadcasting that sees it as purely one-way communication, of a central voice communicating to the masses with an authoritative, or controlling capacity. Such analysis was shared across popular culture (Welles' *Citizen Kane*, Chaplin's *Great Dictator*) and intellectual culture alike, which was apt to dismiss broadcasting as the 'opium of the people' for a secular age (Carey, 1992). However, this conception of television has been revised by more recent theories that explore the capacity of the **audience** to engage actively with television, to bring their own self-knowledge and experience to their interpretation of the television text and to make cultural and identity choices through the viewing experience.

Technological changes in broadcast technology have also challenged previous assumptions about the nature of broadcast media. Digital technology has enabled a greater number of channels, increasing viewer choice and encouraging programming for niche (or 'long tail'), rather than mass, audiences (although narrowcasting and community broadcasting have always rejected the assumption that television was intended only for large audiences of common interest). Furthermore, digital technology allows for two-way communication through broadcasting, enabling interactivity (with the programme or with other people) through the television set.

'Broadcasting' also describes an industry, funded through subscriptions, advertising, sponsorship, donations, government funding or a combination of these sources.

The radio broadcasting industry, which preceded TV as *the* home-based entertainment and information medium, now displays interesting differences from television. Radio has niched, with significant activities that are not common in television, for instance local programming (including rural and remote), youth and music programming (where different stations have very specialised playlists), and broadcasting for minority or community groups. At the international level, radio broadcasting is still supported by national governments for development and propaganda purposes. The latter is dominated by the 'big five' organisations: the BBC, Voice of America, Deutsche Welle, Radio France International, and Radio Netherlands, although most countries add their voice to the global conversation, often via shortwave.

See also: **Convergence, Digital/analogue distribution**

Further reading: Spigel and Olsson (2004); Turner and Tay (2009)

CELEBRITY

Celebrity is the signalling of the semiotics of identity, the mediated performance of the self, organised as a social network market. It is only found in societies where identity is a pervasive socio-cultural and political value. Monarchs from Rameses the Great to Queen Elizabeth I were assiduous in establishing the cult of their own person, but the idea that everybody's personal identity was important was not widely established until **modernity** (this function was carried by saints in medieval Europe), and thus there was no competitive market in signalling identity images.

Celebrity has become more important as contemporary Western societies have evolved towards the status of 'economies of attention' (Lanham, 2006), where identity is seen as more significant than (or causally prior to) decision-making, action, or faith, and the celebrity supersedes the leader, hero, or holy-person. Publicity trumps the public. Tracing what he calls a 'history of fame', Braudy (1986: 4) notes that as 'each new medium of fame appears, the human image it conveys is intensified and the number of individuals celebrated expands'.

Celebrities are individuals who are noted for the attention they command in the media. They can come from any walk of life – musicians, sport stars, models, criminals, film, television and radio personalities, as well as participants in **reality TV**. Sometimes professional experts, like authors, lawyers, artists and even scientists, can achieve celebrity status. But not all famous people are celebrities. As a descriptive category celebrity would not usually include politicians, royal families, or prominent people with specific qualifications. This is because celebrity is not granted on the basis of institutional position or public office but on the basis of desirable personal qualities – roughly, marriageability and its discontents. Even so, it has less to do with the immanent qualities of a person than with the productive apparatus of a social institution with a network of interlocking agents and agencies, all the way from those who produce a given image for a person (stylist, personal trainer, shopper, hairdresser, etc.) via the agencies that produce and circulate images of that image (paparazzi, picture agencies, gossip magazines and TV shows, etc.), through to the market in which these images contend for attention – a market that includes not only 'end users' such as fans but also professionals on the lookout for new talent, which is why celebrities often collude with paparazzi to get noticed. In short, celebrity is a competitive *social network market*.

The concept of celebrity also differs from that of the **star**, because stardom was the product of a different industrial process, controlled by the big movie studios. It was not an open market although the commodity – images of marriageability – may have been the same. Where stardom is all about the centrally controlled producer, and is therefore modern, celebrity is all about distributed hyper-production and competitive marketing where consumers and users set the values, and is therefore postmodern.

Celebrities are set apart from stars in the symbolic or imaginary realm too, for where stars were assiduously protected from any contamination by ordinariness, celebrities are the very embodiment of it. Once established in the market, a given celebrity is available to carry ordinary problems associated with body image, intimate relationships, and day-to-day conduct – the comportment of the self. Less routinely, they are available to adorn social causes. Thus the 'script' of gossip magazines is to find the most beautiful and favoured people and then to construct narratives of risk, danger and dilemma around them, showing that despite their appeal they face the same issues as 'we' do. Their celebrity *function* (rather than status) is to **represent** the vicissitudes of **ordinary culture**.

See also: **Identification, Stars, Subjectivity**

Further reading: Marshall (2006); Turner (2004); Redmond and Holmes (2007)

CENSORSHIP

Censorship is an assault on both truth (public) and beauty (private) in the name of safety (external or military threat) and decency (internal or moral threat). It proceeds through control of published content by official agencies in order to discipline populations, aiming to render docile any dangerous thoughts and desires. In the realm of fact (news, **journalism**, security), censorship is usually connected with the *public* domain of politics, although it can also relate to religious, royal or reproductive matters. In the realm of fiction (drama, **authorship**, imagination), it applies to the *private* domain of sexual behaviour, offensive language and moral conduct.

Censorship is of ancient origin. The word comes from the office responsible for taking the census (head-count and property audit of all citizens) and regulating morality in Rome (Monarchical/Republican period), thereby maintaining state control over both *property* values and *personal* values. Ever since, censorship has overlapped the public and private domains. Roman censors had power to reduce the rank of citizens or senators, since their function was to maintain status-based virtues in the conduct of citizens. Modern censors have power over publications rather than persons; their concern is for the morals of the presumed reader not the writer. Censors may restrict or prohibit the publication of anything they judge to be contrary to 'public morality'. Where once this judgement was their own, in later periods it imposed that of central administrations (monarchs, popes, military dictators); in democracies the judgement is said to be made on behalf of a 'reasonable adult'.

What attracts the attention of censors is entirely contextual and historical. In Roman times it included celibacy or *failure* to marry, thus depriving the state of future citizens (Valerius, n.d.: II, 9.1). More recently it may include *attempts* to marry, depending on the age, race and sex relations of the intended couple. And in between, censorship applied to arguments in favour of *divorce*. Indeed it was this that prompted the publication of the most famous document in the modern history of opposition to censorship, John Milton's *Areopagitica* of 1644 (Figure 2), where the poet of *Paradise Lost* – whose pamphlet on divorce had been censored – defended the principle of a free press. Although a supporter of the Parliamentary cause in the Civil War, which was at its height at the time, Milton protested against Parliament's imposition of an official licensing system for all printed materials, requiring the registration of authors, printers and publishers, granting powers to seize and destroy offensive books and to arrest and imprison offenders. Despite Milton's prestige and the subsequent ascendancy of the notion of 'free speech' (especially in the USA), most

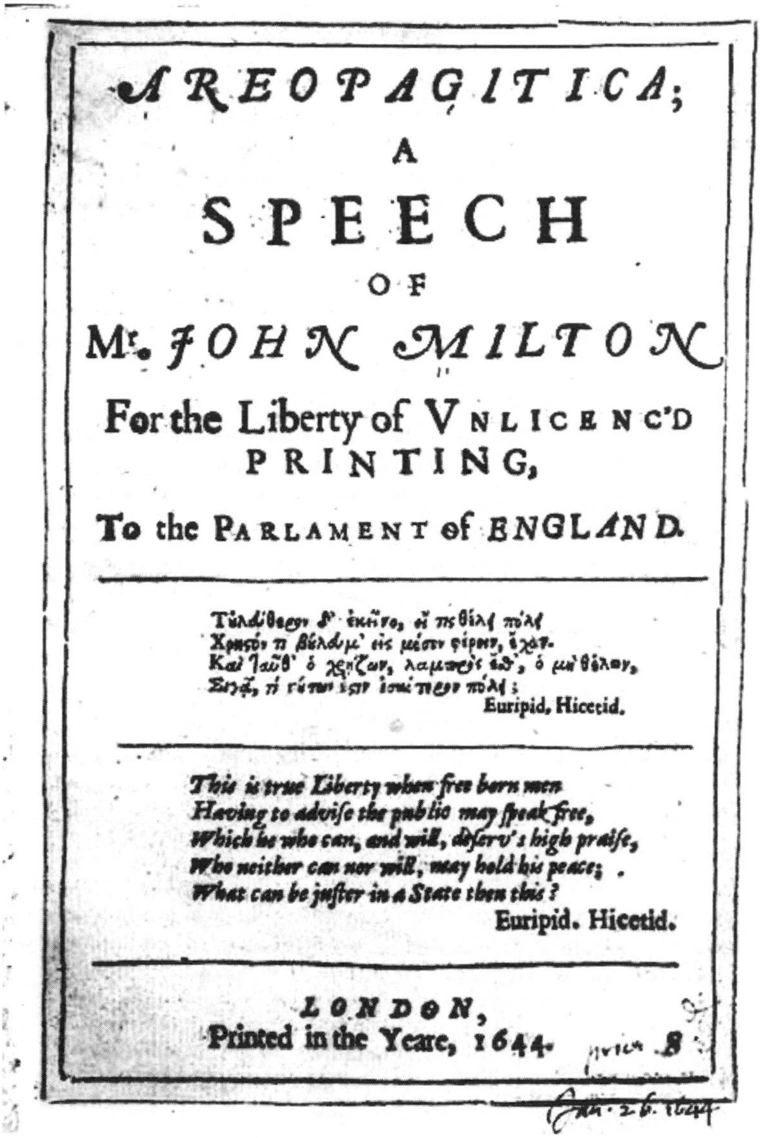

AREOPAGITICA;

A

SPEECH

OF

Mr. JOHN MILTON

For the Liberty of VNLICENC'D
PRINTING,

To the PARLAMENT of ENGLAND.

Τὴλθερον δ' ἐκεῖνο, εἰ τις θέλει πόλι
Χρηστὸν τι βέλδμ' εἰς μέσον φέρειν, ἔχων.
Καὶ ταῦθ' ὁ χρηζων, λαμπρὸς ἐσθ', ὁ μὴ θέλων,
Σιγᾷ, τί τέτων ἐστιν ἰσαίτηρον πόλι;

Euripid, Hicetid.

This is true Liberty when free born men
Having to advise the public may speak free,
Which he who can, and will, deserv's high praise,
Who neither can nor will, may hold his peace;
What can be juster in a State then this?

Euripid. Hicetid.

LONDON,
Printed in the Yeare, 1644.

Figure 2 'Give me the liberty to know, to utter, and to argue freely according to conscience, above all liberties' – Milton's *Areopagitica*. (Public domain image; courtesy of US Library of Congress.)

of these provisions remained within the legislative arsenal of modern countries for centuries, some of them to this day.

Thus a gap has opened between what governments have power to censor and what citizens may believe to be their rights. Powers are not always exercised – publications may not be prosecuted – but it is available for entrepreneurial authorities and modern expert systems to occupy in the name of those who are deemed to be in need of protection from dangers. Here again, times change. Where once the criminal law focused on punishing certain *acts*, a more recent tendency has been for it to criminalise categories of *person*. In Europe this reached its peak during the Nazi period (1933–45), when classifying whole categories of people as dangerous reached its largest scale and most murderous intensity. Although rarely applied since then to ethnic groups, the tendency to criminalise types of person persists, not least in matters of sexuality. In many legal codes (such as the Napoleonic Code widely adopted in modernising Europe after 1810), *no* sexual *acts* were specified as crimes; but, during the nineteenth and twentieth century, certain sexual tastes or drives (i.e. types of *person*) were criminalised, notably homosexuality and (later) paedophilia.

These moves were enabled by the creation of medical and psychiatric knowledge institutions, which claimed to be able to identify both the kind of person likely to pose a danger, and how to 'treat' those in need of protection. The sexuality of children was recognised, but only medical professionals or clinical psychologists could observe it with impunity. Thus an alliance of medical and legal institutions has occupied that gap between censorship powers and practices, producing the knowledge that has shifted the official gaze of the censor ever more unblinkingly to those observing children. Michel Foucault, in a prescient interview given in 1978, foresaw that the production and protection of childhood asexuality was leading to a disciplinary society based on generalised dangers:

> We're going to have a society of dangers, with, on the one side, those who are in danger, and on the other, those who are dangerous . . . . Sexuality will become a threat in all social relations . . . . And sexuality will [be] a kind of roaming danger, a sort of omnipresent phantom . . . . It is on this shadow, this phantom, this fear that the authorities would try to get a grip . . . with the support of the medical institutions.
>
> (Foucault, 1988: 271–85.)

Following the successful production of sexual pathology, censorship entrepreneurs have become active in many countries, especially seeking to ban media representations that depict non–hetero-normative practices, or any material that 'sexualises' children, claiming that such images can be seen throughout the most popular media, including TV, magazines, advertising, music videos and the internet (www. homeoffice.gov.uk/documents/Sexualisation-young-people.pdf). The world of fine art is not exempt, with well-publicised police raids on art and photography galleries in many countries.

Censorship of child pornography is total. Despite the best of intentions, this has resulted in problems when parents' photos of their children in the bath are prosecuted, or when demands for censorship extend into mainstream media. In other words, revulsion against child exploitation may result in over-extending the definition of pornography, putting at serious risk not children but their carers. Public debate routinely defers to medical and psychological experts, the very group with most to gain from pathologising the population. Hence, child pornography – and paedophiles – are suddenly seen everywhere, legislation errs on the safe side, and editors even safer. Thus, role-play and computer animations are banned as if they were directly abusive of real children. Possession of such material attracts lengthy prison sentences. Paedophiles are fair game in the tabloid press; a populist lynch-mentality attracts formal political support, and law-enforcement agencies feel free to entrap certain types of person, using role-playing police officers as *agents provocateurs*. Draconian censorship initiatives are justified on the grounds that everyone is against child abuse.

Censorship is thus a vital and flexible tool in the contemporary armoury of social surveillance for the production of self-monitored decency among the general population. We are encouraged to police our own looking. In the process, popular commitment to freedom of expression is eroded, as psych-complex activists, often with collusion from the very media they criticise, seek to ban 'raunchy' or 'sexualised' girls' magazines, lad mags, advertising, music videos and the like in the name of childhood innocence. Jurisdictions around the world try to extend censorship to the internet, even though much of its content falls beyond the national reach of their regulatory remit. Meanwhile, censorship of slow-process media like movies and publications continues, providing models for attempts to censor the internet, which brings the private (moral) and public (political/security) aspects of censorship back within the same frame.

Censorship *classification* systems have a remarkable longevity, going back 100 years when they were first introduced for film, and back to

1643 for printed materials (in the United Kingdom). The two best-known film systems are the British, known as T. P. O'Connor's 43 Rules, which was introduced in 1916 (www.sbbfc.co.uk/history/1912_1949), and the 1930 American Hayes Code (Jeff and Simmons, 1990: 283–6). Such systems are a revealing expression of the fears of the ruling elite at a given time, from which a later generation does not require protection, for instance:

- *United Kingdom:* prohibition of depictions of the 'relations of capital and labour', ridicule of 'British officers in India', and depictions of 'race suicide';
- *USA:* the use of liquor in American life, miscegenation (interracial marriage), 'white slavery' and 'profanity', including the use of the word 'Gawd'.

Obviously such pernicious nonsense (prohibition, that is) has to be revised to maintain credibility, but the systems themselves persist for generations. Despite their evident ties to a bygone era, many prohibited subjects have carried over into contemporary media, especially an overall caution about showing even consensual sexual relations, whereas violence remains routine.

Community values cannot be the same now as they were in 1916, but the language of classification and prohibition may be reproduced from one code to the next. The Australian Government plans to 'filter' internet content by censoring a list of websites showing material that under film or magazine codes would be 'Refused Classification' (and therefore prohibited from distribution). The legislation simply recycles existing wording from film censorship, refusing classification to online materials that:

> describe or depict in a way that is likely to cause offence to a reasonable adult, a person who is, or appears to be, a child under 18 (whether the person is engaged in sexual activity or not).

This definition is not developed from the actual principles said to underlie it (causing offence to a reasonable adult), even less from the technical realities of an instantaneous medium with a trillion pages, but from a form of words going back to the beginning of film censorship. As a result it will capture material that is not illegal in other contexts (it may have been 'refused classification' on other grounds); and it makes into 'child pornography' material that may not feature children or may not depict sexual behaviour, in other words, where no such crime has been committed. The definition relies on a 'trust me, I'm a doctor' logic, whereby interpretation of what constitutes a child, sexual activity, offence and a reasonable adult is entrusted to anonymous officials – and simultaneously removed from the sphere of personal responsibility among citizens themselves, who are presumably too dangerous to make up their own minds. And yet the regulators' decisions are technically easy to circumvent. Such proposals appeal to popular fears ('community values') among a volatile electorate, and keep censorship as a vital part of the political arsenal of purportedly liberal states seeking to discipline the 'danger' of their own **citizens'** innermost thoughts.

See also: **Media policy, Panopticon, Pornography, Regulation, Violence**

Further reading: Caso and Collins (2008); *Index on Censorship* (journal).

CITIZEN

'Citizenship' is a term of *association* among *strangers*. The term's original link to cities has been lost; as an abstract concept it is effectively a nineteenth-century invention, required to describe associative relations in the rapidly expanding modern nation-state and colonial empire.

Disciplinarily, the concept of citizenship brings with it from *political science* and *history* a focus on the relations between a state and the individual, with connotations of mutual status: rights, duties, conduct, allegiance, obligation, powers and protection. In the study of *communication*, on the other hand, there has been a greater emphasis on the **identity** of the citizen within cultural practices and sense-making systems. But precisely because it is a migrant or inter-discursive term, 'citizenship' cannot choose between *relational status* (mutual obligations) and *individual identity* (personal attributes), but holds these two conceptually distinct features in tension. The result is that the concept can never quite escape from historical contingency (past tense; specific place; documented usage) to become a scientific concept (present tense; generalisable; definitional). At the same time, it is never so completely captured by history that it loses its abstract, universalising potential.

Citizenship is not universal: the very idea of it is refuted in some jurisdictions: e.g. in theocratic states like Saudi Arabia and Iran where sovereignty is said to reside in the deity not the citizen; in Party-controlled ones like China, which recognise 'nationality' not 'citizenship'; and in some philosophies, such as Marxism and feminism, where subjectivity is determined by class or identity not ethno-territorial descent. Indeed, the history of the term's absorption into social science is itself a matter for analysis, because the capture of the concept by science is itself a political or governmental act (Foucault, 1984). The *production* of a seemingly neutral category properly belongs to the *object of study* – i.e. 'regimes of knowledge' in the administration of populations – rather than to the *framework of explanation*.

On the modern evolution of citizenship, T. H. Marshall (1965) proposed three successive stages: *civic* (individual rights); *political* (representative rights); and *social* (the 'welfare state'). Since Marshall's time, the concept has evolved further, with numerous candidates for additional categories, especially **cultural citizenship** (Hartley, 2010).

See also: **Cultural citizenship**

CLASS

Class is a pre-feminist term for naming social distinctions based on hierarchical structures of economic power, status and occupation. People are sorted into groups on the basis of economic factors (income or wealth), but the classes so formed are then made to explain matters external to economics, including values, politics, beliefs and culture.

Pre-modern (feudal) societies sorted people by rank in society based on birth and land tenure. In this universe, 'place' was crucial – both hierarchical (to know one's place) and geographical. People without a connection to a parish were known as vagrants. Their status can be gauged by looking at what happens to Shakespeare's King Lear when he loses his place. In both Rome and medieval Europe, vagrants were non-citizens, and included among them were actors and Jews, who could be harassed accordingly.

The hierarchy of place was overturned by **modernity**, especially the Industrial Revolution and its sweeping social reform. Classes came to refer to the groups produced by their relation to the industrial mode of production. This notion of class was associated with Karl Marx, who identified two new fundamental classes: those who owned the means of production (in capitalist society: the bourgeoisie); and those without capital who owned only their labour power (in industrial society: the proletariat). While Marx's economic analysis has been superseded (economists no longer accept his 'surplus value' theory of growth), his theorisation of the link between the (economic) base and the (ideological) superstructure has remained influential. Marx argued that while both classes were bound by **ideology**, it was the ruling (owning) class who were also the intellectual force in a given epoch. Thus the 'ruling ideas' were those of the ruling class. But at the same time Marx thought that the engine of historical change was provided by a structural antagonism between the fundamental classes, which when acted upon would result in the eventual ascendancy of those whose labour produced wealth – i.e. the organised industrial working class.

Hence the relation of class and ideology was of great importance to those who wanted to speed up history to achieve transformational change. Cultural studies in the Stuart Hall tradition was founded to explain why working people in the older industrial economies were so evidently failing to do the job assigned to their class by history; or, to put it another way: why did the working-class vote Tory? The answer, it was believed, would be found in the way that the 'ideological superstructure' of culture, media, and everyday life was organised by or in the interests of the ruling class. Thus was born the tradition of 'ideology critique', seeking to reveal (or 'demystify') the hidden class interests in popular culture and media.

Max Weber found no reason to dispute Marx's fundamental classes, but argued that the concept could be broken down into subsets that acknowledged status. Managers, intellectuals and journalists (white-collar workers by brain) were privileged over other types of workers (e.g. blue-collar workers by hand) in the skills they could offer the market. In this conception, it is skills and their relation to the market, rather than ownership of the modes of production, that group together individuals. Weber's sociological approach to class allowed for phenomena that Marx's approach did not; especially the dynamism of class mobility and the effect on class of such differences as education, race, and occupation. The sociological conception of class has been modernised by Richard Florida (2002), who argues for the rise of a 'creative class' – 'no-collar' producers of creative value in a globalised, urban, networked knowledge economy.

Class was a major focus of analysis in early 'ideological critique' cultural studies, especially in Britain where class distinction remains a popular talking-point. The Birmingham Centre for Contemporary Cultural Studies theorised that spectacular youth cultures were an expression of and 'magical solution' to class-based tensions among white working-class youth. It was not long before the gendered bias of this approach to **subcultures** was critiqued by feminist analysts, who pointed out that class was no guide to the status of women. For instance, women in traditional marriages tended to be classed alongside their spouse, and thus their class could change overnight (e.g. from 'managerial' to 'welfare dependent') if their marriage came to an end. Furthermore, girls' subcultures were organised around other affinities than those of class.

It soon became clear that identity was formed by much more than class determinations – gender, ethnicity, sexuality and many other attributes were put forward as causal forces; and after Foucault knowledge was seen to be just as important as capital in the productivity of power. Cultural and media studies turned towards identity and power rather than class. Thus, while the concept of class continues to have importance in some branches of sociology, its use in cultural and communications studies has faded.

Its decline as an explanatory category has been hastened by the globalisation of the economy, culture and knowledge. In the light of these changes, Frow (1995: 104) has attempted to reassess the usefulness of contemporary class identity and analysis. He argues that class should no longer be understood as dependent on economic structures, rather it is *relational* among the economic, political and ideological (cultural) spheres. This position recognises the place that other subjectivities have in the construction of identity, and displaces the modernist (Marxist) 'grand narrative' of class. Identities based on gender, nation, ethnicity and sexuality are among the petit-narratives that produce the subjectivity of groups of individuals. Contemporary analysis of this kind avoids essentialist claims, recognising not only differences between classes, but also within them.

See also: **Cultural capital**, **Hegemony**, **Ideology**

Further reading: Wright (2005)

CLUSTER

Urban districts with a concentration of one industry or closely related industries. If the resources you require are close at hand, and if there are others doing similar work in your local area who can assist you, then your work will be easier and more productive. If you are surrounded by people attempting to outdo you – competing for sales or attention – you are likely to work harder. The economist Alfred Marshall wrote of 'industrial districts' in 1890. Cutlery was produced in Sheffield, cotton in Manchester and coal in Newcastle (Marshall, 1961). These are clusters. When there is such a critical mass of related industries, educational institutions, government agencies and community associations located in the same place, innovation and productivity are stimulated. The result is greater prosperity. As Michael Porter points out, competitive advantages in a global economy lie increasingly in local things – knowledge, relationships, motivation (Porter, 1999).

Localisation and industry clusters are proliferating in what US federal banker Alan Greenspan described as the 'weightless' **new economy** (*see* **intangibles**). No longer are *raw materials* (coal, steel, cotton) essential to cluster formation. More important now are computing, information, creativity and ideas. The miniature (practically weightless) microchip, creativity, information, research, talent and networks have replaced coal or steel, manual labour and machinery as the components of the majority of clusters (Florida, 2002).

In 1939 two Stanford University students started an electronic measuring device company out of a car garage in Palo Alto. By 1999 their company, Hewlett-Packard, was one in a cluster within the area, now called Silicon Valley. A high number of companies that make personal computers, circuits, software, 3D graphics and that pioneer internet search engine technology can be found there. It is also the home of Stanford University, where many of Silicon Valley's entrepreneurs, ideas and companies were seeded. It is 'an entire environment, or habitat honed for innovation and entrepreneurship' (Lee *et al.*, 2000).

Cluster policy has influenced urban development around the world, where emergent economies like China may hold a competitive advantage in being able to designate and build large-scale and specialised clusters from scratch, rather than relying on the need to re-purpose declining industrial urban areas, which is what many European cites – like Manchester, Sheffield and Newcastle – have been forced to do.

Cluster research has expanded and challenged previous economic theories. New findings on the importance of cooperative relationships between research, private industry and third sector organisations are arising out of cluster research. Although primarily an economic concept, clusters are focusing attention back to place, lifestyle, localism and community. The assumption that 'nations are the salient entities for understanding the structure of economic life' is being disproved at a macro level through globalisation and at the micro level through clusters (Jacobs, 1984: 30).

See also: **Localisation, Globalisation, Creative industries**

CODE

Tacit or underlying *rules of combination* of recognised elements in any communication system, from language to computer code. Code is a term from communication science, which over the years divided into areas that had little to do with each other (*see* **art–science interface**). Sciences based on 'code' include mathematical and computer sciences, e.g. programming, signal processing and cryptography; communication science applied to telecommunications, etc.; and **biotechnology**, where genetic codes have become a major international focus. Across in the humanities, linguistics and semiotics are also founded on the investigation of language codes.

The work of American information theorists led to the idea that communication was a mechanical transfer process, and that code was simply the means by which messages were put in a form appropriate for transmission through a channel. That model was based on telegraphy (Morse code) and telephony, where the code comprised not what was said by the caller, but the electronic form taken by soundwaves through the phone wire. This scientific/mechanical notion of code has driven developments in computing, notably the writing of code for software applications, and in telecommunications (mobiles, G4).

Code was taken up in linguistics, media studies, and semiotics. A pioneer was the Swiss linguistic theorist Saussure (1974), working in the first decade of the twentieth century. He wanted to study language scientifically, but was faced with an almost infinite jumble and variety of actual speech. So he was looking for whatever it was that enabled utterances to be produced – and 'decoded' – in a coherent and systematic form. Listeners needed to be able to understand sounds that they'd never heard in a given combination before, and to overcome the fact that everyone's voice is unique (including accent, intonation, speed, clarity of diction, etc.), so that *physically* the sounds heard are always unique too. The key was 'code': the generative system of rules of combination (grammar) that allowed elements (lexical items like words) to be selected, combined and used to produce new, hitherto unuttered speech. Hearers, sharing the code, 'hear' what the code says rather than merely what the speaker says, so variations can simply be filtered out.

Codes allow both combination and organisation – words chosen from a **paradigm** or list of possible choices can be strung together in a **syntagm** or chain, but that string is itself rule-governed as to its organisation. A standard English sentence requires, at a minimum, a subject, verb and object. You can choose between different words, but the lexical items chosen have to do the right work in the right order. You can say 'I love you'. But you can't say 'You love I' or 'Love you I': they don't mean the same even though the same words are chosen. Proper 'coding' requires attention to the organisation of elements chosen.

Taking that notion a stage further, many socially organised practices can be referred to as a code: there are *a*esthetic codes, *b*ehavioural codes, codes of *c*onduct, *d*ecency codes ... all the way down to *z*ip codes. In each case what is referred to is an established (shared) understanding of what is appropriately associated with what, according to what *rules of choice and chain*. It may be that some of these codes – codes of conduct for example – are so called because of their *codification* into tabular form, in which case the term 'code' derives from *codex* (Latin: tablet, book).

Codes are dynamic and they evolve. In Saussure's terms they are not only *synchronic* (rules for selecting from a given paradigmatic list) but also *diachronic* (codes change over time). This must mean that there is a code for code-change (*see* **evolution**). Thus codes are hierarchically organised, whereby some operate at the 'macro' level (rules for changing the rules), while other operate at the micro level ('i before e except after c').

The hierarchy of codes extends beyond spoken and written language to cultural codes (customary and creative behaviour), social codes (institutional or organisational behaviour) and historical or contextual codes (codes of knowledge and discourse peculiar to an epoch); again, at both micro (individual) and macro (population-wide) ends of the scale. Cultural studies and computer science may be re-converging in complexity studies, which seek to model the way codes work, using simple models and large-scale computing power to experiment with rules that allow sustainable competition and growth in certain relationships – trading, for instance (Beinhocker, 2006).

COMMUNICATION

Meaning-generating interaction between two systems or organisms by means of mutually recognised signals. Communication enjoyed great vogue in the mid to late twentieth century as a 'master discipline'. Since it was an aspect of virtually all human and quite a bit of non-human activity, it seemed appropriate for an academic discipline founded in its name to harbour similar ambitions. So the study of communication began to assume some of the mantle of philosophy, seeking to explain humanity to itself and link it to the non-human environment. Numerous strands of otherwise disconnected thought contributed to this process:

- From European *structural linguistics* and Russian formalism came the idea that there were fundamental structures underlying *all* human language. Attempts were made to theorise how signifying elements were combined *in general*, not just in a given language (Saussure). Such an approach to language was soon extended to other 'signifying systems', such as literature (Jakobson and the Russian formalists), the narrative structures of folk tales and narrative cinema, etc. (Propp, Todorov), and thence to culture in general – the 'universe of the mind' (Lotman).

- Meanwhile, American *comparative linguistics*, under the influence of Benjamin Lee Whorf and Edmund Sapir, proposed the notion of 'linguistic relativity', suggesting that language organised perception, and different languages organised it differently. Thus, reality was a *product* of how communicative systems ordered the world. Different cultures – Hopi Indians compared with 'standard average Europeans', for instance – therefore experienced different realities, it was argued.

- The French *structural anthropologist* Claude Lévi Strauss connected communication with two other fundamental aspects of culture – marriage and money – suggesting that the *circulation* of signs (in language and art), women (in kinship systems) and money (in the economy) revealed fundamentally similar structures (or **codes**), which Lévi Strauss believed revealed universals of the human mind.

- American *social-science* empirical research into the micro-processes of modern life brought communication into the purview of formal study for the first time. It concentrated on the practical details of how mass society communicated with itself, starting with the unresolvable problem that such a society comprises masses who are anonymous to each other and to commercial and political elites, but who are constitutionally and commercially sovereign as citizens and consumers. In such a paradoxical situation, *mass communication* became of strategic importance, especially the role of advertising (Vance Packard), journalism, PR and political propaganda (Michael Schudson). The **effects** of 'mass' entertainment on unknowable but sovereign individuals were also seen as a big issue.

- It followed that *business* needed communication, the more scientific (i.e. using easily replicated methods to produce findings that were generalisable across large populations), the better. Consumer optimism and behaviour, maximised by the most scientific means possible, were key to the rise and continuing success of the post-Second World War economic boom in the USA, Japan and Europe. Schools of Communication in the USA, founded on the need to train citizens in the public arts of **rhetorical** persuasion so as to democratise the public life of the Republic, prospered as they added media, PR, journalism and advertising to their repertoire.

- The Canadian literary historian *Marshall McLuhan* (1962, 1964), combining his own discipline with cognitive psychology and the communication philosophy of Harold Innes, was also influential in the exorbitation of communication. His aphoristic style appealed not only to many academics, but to people in the business community too, including those in the industries McLuhan seemed to be putting at the centre of the human condition – the media, advertising and television.

- But on the dark side, *governments* were interfering in communication in a big way. Contending ideologies were never more seriously at odds, both in the Cold War's 'mutually assured destruction', and in national liberation struggles from Africa to Vietnam. A serious understanding of how communication worked in practice within and between militarily formidable states seemed timely.

- Raymond Williams (1968) and others, including Herbert Marcuse and Hans Magnus Enzensberger (1970), brought to communications a *critical* perspective that – whatever the virtue of the argument advanced by any one theorist – ensured an important and permanent place for communication on the intellectual and academic agenda.

- Communication *science* gained ground enormously after the Second World War, when inventions ranging from radar to the 'Enigma' code-breaker had shown how important information was in warfare. The invention and commercialisation of computers took that national-military energy and redirected it both to business/government and to imaginative ends. That is, both the IBM 360-50s and 360-65s that sent humanity to the moon and safely back, and Stanley Kubrick's not-so-imaginary red-shifted computer 'Hal' ('IBM' minus one letter of the alphabet spells 'HAL') in *2001: A Space Odyssey*, which did not. Science had the imagination and the means, it seemed, to cause machine-originated communication to transform human life.

- Communications *technologies* for mass commercial and residential uptake proliferated throughout the twentieth century. Several distinct global industries were sustained by them, including telcos, and the media **content industries.**

These different tendencies swirled around each other through the latter part of the twentieth century, sometimes connecting but never fully integrating. The earlier ambition of finding a unified science of communication in which they might all cohere has not been realised. Instead, communication has reverted to 'small c' status: it's an aspect of incommensurable work done in many specialist areas, as appropriate to their needs.

See also: **Mass communication**

COMMUTATION TEST

Substitution as a check for signification. The commutation test originated in European structural linguistics, e.g. the work of Roman Jakobson (1960), where it described the analytic process of substitution of phonemes in a lexical item to determine at what point changes in sound are associated with changes in meaning; as opposed to occasions where changing a phoneme has no such effect. For instance, changing from the unvoiced plosive /p/to the voiced /b/, e.g. 'pier' to 'bier', does change the meaning; but changing /t/to glottal stop /ʔ/or to /d/, e.g. in 'butter', does not.

In semiotics, the commutation test is an experiment where one element of a given text is substituted for a different element, in order to see how choices within a rule-governed set (from single phonemes to entire genres) change the overall signification or meaning. The test works on the Saussurian principle that signs gain meaningfulness only in contrast to each other in a rule-governed system, rather than by reference to an external object. Thus, the word 'tree' gains meaning by being differentiated from other signs – say, 'bush', 'sapling', 'post' – rather than from any properties of perennial woody plants. Changing 'tree' to 'arbre' [English to French] does not substantially change the meaning; changing 'tree' to 'bush' does. This demonstrates the arbitrary ['arbre/tree'] nature of the sign.

The test was applied by Barthes (1967: 48) to visual media, and by him also to the fashion system (1985). If you think of a given fashion ensemble as a **syntagm** – at its simplest, 'hat + top + skirt/pants + shoes' – the choice of each item occurs within the **paradigm** of that item. Changing one item (say, choosing as a top a T-shirt rather than a jacket; or a market-stall garment rather than Chanel) will change the overall meaning of the ensemble. In fact certain style leaders such as Kate Moss pioneered the combination of street-styles with haute-couture, leading to changes in the fashion system itself (where once

'T-shirt' and 'Chanel' could not have appeared together). Taken together, a syntagmatic ensemble may connote second-order or even ideological meanings: thus, 'baseball cap + T-shirt + jeans + sneakers' (combining the four most popular garments in the world) may signify 'American' or even 'freedom' (for instance when worn by musicians). Applying the commutation test to some of these items, especially the hat (e.g. baseball cap to beret, bowler, or Akubra) may change the overall signification to 'French', 'British', 'Australian', etc., whereas changing others (e.g. sneakers to boots) may not.

Thompson (1978) applied the commutation test to actors in movies (i.e. what difference does it make to have – or not to have – a particular actor in a role? For some roles (e.g. Rick in *Casablanca*) a substitution would make a decisive difference. For others – James Bond, Dr Who, and persistent characters from Batman to King Lear – substitution of different actors may be routine.

The commutation test is good for classroom exercises, for instance in the analysis of advertisements, and in media research where the rhetorical, ideological, or polemical purpose of a given text is under scrutiny. Substitution can often reveal what is significant and what is not. At the level of design, colour is often used to signify colourless commodities like gin or bottled water. The choice between blue and green (the colour of the bottle rather than the contents) becomes the most significant distinctive feature of the product, even though such colours have nothing to do with the actual commodity. At the ideological level, choosing what a model wears in an advertisement is crucial. It can also be politically explosive, as occurred in the 2010 Senate elections in West Virginia, USA, where a campaign ad apparently featuring disgruntled blue-collar voters from that state was revealed instead to have been made using actors from elsewhere, dressed to look 'hicky':

> The casting call listed clothing options including trucker or 'John Deere' hats that are 'not brand new, preferably beat up', as well as jeans, down filled vests and 'Dickie's type jacket with t-shirt underneath'. 'We are going for a "Hicky" Blue Collar look', it said. 'These characters are from West Virginia so think coal miner/trucker looks'.
>
> (Associated Press via Google News)

In a sense the ad agency had done its job too well. It chose the *most meaningful* garb for a 'typical West Virginian voter', but the intended signification of the plaid shirts and old caps converted 'authenticity' to 'stereotype' as soon as it was revealed as artifice. Voters could perform a mental 'commutation test' to see how the Republican Party's image of them was far from reality. The Republican Party immediately cancelled the ad.

Further reading: Chandler (2007); www.aber.ac.uk/media/Documents/S4B

COMPLEXITY

Complexity is not just a word in the language to denote *unorganised entanglement*, it is a science: the study of complex adaptive systems, whether these are found in artificial, human or natural systems. A leading research centre in this field is the Santa Fe Institute (founded in 1984), whose website hints at the ambition motivating complexity science: 'if we understand the fundamental principles of organization, we will gain insight into the functioning of cells in biology, firms in economics, and magnets in physics' (www.santafe.edu). Hence complexity science is necessarily profoundly interdisciplinary, linking physical, biological and social sciences. It relies to a large extent on computational methods and mathematical theory to show the under-lying commonality of certain systems and processes.

The importance of complexity theory for communication, cultural and media studies is that communication and social networks are among the most dynamic and intensively studied such complex dynamic systems. How social networks themselves emerge, self-organise, become reflexive, adapt and change; how they link or do not link with their environment and with other systems, and how agency and creativity within such systems may produce innovation or over-complexity, are all questions of moment not only to mathematicians but also to entrepreneurs. Hence, there is a branch of management science devoted to understanding two different types of complexity – the sort that *adds value* (emergence of the new; innovation) and the sort that *decreases value* (over-complex organisation or control, often called bureaucracy).

Complexity science is itself one of the most dynamic and strongly growing fields of intellectual endeavour (see a 'map' here: www.art-sciencefactory.com/complexity-map_feb09.html). It uses both formal academic procedures and the less formal affordances of the internet (crowd-sourcing, cloud-computing, and online social networks) to address problems that cannot be solved by single-discipline academic specialisation alone. Hence complexity science is having an impact on how academic work itself is conducted, via collaborative programmes built around emergent 'problems' (rather than around traditional 'disciplines' or 'funding bodies').

Further reading: Chouliaraki and Fairclough (2000); Lee (2003)

CONNECTIVITY

Connectivity isn't so much a condition (steady state) as a phase, part of the **convergence** process in the general domain of media and communications technologies that occurred in the advanced econo- mies of the West from the 1980s to 2000s, where computing power, telecommunications and media (previously separate technologies and industries) intersected and integrated with each other. Each phase required a different kind of investment and spawned a different kind of industry uptake, including new industries. The phases are:

- *Infrastructure* – the information technology (IT) revolution in busi- ness, when firms invested in computing power to process informa- tion; and the subsequent extension of information and communications technologies (ICTs) from organisations to resi- dences (think IBM and Microsoft ... 1980s);
- *Connectivity* – the linking of IT to telecommunications networks (think World Wide Web ... 1990s);
- *Content* – the shift from 'information' to 'creativity' and from distinct 'producer/consumer' to 'user' via the use of connected computing networks for making and publishing elaborate mediated audio-visual material (think YouTube, Wikipedia, Facebook, etc. ... 2000s).

One of the big differences between 'media' and 'telecommunica- tions' in the analogue era was that the telecommunications industry worked by seeking universal networks (in principle at least) in which *traffic* was the driver of profit, and where the 'content' of any given message was of no value in itself, whereas the media industry worked by using high-cost restricted channels (broadcasting, publishing, cinemas) to distribute high-value content to 'mass' audiences. The quality and accessibility of telecommunication messages was low but their salience to each individual user was high; the downside of mass media was that 'messages' were one-way and said the same thing to everybody. *Connectivity* was the mechanism that allowed these two systems to leak into each other, such that elaborate, self-made creative content could be 'published' by any user, tailored for the use of any other, in networks that were – again, in principle at least – universal.

Connectivity as a term has been extended metaphorically to describe any society characterised by thick bundles of networked information flow. It foregrounds the aspect of society that ties people together through complex flows of inter-relationship and dependency (Mulgan, 1998). Thus, a city exists in a state of connectivity. People congregate in places where they can meet others who share their values; at other times they travel through places where they may encounter difference (Certeau, 1984). Connectivity is a state of inter-dependence, of links that tie people together in communicative networks and coordinating systems. 'Connectivity' in this context may denote a particular cosmopolitanism, a sense of 'being connected' rather than being constrained by parochialism or regional isolation. Social connectivity is amplified by globalisation, and vice versa.

See also: **Internet, Network society**

CONNOTATION

In Barthes' version of Saussurian semiotics, connotation is 'second-order' **signification**, to be contrasted with first-order signification, which he called **denotation**. Thus, first-order denotation is where a sign signifies its referent, e.g. 'tree' signifies a specific woody perennial; or 'if' (the word) signifies a 'conditional' utterance. The second order of signification occurs when a simple denotative sign is appropriated, as it were, to connote something more abstract – 'tree' may connote 'Nature', as in many paintings; 'if' may connote 'possible futures', as in Kipling's poem or Lindsay Anderson's film *If*. There is also a third order of signification, which Fiske and Hartley (1978) called **myth**, where clusters of second-order connotations are linked syntagmatically to use apparently denotative signs for the purpose of reproducing an **ideology**.

See also: **Denotation, Myth, Signification**

CONSENSUS

Consensus – government by consent of the governed; or decision-making by agreement – is a term much used in the field of political communication, and thence in the study of journalism and political media, where it is often distinguished from its apparent opposite, *coer-*

cion. Both terms derive from the idea that government operates on the basis of **power**, and that power is either exercised directly (coercion) or ceded to the sovereign authority by agreement of the population being governed (consent).

Government by consensus is strongly associated with what Foucault (1984) identified as the 'administration of life' through knowledge-producing bureaucracies such as medical or penal authorities, in contrast to an older (pre-modern) form of government through 'pain of death', where sovereignty is both legitimated and exercised by coercive force over a population's bodily security. Thus, after Foucault, 'consensus' is a form of 'governmentality' where order is achieved by means of learned self-discipline among populations, rather than at the point of the sword. In this it is closely associated with the Gramscian notion of **hegemony**, where power is exercised by a dominant state or social class through social leadership rather than military conquest. In short, 'consensus' does not necessarily suggest the free-will consent of the population, but rather it describes an apparatus in which consent can be said to be 'manufactured' – and one of the chief means for 'producing' consent is said to be the mass media, especially in the form of news, when this is taken to be partisan on behalf of a dominant social class or tendency.

Such 'produced' consensus can operate in democratic as well as authoritarian countries, producing an imagined or mythic 'centre' of society for otherwise disparate and even antagonistic groups. The famous American journalist Walter Lippmann (1922) coined the phrase 'the manufacture of consent' to describe the growth of the public opinion industry in the USA; the term was taken up in an influential book on news media by Herman and Chomsky (1988). In these accounts, the very impartiality or neutrality of news is the means by which a hegemonic group can 'manufacture' a consensus that serves their interests rather than those of the audience.

CONSUMPTION/PRODUCTION

Both consumption and production – which imply each other as relative or comparative concepts (neither makes much sense on its own) – have attracted bodies of scholarly literature and even entire sub-disciplines around themselves, often in strange isolation from one another. Thus, there is a strand of 'production studies' in media studies. It focuses on the industrial production process and the personnel who work in the industry. The work of John T. Caldwell on Hollywood as a production apparatus exemplifies this approach.

Meanwhile – and in another part of the academy – consumption has gained increasing prominence. It focuses on the culture and practices of consumption, especially the consumption of media content via communications technologies. It extends to shopping malls and suburbia as cultural spaces, to ethnographic studies of consumption practices (see the work of Daniel Miller), and to studies of specific types of consumption (tourism, mobile devices, music, etc.). Separately, a branch of behavioural psychology, often working closely with marketing, studies what motivates individual consumer behaviour.

Thus a peculiar fissure has developed and remains between disciplines that study production and those that study consumption. In the context of media, cultural and communication studies, consumption was almost completely neglected in classic political-economy approaches, on the grounds that consumption is an ideological effect of causal processes that can only be explained in the economic domain. If consumption was mentioned at all, it was via a critique of consumerism. In the 1970s, consumption began to attract scholars interested in culture, especially feminist writers who critiqued the implied hierarchy of industrial production as a predominantly male domain and domestic consumption as a feminised one.

Part of the problem early theorists faced was that media consumption was regarded as an *unworthy* activity – and it was overwhelmingly *feminised* into the bargain. Thus, marketing routinely identified the consumer as the 'distracted housewife' – and the duty of communication scholars was to find scientific ways to influence, modify and direct her spending behaviour and choice-making processes at the supermarket shelf. At the same time, consumption of 'trash' or 'pulp' literature was frowned upon by cultural critics, and the media forms singled out for scorn were frequently women's fiction like Mills & Boon, girls' magazines (Angela McRobbie), and media forms most clearly associated with identity formation (sitcoms and TV drama for girls).

The consumption/production pair of terms has undergone radical transformation in the digital era. Hitherto, production was the sphere of industry, populated by firms, and characterised by large-scale manufacturing processes for anonymous mass markets. Consumption, conversely, was the private sphere of the household, often feminised in the guise of the housewife, and characterised by individuated consumption of commodified goods. The reality was never quite this simple, but the implied opposition or polarity between production and consumption has become axiomatic common sense. However, it has been thrown into turmoil in the digital environment, where 'the user' may be a producer and a consumer at the same time. In other words, anyone who uploads content online is a publisher (previously an activity exclusively done by producers); anyone who downloads is a consumer. Thus private individuals are producers; but equally, firms or other organisations are consumers – networked communications erases the industrial distinction associated with factory production, and reinstates a model of causation that is much closer to that of language, which is dialogic, turn-taking, and cumulative, with creativity and productivity shared among speakers (who are also listeners) in the overall performance of a speech act.

Further reading: Trentmann (2006); D. Miller (2008)

CONTENT ANALYSIS

As developed in communication sciences, content analysis measures frequencies of lexical items (i.e. words) in texts, along with other quantifiable measures such as space (press) or time (broadcasting), to make replicable and valid inferences about the themes and context in which such frequencies occur. It is routinely used by researchers interested in how the media represent certain topics, from politics to sexuality. Content analysis is a tricky method to get right, because it is a perfect example of the 'garbage in, garbage out' problem. If you ask stupid questions, your results will be stupid. First of all, then, it is important to ask *yourself* some questions (Krippendorff, 2004):

* Which data are analysed?
* How are they defined?
* What is the population from which they are drawn?
* What is the context relative to which the data are analysed?
* What are the boundaries of the analysis?
* What is the target of the inferences?

In other words, the quality of your findings will depend on how you have isolated what it is that needs counting. More important, whether or not your findings are *descriptive* or *inferential* (Trochim, 2006) will depend on how you set up the analysis. Descriptive statistics simply summarise what you have counted: e.g. when counting representations of swans, we found x occurrences of the colour 'white' and n of the colour 'black'). Inferential statistics are those which entitle you to conclude something about the world beyond the sample: e.g. because we found infinite white swans and zero black ones, we conclude that *all swans are white*. But numbers, even large ones, do not warrant universal claims. This is the famous 'black swan' problem, where repeated observations of white swans (in Western thought, from antiquity onwards) do not warrant the universal claim that 'all swans are white', since at any moment – in this case when the Australian black swan *Cygnus atratus* was discovered by Europeans in 1697 and described scientifically in 1790 – a universal truth can be falsified by a single counter-example.

Phillip Bell extends content analysis to visual images, and warns about the use of 'commonsense social categories, such as "roles" depicted, "settings" shown, gender and age of represented participants in images' (2001: 24). He notes that 'coding categories used in research [are] frequently moralistic and decontextualized' (p. 24). He points out that quantification of conventional images may 'imply that the greater their frequency, the greater their significance' (p. 25). But caution is advised: 'the easy legibility of clichés makes them no more than short-hand, stereotypical elements for most viewers who may not understand them in the way that codes devised by a researcher may imply' (p. 25). Therefore he recommends elaborate training, cross-checking, statistical techniques and other tests to check the reliability of coders. He concludes that content analysis cannot be taken to reflect any reality beyond the content analysed; it cannot be used to determine 'true' or 'false' representations; and 'generalising from content analysis can be difficult' (p. 25).

Central to content analysis is that the method is undertaken systematically, is able to be replicated in other contexts, and may rely on a proprietary computer program such as NU*Dist. Casey *et al.* (2002: 41) argue that one of the advantages of content analysis 'is that it requires adherence to systematic rules and procedures'. Preliminary or diagnostic research using a small pilot sample may be prudent, especially prior to longitudinal trend analysis of content across a large dataset over a number of years with full statistical safeguards.

Even when done well, the classification of content is necessarily open to challenge. This is why Casey *et al.* (2002: 42) note that content analysis 'tends more often to be used as a starting point or in conjunction with other methodologies than as a method standing alone'. Content analysis is reassuringly quantitative, but it is best done in conjunction with both **textual analysis** and audience research to show how the findings about frequency of occurrence connect with the form in which such content is actually experienced by readers and viewers.

See also: **Methodology**

Further reading: Riffe *et al.* (2005)

CONTENT INDUSTRIES

Also known in the USA as the '**copyright** industries'. Businesses based upon the value of intellectual property, trading in intangible, creative, and information-based products. The content industries include, for instance: Advertising, Book Publishing, Cinema, Computer Games, Corporate Communication, Magazines, Music, Newspapers, Online Publishers, Performance, Radio, Software, TV and Video, Theme Parks, Web Design.

It is a commonsensical term rather than analytical concept, with two important flaws. First, it seeks to describe a 'sector' of the economy, but thereby leaves out of account the extent to which content production is embedded in businesses that are not classified as 'content industries' as such, like tourism, government, etc. As a result, the full economic scale of the 'content industries' and the extent of employment in content-making occupations are underestimated if they are regarded as an industry sector. The second flaw is that there are very different types of 'content industry', including both content originators (production companies, creative artists and authors, software and games designers) and content distributors (e.g. broadcasters, publishers, internet service providers, telcos).

See also: **Creative industries**

CONTEXT

Context in communication and media may describe:

- the *discursive surroundings* in which a given utterance or text is encountered; roughly, the genre or register of communication within which it makes sense;
- the *social situatedness* of the communicative event with respect to its participants, e.g. identity, sexuality, class, gender, nationality, age group, or family-setting;
- the *spatio-temporal location* of the utterance itself; or
- the *'definition of the situation'* brought to bear on a communicative event by participants themselves (using 'context-appropriate' language or other signifying system, for instance dress codes).

Thus, you wouldn't dress or speak for an encounter with a judge in a court of law in the same way that you might for one with your peers in a café, for all four reasons above. It follows that context is a strong determinant of meaning in communication.

For some commentators, the study of culture in the contemporary tradition is 'radically contextual' (Grossberg, 1996). Cultural studies is *defined* by its attention to context. This is because cultural studies is primarily interested in identity-formation, social relations, and difference, all of which can be calculated only *in context* – not by reference to universal characteristics. This sets such studies in opposition to positivist social science, especially experimental psychology, which proceeds on the basis of context-free 'methodological individualism'. In this latter environment, people are stripped of their *specificity* and treated as 'subjects' in order to produce generalisable results. But in cultural studies that is itself a political – literally a subjugating – move. Recently, sciences like economics and even the biosciences have become more sensitive to the cultural context of human 'behaviour'.

CONVENTIONS

A term borrowed from literary history, especially the study of drama, where it describes the generic and staging norms of a given period or place. Conventions are those aspects of a cultural form that may safely be taken for granted by the audience while they attend to what pleases them – the characterisations, action and plot of a given story. Thus speaking English is conventional in Anglophone drama, even when the action is set in a time (past or future) when the English language did not exist. People singing to each other in musicals is conventional, albeit rare on the street.

In terms of realism, there is a gradient from 'conventional' to 'naturalistic' or 'transparent'. One generation's 'realistic' may be the next's 'stilted'; and each new popular medium seems more transparent than its predecessor. So screen media (film) seemed more realistic than staged drama or the printed page; live TV was welcomed as more transparent (less artificial) than the movies; and more recently, social network sites seem less 'produced' and controlled than broadcast media. Modernity is characterised by progressively *less* conventional media forms.

Aesthetically, from the form of a poem (or lyric) to the design of a palace (or paper cup), a different anti-conventional impulse seems to be at work. Here the gradient is from 'conventional' to 'avant-garde' or 'original'. The new is preferred over the known. As a result, the term 'conventional' acquires a pejorative connotation, as if only emergent and 'difficult' forms are worthwhile, and established conventions are repetitious. This is a prejudice associated with modernist art-forms, where originality is prized over transparency.

However, from the point of view of 'getting the message across', the apparent 'transparency' of a realistic or naturalistic text is often achieved precisely because of the conventions in which it is couched. From information theory we learn that **redundancy** is vital to communication, so repetition, reinforcement, and recognition – the stuff of conventions – are all necessary for people to make sense of each other and the texts they encounter. And history tells us that new or avant-garde media forms often experience a time-lag before they achieve maximum social impact. It is arguable that a certain degree of conventionality has to be established before revolutionary messages can be heard. In other words, the tension between conventions and their opposites (naturalism, the new, transparency) is a continuing and productive dynamic, not a 'problem' that can be fixed.

Further reading: O'Shaughnessy and Stadler (2009)

CONVERGENCE

The integration of telephony, computing and media (broadcasting) technologies, and thence the integration of the businesses, markets, and social interactions associated with them. Responding to a television programme (broadcasting) through an online (telecommunications) website that measures viewer responses and votes (computing) is a basic form of convergence. Being able to do all of this through the one device is also a result of convergence, which is now characterised by mobility as well as integration – convergence has migrated from the office to the home and thence to the street, or wherever a user happens to be.

The adaptability of digital information has enabled a particular type of industry restructuring. Service industries, including broadcasting and telecommunications, have traditionally operated in domestic markets with industries centred on standardised services delivered to mass markets. These structures have been assumed in policy-making arenas in the past. As convergence linked these traditionally separate industries through digital networks, traditional industry structures were no longer viable. Industries and markets are integrating, as well as technologies, so print, screen and website can now be seen as platforms for the same content-provider. Convergence has resulted in 'transmedia' production.

Some of the possible consequences of these changes involve: networks supporting a range of services, new competition between previously distinct businesses, service innovation with a focus on

customisation and flexibility, the potential for niche markets and a greater scope for international trade in services and goods.

Convergence is causing a number of countries to revisit their communications policies. Because the same content can now be received across once separately regulated media – television, radio and the internet – governments are considering the extent to which **regulation** will need to be rethought to deal with these changes. For instance, the United Kingdom has brought together its formerly separate regulatory bodies for telecommunications, television and radio under one umbrella agency (Ofcom).

Changes brought about by convergence mean that the traditional one-to-many information distribution structures will no longer be preserved because of technological constraints. To continue to receive information from singular, 'closed' or inaccessible sources, without entering into participatory dialogue and production, will be the result of industrial, political or cultural forces rather than technical constraints. Meanwhile, such choices will become more difficult to sustain in a competitive consumer market, as technological affordances put continuing pressure on unconvergent media. Thus, 'the book' is now on a convergent path with iPads, Kindles and e-books.

Further reading: Jenkins (2006a)

CONVERSATION ANALYSIS

The search for patterned regularities in the details of apparently unstructured or spontaneous conversational behaviour. The approach has its roots in a branch of sociology known as ethnomethodology, which was concerned with identifying the fundamental categories and forms of reasoning used by members of society to make sense of their everyday social world. It was part of a continuing reaction in the human and social sciences against ill-considered and over-optimistic uses of quantitative and statistical method.

True to its sociological origins, conversation analysis is interested in verbal interaction primarily as evidence for the situated social order. Practitioners of this approach study conversation as a rich source of observable material on how members of society achieve orderliness in their everyday interactions with each other. They view conversations as jointly constructed, practical accomplishments, and seek to display from the close analysis of transcribed talk the methods adopted by participants in achieving this orderliness – the conversational structures to which participants attend and the interpretative work that they undertake.

In line with this project, conversation analysis has provided detailed accounts of how the taking of turns is managed in conversation and how turns are linked together in coherent ways. Some types of utterance are predictably related to each other in pairs such as *summons* + *answer*, *question* + *answer* or *greeting* + *greeting*, and related pairs such as these provide strong linking formats as part of the sequential organisation of talk.

See also: **Pragmatics**

Further reading: Have (2007); Hutchby and Wooffitt (2008)

COPYRIGHT

Copyright is a form of **intellectual property** covering creative work and providing a legal framework for regulating its dissemination and exploitation. In other words, copyright is the means by which creative work can be commodified and traded. Copyright covers songs, books, artworks and designs, but also less obvious properties such as a star's name or the design of a form.

The 'information age' has brought about new issues in copyright. Not only is information now recognised as a valuable asset (not just a management tool), but also its availability and the means by which we access and order it are undergoing immense change owing to the emergence of new technologies. Digital media allow for perfect and unlimited copying of data, enabling the virtually cost-free replication and distribution of highly desired materials. As a result, some argue that copyright has had its day (see especially Boldrin and Levine, 2002, 2005, 2008; Vaidhyanathan, 2003; Van Schijndel and Smiers, 2005).

The creator of a piece of software may spend significant time and effort to produce a useful application. That software could potentially be freely shared with millions around the world. Or the producer of could claim copyright (i.e. license usage), restricting the ability of others to reproduce the information without paying a fee or incurring legal penalty. There are several issues here:

- Digital information can be reproduced without losing quality in the process. That is, digital information is easier to pirate than previous technologies.
- The benefit of copyright is that it allows the creator of a sought-after information asset to reap a reward for its exploitation. If software or any other creative or inventive information were to be

distributed without such reward opportunities, then many – so it is claimed by intellectual property rights lobbyists – would be discouraged from creating it in the first place.

• However, protecting and restricting the flow of information also presents significant problems. To some extent, information is a public resource. If people cannot gain access to it then their own ability to innovate and produce, or to discuss and debate, will be limited. Business opportunities will be diminished and a 'democratic deficit' will ensue. The 'information commons', where the collective exchange of ideas takes place, can be potentially confined by legalistic protections that deny access to information, especially when copyright is aggressively pursued by big corporations against private individuals or public educational institutions.

The free-software or open-source movement, integral to the development of the internet, was founded on the principle that innovation required collaboration and access to information. If legal or technological measures had been put in place to ensure that code or software could not be used without permission from the creator/owner, then the development of the internet would have been substantially slower. It also may have developed an entirely different character as a result.

Potential profits are often the central motive behind legalistic controls on information. As Boyle (1996) and others have pointed out, large companies have taken advantage of laws intended to assist independent creators to gain a market advantage, with the implication that their 'ownership' becomes so expansive that it restricts the ability of others to create. In fact the information economy is subject to monopolistic tendencies just as the industrial one was. Aggressive law firms can be more hard-line than copyright-holders themselves, finding ways to profit from chasing those who breach licensing conditions that may never have been countenanced by the creator of the work. But at the same time, many argue that the 'copyright industries' or **content industries** that are now so important to the world economy cannot exist without copyright. One proposed partial solution is a two-stage process, where the copyright-holder may enforce their rights on first publication, but subsequent sharing is not impeded. Another solution has been implemented in the form of the Creative Commons movement (Fitzgerald *et al.*, 2007). But it has been argued that copyright in the Western tradition may not suit the economic and cultural circumstances of emergent and developing economies like China (Montgomery, 2011). The future of *innovation* suggests an uncertain future for copyright.

See also: **Analogue/digital distribution, Author, Convergence, Intellectual property**

CREATIVE DESTRUCTION

The process of incessant disruptive renewal associated with economic innovation. 'Creative destruction' is Joseph Schumpeter's term for the restless renewal of capitalism via entrepreneurial risk-taking innovation. It seeks to explain economic activity as a dynamic force for change (rather than as a system seeking equilibrium, as for instance between supply and demand). Thus, 'creative destruction' is the process of transformation associated with innovation. It is 'creative' because it opens up new industries; 'destructive' because it results in the decline of previously dominant firms, often accompanied by severe social disruption in the workforce and cities associated with the 'old order'. For Schumpeter, creative destruction is a defining internal feature of capitalism, not a periodic misfortune. It is thus 'endogenous' to the system of capitalism itself; not an 'external shock':

> The opening up of new markets and the organizational development from the craft shop and factory to such concerns as US Steel illustrate the process of industrial mutation that incessantly revolutionizes the economic structure from within, incessantly destroying the old one, incessantly creating a new one . . . . It must be seen in its role in the perennial gale of creative destruction; it cannot be understood . . . on the hypothesis that there is a perennial lull.
>
> (Schumpeter, 1976)

Applying this notion to culture, Tyler Cowen (2002) argues that while cultural globalisation may diminish differences between societies around the world, it can be argued to have increased diversity within them, by promoting greater cross-cultural trade and richer individual choices: this process is dynamic and disruptive – but it does not have to be seen in apocalyptic terms as the demise of culture, which has always been stimulated by exchange and renewal, rather than by protection and preservation.

However, the radical, progressive and 'emergent' character of 'creative destruction' has been neglected in critical cultural studies, because Schumpeter himself was a conservative economist and his work became associated with 'neoliberal' ideologies associated with Thatcherism-Reaganism. As late as 2010 Rupert Murdoch was still quoting Mrs Thatcher (as if she'd foreseen the Global Financial Crisis) for having said: 'what Schumpeter famously called the "gales of creative destruction" still roar mightily from time to time' (www.cps. org.uk – Search: 'Rupert Murdoch's Inaugural Margaret Thatcher Lecture').

But the political uptake of the idea should not diminish its explanatory power, which foregrounds innovation and entrepreneurial leadership as the driver of economic growth. In other words, rather than seeming to approve of the *destruction*, the term seeks to explain *creativity* as the source of emergent ideas.

Further reading: Metcalfe (1998)

CREATIVE INDUSTRIES

Since the emergence of the concept in the 1990s, three different models of the creative industries can be identified. Each phase has supplemented – not supplanted – the one that went before, so that while the three types may have come into economic and analytical prominence one after another, they are all present simultaneously in various states of development.

CI-1: Creative clusters (industry) – closed expert system

- *Industry* definition – the original UK usage of the term (Culture, Media and Sport, 2001).
- 'Creative clusters' of different 'industry sectors' – advertising, architecture, publishing, software, performing arts, media production, art, design, fashion, etc. – that together produce creative works or *outputs*.
- 'Provider-led' or supply-based definition.
- The sector is reckoned to be anywhere between 3 and 8 per cent of advanced economies (United Kingdom, USA, Australia), also important to emergent economies (e.g. China, Indonesia, Brazil).
- High-growth.
- Economic multiplier effect (creative industries stimulate growth in general).

CI-2: Creative services (economy) – closed innovation system

- *Services* definition.
- 'Creative services' – creative *inputs* by creative occupations and

companies (professional designers, producers, performers and writers).

- Creative services expand the creative industries by at least a third, because of creative occupations in other sectors.
- Creative input is high value-added.
- Adds value to the economy as a whole, boosting the innovation of otherwise static sectors (e.g. manufacturing).

CI-3: Creative citizens (culture) – open innovation network

- *Cultural* definition (emergent).
- 'Creative citizens' – population, workforce, consumers, users, and entrepreneurs, artists.
- User-led or demand-side definition.
- The energies of everyone in the system can be harnessed, adding the value of entire social networks and the individual agency of whole populations to the *growth of knowledge*.
- Domain of experimentation and adaptation, where individual agency may have network effects.

The first two models – CI-1 and CI-2 – are based on the **new economy**; CI-3 is based on **culture**. CI-3 extends the idea of the creative industries from firms to the whole population (Shirky, 2008). Everyone's creative potential can be harnessed for **innovation**, which can come from anywhere in the system. Rather than being seen as the output of an industry, creativity becomes a property of complex systems, socially networked relations, and the interaction of cultural and economic activities. Furthermore, social networks themselves are sources of innovation; they are not simply distribution media. The policy emphasis shifts from **copyright** (CI-1) to *innovation* (CI-2 and CI-3); from **intellectual property** to *emergence*.

The creative *industries* (CI-1) are those that take traditional creative talents in design, performance, production, and writing, combine these with media production and distribution techniques (for scale) and new interactive technologies (for customisation), in order to create and distribute creative content throughout the service sector of the new economy (CI-2). The mode of production is 'Hollywood' not 'Detroit' – project-based and innovative, rather than industrial and standardised. It is characterised by networks and partnerships. Consumers have given way to **users** – interactive partners in further development of the creative product (CI-3).

The creative industries provide content products to the new

knowledge economy (CI-2). It is here that the major social and consumer impact of new interactive media technologies is felt, since audiences are much more interested in content than in technologies as such. The appeal is in the story, sight, song, or speech, not in the carrier-mechanism. This is increasingly true where the potential for 'transmedia' distribution of creative content via the internet and other new interactive communication forms is being realised. In addition, audiences increasingly expect high-tech content, interactivity and customisation in traditional arts, media and entertainment forms.

In this context, creative content is not confined to leisure and entertainment products, but extends to commercial enterprises generally. As the new interactive media technologies evolve from business-to-business to business-to-consumer applications, creative content will be the central requirement, whether the application is for a bank, an educational institution or an entertainment provider, or whether the user is in 'sit-back' or 'sit-up' mode.

Previously distinct industries have rapidly **converged** and integrated. Advances in technology and increases in network performance have created a fertile environment for the incubation and growth of new sectors and the opportunity for existing disciplines to find new commercial applications. For instance, animation and creative writing both find new application in the development of computer **games**, which themselves evolve from one-person to interactive games, with multiple players, via the internet.

The stimulation of the 'intangible' sector (CI-2) relies more than ever on creativity, flair, and risk-taking imagination – on creative enterprises feeding constantly updated new content into technologically advanced knowledge-based industries. But content providers no longer need to be located in metropolitan centres or one of the many 'silicon valleys' to play a global role. Music, animation, design, publishing, interactive media, e-commerce and entertainment are all cottage industries on the creative or supply side, relying on small/medium enterprises (SMEs) and freelance creative talent working via short-lived projects. The need in this context is for interdisciplinary clusters, flexible and highly porous teams, creative enterprises rather than large-scale vertically integrated industries.

The creative industries (CI-1) are a significant sector of the economy. The UK government has identified the following cluster as the creative industries:

- Advertising
- Architecture

- Arts and antiques market
- Crafts
- Design
- Designer fashion
- Film
- Interactive leisure software
- Music
- Performing arts
- Publishing
- Software
- Television and radio

In the United Kingdom these creative industries generated revenues of around £112.5 billion and employed some 1.3 million people in 2001. Exports contributed around £10.3 billion to the balance of trade, and the industries accounted for over 5 per cent of GDP. In 1997–98, output grew by 16 per cent, compared to under 6 per cent for the economy as a whole (Culture, Media and Sport, 2001).

In addition, the following sectors were recognised for their 'close economic relationships' with the creative industries:

- Heritage
- Hospitality
- Museums and galleries
- Sport
- Tourism

It may be argued that the 'creative industries' extend and dissolve ever further into the services sector, and that this entire sector is faced with the challenge of using creative inputs to support core business. Furthermore, entire industries have emerged to support the creative sector, including impresarios, agents, management companies, publicists, events and exhibition managers, and knowledge and cultural entrepreneurs (Leadbeater, 1999).

As **user-created content** or consumer co-created content, and what Henry Jenkins calls 'spreadable' media, have burgeoned since the mid-2000s, CI-3 or 'creative *culture*' has become increasingly important in economic calculations. Industries like games have led the way in showing how users are as much a part of the business plan as are developers, and media platforms based on user-created content (UCC) (OECD, 2007) like YouTube have challenged the dominance of traditional mass media. In CI-3, 'creative citizens' are productive and creative partners in the growth of both economic and cultural value; they are not simply potential consumers or audiences.

Further reading: Anheier and Rajisar (2008); Hartley (2005)

CULTURAL CAPITAL

Cultural 'habits and dispositions' that together compose a resource from which individuals and groups (especially classes) can benefit compared with others. In economics, capital is 'spare money'; more precisely, assets that are available for use in the production of further assets. The word can be extended to factors of production other than money, as long as these are used for further production (wealth creation) not immediate personal consumption. Thus, 'capital goods' (goods used to produce other goods) include factories, machinery, tools and equipment. By extension, 'capital' can be applied to *any* productive 'asset', and so over the years terms such as 'cultural capital', 'social capital', 'intellectual capital' and 'human capital' have become familiar.

The idea of 'cultural' capital therefore needs to be understood in these *productive* terms – it does not simply describe a person or place with culture to spare. It points to the possibility that the 'possession' of certain cultural assets enables certain individuals to prosper more than others in the same circumstances. The classic case, dating from the 1960s when French sociologist Pierre Bourdieu coined the term (Bourdieu and Passeron, 1979), is where educational attainment (school performance) is differentiated according to class. Bourdieu proposed that certain students possessed cultural capital (habits and dispositions gained in the family environment, not at school), from which they were able to 'profit' by achieving consistently better results in competitive examinations compared with students from different social classes, and thence improved life chances through higher education, employment, etc.

The emphasis on class in Bourdieu is important because it suggests that cultural capital, like its economic counterpart, can be monopolised by groups as well as individuals, and it can be transmitted through the generations as a kind of Lamarckian inheritance, as middle- and upper-class families seek to reproduce the conditions for their own continued prosperity. Thus, supposedly neutral or impartial examinations (such as the Oxford/Cambridge University entrance exam) consistently favour class-based candidates, in a two-step transformation of class background to economic advantage, where family background

72

predisposes certain families to opt for private/independent schooling; and the entrance exam disproportionately favours private-school candidates (who know how to play the game). Class difference, encoded in cultural habits and dispositions, is parleyed into economic advantage on a defensibly 'impartial' stage. The theory of cultural capital suggests, then, that culture is intimately caught up in power. Culture, taste, art and education are not *consumed* by those who possess cultural capital, but are themselves productive sources of power in the economic and political domains.

Fiske (1987: 18–19), following a similar path to that of Giroux (1983), attempts to overcome the dystopian nature of Bourdieu's thesis by introducing the term popular cultural capital. Here the idea of culture as a source of resistance is introduced. Fiske argues that this form of capital 'is an accumulation of meanings and pleasures that serves the interests of the subordinate' classes. With 'popular cultural capital', individuals are able to form subjectivities based on an opposition to dominant values or, as he puts it, they find 'power in being different'. For Fiske, television and its traditional genres are symbolic of this process. This populist tone is absent in the work of Bourdieu himself, and subsequent studies that have followed his approach (e.g. Bennett *et al.*, 1999).

See also: **Class**

Further reading: Bourdieu (1984)

CULTURAL CITIZENSHIP

Citizenship is well-established in modern states in three important spheres of life:

- *the civic* – personal liberty; freedom of speech; property rights; access to justice;
- *the political* – freedom of association; rights of representation; the vote; right to hold public office;
- *the social* – education, employment, and welfare rights (Marshall, 1965).

Cultural citizenship is the extension of these notions of citizenship into the cultural sphere of life, especially in relation to (a) voluntary association and affiliation in the domain of *identity*; (b) communities arising from shared symbolic, discursive and mediated *meaning*.

The pursuit of self-organising, reflexive, common purpose among voluntary co-subjects, who learn about each other and about the state of play of their interests through the media, has led some commentators to posit the emergence of *media citizenship* and what Hartley calls *DIY citizenship* (Hartley, 1996, 1999, 2010). This is based on the *use* of popular media by lay audiences for identity-formation, associative relations, and even for periodic actions that reverse 'consumer demand' from a corporate strategy to a popular movement. These 'active audiences' and **fans** use leisure entertainment to inform themselves and to connect with co-subjects. They learn civic virtues (neighbourly comportment and care for the community) from media entertainment. In the very process of consumption of commercial pop culture, 'citizens of media' also act as *producers* of 'imagined communities' – and real associations – that cut across formal citizenship.

'Identity politics' is the arena in which cultural citizenship is contested. It is possible to see a spectrum or gradient of civic, political and social rights that have been won for various types of identity: some are enshrined in law; others are barely recognised. Thus, since the Second World War, the ethnic, racial and linguistic identity of significant minorities within larger states has increasingly been recognised as a basis for civil rights; in some jurisdictions gender and sexual-orientation identities have won similar protection; it is less common to see disability and age-group-related identities in these terms, although there are important activist movements related to both; it is rare indeed to find examples where class or subcultural identity is accorded civic status.

Citizenship theory has experienced a revival in political theory over the last decade in relation to unresolved questions surrounding identity politics and group rights. As Kymlicka and Norman write, 'it is a natural evolution in political discourse because the concept of citizenship seems to integrate the demands of justice and community membership – the central concepts of political philosophy in the 1970s and 1980s respectively' (Kymlicka and Norman, 1994: 352). Furthermore, globalisation has brought into question the nation-state's claim to be the sole provider of citizenship rights, owing to the increasingly global nature of economics, human rights (treaties) and the movement of people across borders for work, exile or refuge. Whether citizenship remains a concept that should be pursued and reconceptualised as a result of the changing political landscape or whether we are experiencing a 'breakdown in citizenship' is a key theoretical problem of our time.

The 'new social movements' of the twentieth century brought increasing demands for rights based on identity and group cultures into the political arena: feminism, gay rights, Indigenous rights and the black civil rights movement in the United States, to name a few. The notion of a unified and homogenous citizenry, dedicated to a singular cultural and political project, was contested. The political community consisted of fragmented, competing and culturally diverse groups. Citizenship had to be conceived within the realities of contemporary democracies: namely that 'the security provided by the authorities cannot just be enjoyed; it must itself be secured, and sometimes against the authorities themselves' (Walzer, 1989: 217). Where democracy comprised a changing cultural landscape under a continual process of negotiation and dispute, citizenship could no longer be seen as the possession of a common culture and heritage.

'Differentiated citizenship', as Young named it, entailed that certain groups be recognised not simply as individual citizens, but as possessing certain rights as a result of their status within a group (Young, 1990). Although as individuals, members of minority groups may possess the same rights as others, they may have less political power. Only by recognising such groups is it possible actively to pursue a diverse and equal society. Claims for Indigenous land rights, quota systems to encourage more women in political or executive positions, or the institution of **multiculturalism** as a government strategy, are legislative concessions to the need for cultural rights.

However, cultural citizenship has not gone without its critics. Some maintain that cultural groups are in a constant state of change owing to political, economic and social forces (Kukathas, 1995). Although people may collectively gather to influence political structures, it is their rights as individuals that must ultimately be protected. To protect the group may be at the expense of those that chose to differentiate themselves from the group. Furthermore, with the complex, shifting terrain of culture and identity, the potential terrain of citizenship theory is becoming potentially limitless. If, as Toby Miller puts it, *cultural citizenship* is 'the right to know and speak', which he adds to political citizenship ('the right to reside and vote') and economic citizenship ('the right to work and prosper') (2006: 35), then it is hard to decide where citizenship differs from humanity in general.

See also: **Media citizenship, Multiculturalism**

CULTURAL SCIENCE

The attempt to align cultural studies with evolutionary theory and complexity theory: http://cultural-science.org.

See also: **Complexity, Evolution, VSR**

CULTURAL STUDIES

Cultural studies is the study of the asymmetric relations between addresser and addressee in modernity, especially via:

* the nexus between *consciousness* and *power*: culture as politics;
* *identity*-formation in modernity: culture as *ordinary* life;
* *mediated* popular entertainment culture: culture as **text**;
* the expansion of *difference*: culture as plural.

Cultural studies developed in the United Kingdom out of Marxism, structuralism and feminism in the intellectual sphere, and from literary, sociological and anthropological studies in the disciplinary domain. It took culture to be the sphere in which class, gender, race and other identity-based and relational inequalities were made meaningful or conscious, and lived through either by resistance (subcultures) or some sort of 'negotiated' accommodation (audiences). Culture understood this way was the terrain on which **hegemony** was struggled for and established.

Clearly this approach to culture differed markedly from that of the traditional literary and art critics for whom culture was the sphere of aesthetics and moral or creative values. Cultural studies sought to account for cultural differences and practices not by reference to intrinsic or eternal values (how good?), but by reference to the overall map of social relations (in whose interests?). The 'subject' of cultural studies was no longer 'the human condition' but 'power'. The shape of cultural studies has been directly influenced by its own struggle to decolonise the concept that had been inherited from literary and art criticism, and to make criticism itself more self-reflexive.

Cultural studies has developed a body of work that attempts to recover and place the cultures of hitherto neglected groups. Initially this entailed attention to the historical development and forms of working-class culture, and analysis of contemporary forms of popular culture and media. Partly in response to the intellectual and political upheavals of the 1960s (which saw rapid developments internationally in structuralism, semiotics, Marxism, feminism) cultural studies entered a period of intensive theoretical work. The aim was to understand how culture (the social production of sense and consciousness) should be specified in itself and in relation to economics (production) and politics (social relations). This required the elaboration of new theoretical models, and the reworking of certain central organising concepts (for example, class, ideology, hegemony, language, subjectivity). Meanwhile, attention at the empirical level was focused on ethnographic and textual studies of those cultural practices and forms that seemed to show how people exploit the available cultural discourses to resist or rework the authority of dominant ideology.

Thereafter, a series of intellectual and political encounters progressively remodelled the shape and direction of cultural studies. Serious dialogues were conducted with feminists (attention to subcultures ignored women); sociologists (problems of method and generalisability); psychoanalytical theorists (identity and subjectivity); anthropologists (ethnographic method); postcolonial and 'subaltern' writers (multiculturalism, the Anglo-American bias of cultural studies); Foucauldians (debates about power); policymakers (the ability of cultural studies to engage in public policy formation); cultural activists (**culture jamming**).

Throughout its short history, cultural studies has been characterised by attention to the politics of both methods of study and academic disciplines. It makes explicit what other academic disciplines often leave implicit – that the production of knowledge is itself a 'ruse to power'.

Further reading: During (2005); Hartley (2003); Lee (2003); Rojek (2007); Turner (2003)

CULTURE

The production, circulation, experience and transformation (over time and space) of meaning (language), identity (consciousness), and relationships (social networks). The sphere of culture can be distinguished from – while at the same time it unifies – the spheres of economics and politics. Culture reproduces not goods but human life; it is the domain where meaning, identity, and relationships are, with the aid of various technologies, established, conducted and transformed.

In many disciplines, culture is associated with *values, beliefs, and ideas*. However, in **cultural studies** these positive but nebulous notions are understood not as things but as the outcome of processes, especially **discursive** practices that are institutionalised and ordered in rule-governed dynamic systems (of which the paradigm example is language), which may range from micro-level everyday routines (where identity is established in relation to class, gender, race, etc.), via intermediate institutions (broadcasters, schools, museums, markets) to large-scale cultural forms (e.g. art, religion, knowledge).

Culture as an analytical concept is **context**-dependent. It will often be possible to use or read the word clearly and uncontroversially: high culture, Welsh culture, youth culture, a cultured person, Chinese culture, working-class culture, intellectual culture; or even, referring back to earlier definitions of 'culture', to mean the breeding of improved stock, a cultured pearl, bacterial culture, agriculture, cultivation of the soil. Although it makes sense in each usage, the sum of all usages does not amount to a coherent concept. Thus the term *culture* is multi-discursive; it can be mobilised in a number of different discourses. It may be the discourse of nationalism, fashion, anthropology, literary criticism, viticulture (wine making), Marxism, feminism, cultural studies, or common sense. In each case, the word's meaning will be determined relationally, or negatively, by its differentiation from others in that discourse; and not positively, by reference to any intrinsic or self-evident or fixed properties.

This is because culture as a concept is historical. Its established senses and uses result from its usage within various **discourses**. It stems, originally, from a purely agricultural root; culture as cultivation of the soil, of plants, culture as tillage. By extension, it encompasses the culture *of* creatures from oysters to bacteria. Cultivation such as this implies not just growth but also deliberate tending of 'natural' stock to transform it into a desired 'cultivar' – a strain with selected, refined or improved characteristics.

Applying all this to people, it is clear that the term offers a fertile metaphor for the cultivation of minds; in particular, the deliberate husbandry of 'natural' capacities to produce perfect rulers. It is not without significance that just this usage of the term roughly coincided with the establishment of the first stage of the modern market economy in Britain – agrarian capitalism in the seventeenth and eighteenth centuries. The production of a strain of men who are not 'naturally' (by divine right of succession) fitted to rule but who are nevertheless powerful, is made sense of by those men themselves and for the benefit of others, by the systematic dissemination of the metaphor of culture. Merchant adventurers turned their capital gains into land; and landowners turned their houses into classical palaces, using 'culture' to signify social leadership.

However, the early hegemony of the aristocratic landowning capitalists and merchant adventurers was subjected by the nineteenth century to the altogether more disruptive development of urban, industrial, commercial capital. No sooner was culture established as a term that referred freely to desirable qualities in leading personages, without reference to plant-breeding, than economic and political changes began to challenge the naturalised right of the cultured aristocracy to rule. Entrepreneurial and imperial capitalism appeared to be no respecter of culture, which seemed to lag behind economic change, instead preserving heritage values and legacy properties. At the same time, the term was denounced by Marx, for whom the culture which meant works of wonder for the rich entailed rags and corruption for the poor; and it was apparently ignored by the capitalist and middle classes alike, who were accused of philistinism by those who valued the established cultural heritage of the day. It was left to the intelligentsia, especially its liberal–conservative, moralist–humanist, literary element, to take up the concept. Here, during the mid-nineteenth century, it began to be honed into quite a precise notion, which is still influential today.

Culture was established, especially by Matthew Arnold and his followers, as the pursuit not of material but of spiritual perfection via the knowledge and practice of 'great' literature, 'fine' art and 'serious' music. Since the goal was perfection not just understanding, and spiritual not material, culture was seen as the training of 'discrimination' and 'appreciation' based on 'responsiveness' to 'the best that has been thought and said in the world'. The cultural critics then strove to prescribe and establish a canon of what exactly could be counted as the 'best'. But such critics also tended to see themselves as an embattled community struggling against the encroachments of material civilisation and scientific technology to preserve the 'sweetness and light' of culture and disseminate it to the benighted denizens of mass society. In such a climate it is not surprising to find that the 'treasures' of culture are assumed to belong to a pre-industrial past and a non-industrial consciousness: Matthew Arnold asserted that the 'wealth' of England (by which he meant the British Empire) comprised 'culture not coal' – spiritual and aesthetic values rather than economic values and trade.

Modern proponents of this concept of culture-as-embattled-perfection have been influential in offering an ideology to highly placed elites in government, administrative, intellectual and even broadcasting circles, within which their *sectional* interests can be represented as *general* interests: 'minority' or 'high' culture is good for *everybody*, even those who have no share in it beyond paying the taxes that support its publicly subsidised continuation despite its manifest 'market failure'.

Early post-Second World War cultural studies sought to decolonise the elitist concept of culture that dispossessed most people, leaving a 'cultured' few and an 'uncultured' majority, pointing to the degree of fit between this division of culture and other social divisions such as those of class, gender and race. The critical discourse of 'excellence' worked not so much to preserve timeless and universal treasures but, much more immediately though less obviously, to translate class and other kinds of social primacy into **cultural capital**. The struggle to dismantle the supremacy of elite, high English culture was championed first by Hoggart (1957) and Williams (1958a). Their initiative was taken up in cultural studies, in which the concept of culture underwent a radical transformation, based not on the intrinsic merits of artworks but on the politics of culture in class-divided societies. Since the late 1960s this class-centric notion of culture has been reworked in terms of Marxist, feminist, queer and multicultural approaches, among others. Culture came to be seen as a determining and not just a determined part of social activity, being the sphere where identity was formed and therefore where identity politics was grounded. Thus culture was seen as a significant sphere for the reproduction of social power inequalities, and a major component of the expanding world economy.

At the same time, the study of culture in academic disciplines began to spill out of its traditional home in departments of anthropology ('traditional' culture) and the 'high' humanities (aesthetic and national cultures). In particular, the study of contemporary popular culture required attention to *technology* (the platform of culture), *social relations* (institutions of culture), and *political economy* (the business of culture). Thus, cultural studies began a long series of interdisciplinary encounters with technology (e.g. information theory), social sciences, and economics; and these fields also developed their own sub-fields, such as the sociology of culture and cultural economics. *Mediated* culture has developed into a distinct multidisciplinary field in its own right, frequently designated as 'media and communications'.

More recently, the natural sciences have taken a renewed interest in culture. In the biosciences, advances in evolutionary approaches such as genomics have spurred interest in the evolutionary and biological bases of culture. In the physical and mathematical sciences the growth of computing power, and digital and online media, has led to the aspiration that cultural choices and behaviour can be modelled and measured using massive-scale data. Thus, cutting-edge research centres like the Santa Fe Institute are working on a 'physics of society', in which culture is treated as a complex open adaptive system.

See also: **Class, Difference, Discourse, Hegemony, Ideology, Language, Nature, Popular, Signification, Structuralism, Subjectivity**

Further reading: Eagleton (2000); Turner (2003); Williams (1981)

CULTURE JAMMING

Anti-corporate activism using contemporary marketing, design and media techniques to propagate countercultural ideologies. Culture jamming often appropriates well-known logos and trademarks to undermine brand images and to draw attention to acts of commercial delinquency, especially in relation to social justice (e.g. sweatshops and child labour) and environmental sustainability (eco-activism). Culture jamming is media-savvy and streetwise, sharing semiotic and cultural values with street theatre, student demonstrations, graffiti art (e.g. Banksy), and pop festivals.

Named 'culture jamming' by San Francisco band Negativland in 1984, but also known as 'guerrilla art' or 'citizens' art', this is high-tech and low-tech interactive media. One strategy to 'unswoosh' the Nike advertising campaign was to change the slogan 'Just Do It' to 'Just Stop It'. A separate attempt to jam Nike saw MIT graduate student, Jonah Paretti, try to take advantage of Nike's offer to personalise shoes by having the company stitch the word 'sweatshop' onto his order of a pair of Nike shoes. Although Nike refused, the email correspondence between Paretti and Nike over the incident was sent to millions of people around the world. Other jams have included changing the Apple logo to a skull and transforming the word Shell to read $hell (with the 'hell' emphasised). Internet hackers redirect visitors to subversive sites. Every year, people in America, Canada, Australia, Japan and Europe participate in 'Buy Nothing Day' in order to highlight their country's over-consumption compared with the third world. In an inversion of shoplifting, zine makers surreptitiously place their zines in between other publications in bookshops in the hope that someone will read what otherwise is unacceptable to the publishing industry.

As these examples highlight, culture jamming is about doing rather than theorising the media. Or as Naomi Klein puts it, culture jamming is 'writing theory on the streets' (Klein, 2000: 284). Adbusters' founder, Kalle Lasn, writes that 'communication professors tell their students everything that's wrong with the global media monopoly, but never a word how to fix it' (Lasn, 2000: 116). Texts on culture jamming are generally 'how-to' guides that celebrate the public's right to utilise public space in order to interfere with corporate messages. They openly assert the audience's engagement with texts, refusing to accept that any medium is a one-way communicative device, adding a whole new dimension to media theory's 'active audience'.

See also: **Anti-globalisation, Internationalisation**

Further reading: Hazen and Winokur (1997); Branwyn (1997), rtmark.com

CULTURE WARS

The name given to politicised debates about the contemporary condition and prospects of Enlightenment concepts of art, truth and reason. The debates circulated within and between academic, intellectual and journalistic domains in the 1980s and 90s, in the USA and other countries such as Australia and the United Kingdom. The culture wars were a form of political ventriloquism, amplified in partisan media, where right-wing vs left-wing agendas were pursued in cultural contexts, politicising history, literary studies, and philosophy, where reality, truth, and reason were said to be undermined by those who introduced 'relativism' into the study of human activity. The latter included **postmodernists**, advocates of political correctness, theorists, **deconstructionists** (i.e. followers of continental rather than empirical philosophy), feminists, **postcolonial** critics and anyone doing media or cultural studies. What was at stake was a shift

from (Hooray!):	*to (Boo!)*:
modern	postmodern
universal	relative
reason	emotion (or else 'irrealism')
production	consumption
imperial	postcolonial
urban	suburban
government	identity
decision–maker	celebrity
public life	private life
men	women
information (or else art)	entertainment
words	pictures
literature	media

The culture wars were a public attempt to think through how such opposites did and should *interact*. The wise observer watched the interaction, and did not seek to choose between the opposites.

CUSTOMISATION

Customisation is a response to increasingly fragmented, specialised niche markets, whereby businesses are replacing old strategies organised around *mass* consumption habits with services aimed at more selective, or *personalised*, buying choices. For instance, where cultural choices such as broadcast media were once limited to only a few channels directed at large audiences, subscription TV and internet programming can be directed at smaller, more specific audiences.

In the media industries, customisation is said to be a result of **convergence**. Instead of buying the paper that everyone else reads, online news service subscribers can now customise what they receive into a 'Daily Me' version of events. This can be seen as an empowering development. It assumes that greater diversity of products and media will be on offer, including new content for once marginalised or excluded groups. However, people can avoid what they don't already like. As a result, *exposure* to the unfamiliar – cultures, ideas and information – may be reduced. This has caused some to regret the passing of standardised mass communication, which forced readers and viewers to see what they didn't choose or desire to see, in news bulletins, etc. However, customisation may simply be a formal recognition of what people do anyway, since no-one reads the whole of a newspaper or watches everything broadcast on TV, and they take away what they want, rather than necessarily accepting what they're told, so 'avoidance' and **aberrant decoding** are structural whether at the supply or the consumption end of the communication chain.

See also: **Convergence**

CYBERCULTURE

The culture of the networked human–computer interface, incorporating gaming, social networking, the blogosphere, and cultural practices associated with internet use. The term owes something to Donna Haraway's (1990) notion of the **cyborg** (the organism–machine as an integrated circuit) which was itself an attempt to shift feminist politics beyond humanist questions of intrinsic or organic identity. Thus, cyberculture is the domain of *system-based* identity-formation, *networked* agency and relationships, and *technological* sense-making practices.

Further reading: Nayer (2010)

CYBERDEMOCRACY

Self-governing virtual communities. Cyberdemocracy is a concept that sees the internet as a technology that has a transformative social influence: participation extends democracy (rule by those involved) either within its own social space or in society at large.

According to Mark Poster, asking what *impact* the internet might have upon the society, culture and politics is to ask the wrong question. The internet is more like Germany (a social space that turns people into Germans) than it is like a hammer (a tool that has an *impact* on nails, but doesn't turn people into hammers) (Poster, 2000: 403). Looking at the internet as a tool, to determine what its effects on democracy are, sees it merely as creating an impact upon the existing social surface. For Poster, this denies the possibility that the internet brings *new social spaces* within which identities and communities can exist; turning people into 'Netizens', in effect.

One of the questions of cyberdemocracy is whether it is a given result of technological development or whether it requires a commitment to developing particular types of forums and networks that are inclusive and constructed with democratic principles in mind (Calabrese and Borchert, 1996). It has been argued that the majority of online forums more accurately resemble either anarchy or dictatorship than democracy (Smith and Kollock, 1999).

As Calabrese and Borchert have pointed out, *instances* of cyberdemocracy have existed and will continue to exist. Whether they are random, institutionalised or commonplace is perhaps 'not what is most important about democracy' (1996: 264). From this angle, cyberdemocracy is not about asserting that cyberspace is *inherently* democratic but that cyberdemocracy can exist where people choose to make it.

See also: **Digital divide**, **Public sphere**

Further reading: Boler (2008); Shane (2004)

CYBERNETICS

Cybernetics is a science of communication concerned with the controlling of information within biological or human-made systems. Its primary focus is the adaptive or self-controlling abilities of systems – from how people perform logic to the possibilities for artificial intelligence or problem-solving (heuristic) computer programming. As such, it is an interdisciplinary pursuit ranging across mathematics, biology, psychology, logic and communications.

Central to the science of cybernetics is the principle of feedback whereby the output is relayed back to modify the input. For example, automatic systems within a car may have sensing devices that change the temperature inside the car according to signals received from the environment. Cybernetics often focuses on intelligent, or human-like behaviour, as well as technological and biological innovation.

See also: **Cyborg**

CYBORG

The image of the cyborg describes a fusion between human and machine, the organic and the technological. Cyborgs exist now in our everyday lives in such forms as artificial limbs, immunisation, pacemakers and internet chat rooms. In all of these technologies the exact point of distinction between the body and the machine is difficult to locate. Culturally, the cyborg allows for the creation of strategic identities in a technologically mediated society.

The cyborg was first invoked in the cultural studies context by Donna Haraway in her 1984 essay *A Manifesto for Cyborgs* (Haraway, 1990). Haraway's concept of the cyborg was a provocation, intended to open up feminist dialogue by moving it beyond the assumption of an organic or natural state of femaleness. In cyborg theory, technology is not seen as a threat but accepted as having merged with the natural to the point where the boundaries are no longer fixed but are instead recognised as constructs and tools of domination that can be shifted and challenged. As a hybrid organism and machine, the cyborg is 'the illegitimate offspring of militarism and patriarchal capitalism', but one which is not faithful to its parent. It takes science and technology beyond a masculinist tradition of progress and breaks down the binaries of culture/nature, civilised/primitive, mind/body. It therefore provides a means to overcome an imposed 'natural' state of being that confines the individual to oppressive power relationships. The cyborg is transformative and **postmodern**, as 'the certainty of what counts as nature – a source of insight and a promise of innocence – is undermined, probably fatally'.

Although Haraway's vision of the cyborg is not restricted to cyber-space, it implies that online expression – through and within tech-nology – will have ramifications for real-world politics and personal identity.

See also: **Art–science interface, Cyberculture, Cyberdemocracy, Virtuality**

Further reading: Kirkup *et al.* (2000)

DECONSTRUCTION

A philosophical–pedagogical procedure that uses language to criticise language's capacity to mean, by finding that the terms upon which texts are founded – especially philosophical texts pretending to reason – undermine what they say. Deconstruction, which was elaborated by continental philosopher Jacques Derrida, became very influential in certain branches of literary criticism in the 1970s and 80s (Culler, 1982, 2003).

The *word* 'deconstruction' has also permeated media and cultural studies, often with very little reference to or understanding of the Derridean enterprise (Lucy, 2003), to refer to the use of textual anal-ysis techniques to reveal hidden ideologies and biases in media texts.

The Shakespearean critic Terence Hawkes (2002) has shown how deconstruction works. He discusses Derrida's (1974) book *Glas* ['Knell'], where the pages are divided into two parallel columns of print, separated by numerous quotations in a different font. On the left, the text is about the philosopher Hegel's 'rational analysis of the concept of the family, the Law and the state', while on the right, the text is about the writer Jean Genet, 'a notorious thief, homosexual and transvestite'. Hawkes comments:

> In *Glas*, one kind of rationality – Hegel's – literally confronts, even glares at, its opposite, that of Genet …. What first appears as a radical disjunction between the two columns turns gradually into a kind of fruitful connection, something that plunges the very notion of 'text' into a revealing crisis, exposing and bringing into question the process of 'smoothing over the joints' in which our production of meaning has such a massive invest-ment.
>
> (2002: 23–4)

Here, deconstruction is literal – the texts Derrida analyses are torn to pieces. But the process is not destructive, in the same way that an anatomical dissection is not destructive of *knowledge*, even though it 'deconstructs' a cadaver that is itself, for this purpose, a text. The very act of reading one kind of reason against its opposite reveals how co-dependent they are, and how caught up in language is 'pure' reason. Hawkes goes on to discuss another such 'text': 'with upholders of reason and law on the one side, and with thieves and subversives on the other, that text – to this day – is called 'Great Britain'. He proceeds to analyse this 'text' by reading it against the grain of its own Shakespearean and historical opposite – Wales.

See also: **Culture wars, Structuralism, Text**

DEIXIS

In language, deixis (adjective = deictic) describes words or expressions that point 'outwards' from the text to the extra-linguistic context. There are three major categories:

- *person deixis*, such as I, you, he/she/it, we, they, me, mine, us, ours, them, theirs;
- *time deixis*, such as now, then, yesterday, today, tomorrow;
- *place deixis*, such as here, there, away, this, that.

Part of the interest of such apparently commonplace items is the way they shift in meaning from context to context by referring to different entities: thus 'I' refers to whoever is speaking at the moment of utterance. This can pose problems during early language development. Children take time to identify the meaning of deictic terms, e.g. saying, 'pick you up, Daddy' instead of 'pick me up, Daddy'. Deixis is also interesting for the way in which it raises crucially important issues about language and meaning. Consideration of deixis terms helps to show how the meaning of many utterances does not reside purely in the words themselves, but depends also upon the **context** in which the words were uttered.

DEMOCRATAINMENT

In commercial democracies, public participation in public affairs is increasingly conducted though highly mediated entertainment media and commercial rather than public institutions. Deliberation, debate and even voting are part of an entertainment experience, and not separated out into a separate 'sphere'. The term was coined by Hartley (1999), as an extension to already-identified hybrids such as **infotainment** and **edutainment**. It has been criticised as merely 'demotic' rather than 'democratic' by Turner (2010).

Further reading: Hartley (2008)

DENOTATION

In Saussure–Barthes **semiotics**, denotation is the 'first order' of **signification** – the relation between a *signifier* and its *signified* that generates a denotative **sign**, most readily understood where language is used as a nomenclature that names things external to it: the sign 'fly' *denotes* that thing buzzing irritatingly around my head (while differentiating it from other signs, like 'mozzie'). Denotation is rarely encountered without **connotation** or second-order signification, where a sign ('fly') signifies something more abstract; say, 'summer'; or conversely 'rottenness', depending on context.

See also: **Connotation**

DEREGULATION

Deregulation is the reduction or rejection by government of existing rules (in the form of **regulation**) on both private industry (e.g. media corporations) and public institutions (the BBC, for instance), in order to stimulate competition and efficiency through the removal of bureaucratic and legislative barriers. Deregulation was the political buzz-word of the Reagan–Thatcher era in the 1980s, when free-enterprise foundations commissioned economists to produce studies hostile to regulatory activity and 'targeted the media to be conquered, second only to direct political power itself' (Tunstall, 1986: 12). Since then it has developed into a much more general policy direction for governments of all persuasions.

In the USA, deregulation of the communications industry was justified by technological convergence. As technological barriers between distinct industries began to dissolve, companies were encouraged to diversify their markets in order to increase efficiency and innovation. This in part required a relaxation of antitrust laws (regulation designed to prevent monopolies). It was assumed that competition, rather than regulation, was an appropriate means to overcome market bottlenecks. However, regulation of the marketplace is needed even here, because competition can produce monopolistic concentration (dominant firms buy competitors) and sameness of product (programming of TV networks or news channels), rather than diversity of market choices. Competition through deregulation may also lead to the abandonment of community obligations (e.g. locally sourced content) and public-interest requirements for the benefit of industry profitability.

Recent thinking on effective policymaking seeks to overcome the intellectual stalemate of the pro-market (deregulation) vs pro-public (regulation) positions by looking to responsive policy process that seek cooperation between government regulation, industry self-regulation and community mobilisation. Known as 'the third-way' or 'new progressivism', the intention of such an approach is to foster wealth-creation and innovation through the provision of education, health-care reform and urban regeneration (Giddens, 2000).

As Tunstall has argued, deregulation does not remove an industry from politics or political attention. To deregulate is to release an industry from centralised bureaucratic control, making it subject to commercial interests and the attention of political lobbying. When there are fewer rules, the significance of the rules that remain becomes greater. But, 'the abolition of some rules also makes the surviving rules seem more ambiguous and more vulnerable to alteration or abolition' (Tunstall, 1986: 6).

Deregulation became a political hot potato in the wake of the 2008 Global Financial Crisis, which was said to have occurred because the regulation regime for banks and the financial services industry had proven to fail at the very moment when it should have been most intrusive.

See also: **Globalisation, Privatisation, Regulation**

DIACHRONIC

To study something diachronically (throughout time) is to study it as a dynamic or changing system. The term is associated with Ferdinand de Saussure (1974), whose science of semiotics set up a distinction between studying language as a system of meanings at one moment in time (*synchronic*) and studying changes in the system of meanings from one temporal point to another (*diachronic*). The linguistics of his day (the turn of the twentieth century) was still primarily concerned with historical analysis of the origins of languages; with changes in pronunciation from one period to another; and with tracing changes in the meaning of individual words from their origin in a source language. Saussure regarded these endeavours as fundamentally flawed, because they were atomistic and neglected the interrelated rule-governed components of the system by focusing on isolated elements. The proper historical study of language, for Saussure, depended on initially describing the overall shape of the language, synchronically, before proceeding to the description of its change over time. Thus, for Saussure, synchronic study was logically prior to diachronic. Combining the two would eventually be possible – he called this *panchronic* – but Saussure himself died before he could attempt panchronic linguistics. In this sense, Saussure was not, as has sometimes been assumed, *against* the historical study of language. On the contrary, he was concerned to establish the historical study of language on a sounder footing. However, one effect of his *Course in General Linguistics* (1974, first published 1911) was to re-orientate the whole direction of linguistic research away from the study of historical change and on to the current state of the language, so that historical linguistics has, until recently, suffered a long period of neglect. Diachronic explanations of language have recently been boosted by means of **evolutionary** studies (Pinker, 2003; Deutscher, 2006).

DIALECT

A dialect is a socially or regionally marked variety of a language, made up of distinctive patterns of sentence construction, vocabulary and pronunciation. It is an example of variation within a single language, although dialects can 'speciate' into new languages (e.g. regional Latins into the Romance languages). The use of one dialect rather than another indicates the social class and regional origins of the speaker. Everyone speaks a dialect. The standard UK dialect evolved out of a particular regional dialect of the south-east English Midlands and gained pre-eminence not because of any intrinsic linguistic superiority, but simply because it was the dialect spoken in a part of the country that was influential in the emergence of the modern UK nation-state. Its adoption as the standard form, particularly for written communication, and more recently for broadcasting (as in 'BBC-English'), has led to normative pressure on other regional and class dialects. This gives rise to the mistaken view that the standard dialect is inherently more correct than others – a judgement which is founded in social prestige and status distinctions. From a linguistic viewpoint all dialects are equal, even though a particular dialect can become identified with a particular communicative role.

In some countries the word 'dialect' can be used to refer to completely separate languages, especially where these enjoy lower prestige as a group than a dominant language. Thus in Australia, Aboriginal languages are routinely referred to as 'dialects', even by activists, e.g.: 'Do we know how to say "yes" in any of the 360 Aboriginal dialects in this country?' (Ernie Dingo, Aboriginal actor and Yamatji man. *Koori Mail* No. 469, p. 11: www.creativespirits. info/aboriginalculture/language). Thus there's a politics of dialect, where evaluations based on privileging one variety of language over others contributes to an often unwitting process of reproduction of hierarchies of subordination.

DIALOGIC

A property of all signification, that of being structured as dialogue. The term was coined by Valentin Volosinov (1973, first published 1929) in order to stress the continuous, interactive, generative process of language, as opposed to the Saussurian emphasis on its abstract, structural form. Volosinov argues that all language is expressive of social relations, and hence that every individual utterance is structured as dialogue. That is, the way an utterance is organised by a speaker/ writer is oriented towards an anticipated response in the hearer/reader. Furthermore, once the utterance is received by its addressee, it results in meaning and understanding only through a dialogic interaction with what Volosinov calls 'inner speech' – a kind of internal dialogue that not only renders signals into sense, but simultaneously takes the process further by generating a response that is capable of being uttered as the next turn in the dialogue.

Volosinov argues that this dialogic feature of signification is not tied to speech alone, but characterises all utterances. Even monologues or soliloquies (speech without an addressee) are internally structured as dialogue. The same goes for utterances whose addressees are neither present nor known to the addresser – for example, books and media output.

See also: **Author/ship**, **Multi-accentuality**

DIASPORA

The original Diaspora was worldwide Jewry. The term has lost its capital letter and been generalised in cultural theory to refer to any migrant or cosmopolitan community and experience (Clifford, 1997).

Diasporic communities are groups of people who are distanced from their homeland, as political or economic migrants, or refugees. The experience of exile may be accompanied by a sense of belonging to the former homeland and a continued allegiance to that remembered culture within a host country. For some communities, such as the Iranian community in Los Angeles or the Vietnamese in Melbourne, the homeland is a denied concept owing to its occupation by a regime of which they are not part (Cunningham and Sinclair, 2000). Diasporas are therefore heterogeneous cultures, spatially separated from their place of origin yet living between places in their identity and cultural life. The psychological and cultural experience of diaspora can be one of hybridity, exile, nostalgia, selective adaptation or cultural invention.

The term is useful for moving beyond conceptions of **ethnicity** that depict unitary notions of culture that are contained within national borders. Diasporas present a complex picture of ethnic identity, whereby groups participate in activities that maintain aspects of their homeland within the host country while at the same time participating in the lifestyle and culture of their new home. The experience of diaspora is one of group memory, a desire to preserve and carry the languages, tastes, dress and rituals of home within a new temporary or permanent space. It is therefore a notion of ethnicity that involves the movement of people, and cultures. It is not only a 'looking back' to the past, but the making of new communities and the transformation of traditions, neighbourhoods and cultures.

Only some migrant groups attract the term. It seems that 'diaspora' applies to migrants who have dispersed under some sort of duress, whether military–political or economic. There are said to be Vietnamese and Chinese diasporas throughout the world, but no British or American ones: overseas 'Brits' are called 'expats' (among other things).

Further reading: Naficy (1993); Cunningham and Sinclair (2000); Braziel and Mannur (2003)

DIEGESIS (DIEGETIC), HYPERDIEGESIS

A term describing the total fictive world inside a **narrative**. Aristotle used it to describe how literature was a process of *telling* a story that did not involve *showing* it. The ideal was to tell a story so artfully that the art was not noticed by the audience; everything would appear to be diegetic, or inside the story, not exegesis, or the external explanation of the storytelling. Film theorist Christian Metz developed this definition in his **semiotic** analysis of cinema where he described diegesis as 'the signified of the narrative' (Stam *et al.*, 1992: 38).

Diegesis recognises that **codes** and **conventions** give a film text its meaning, and that these are shared between filmmakers and their audiences. For example, if a character in a film turns on a radio and music is heard, it appears to be part of the character's world in the narrative – the music is diegetic. In contrast, if music is played *over* the action (e.g. the 'soundtrack'), this is a non-diegetic technique. Non-diegetic conventions also include voice-overs, credit sequences, editing, camerawork and those rare occasions when characters directly address the camera.

Diegesis is central to realist representation (everyone stays in-character). But there have been many sophisticated challenges to realist conventions. Baz Luhrmann's *Romeo and Juliet* employs a series of non-diegetic conventions to reinterpret a well-known narrative. The film uses a contemporary soundtrack, an urban setting and radical camera movement, yet retains Shakespearian verse. In this instance, playing with diegetic conventions forms part of the pleasure of the text.

Matt Hills (2002: 137–42) has coined the term 'hyperdiegesis' to refer to 'the creation of a vast and detailed narrative space'. Cult texts tend to be those with 'endlessly deferred hyperdiegesis'. This term can be applied to the extension of the narrative universe into cross-platform or 'transmedia' spaces, including fanvids placed on YouTube, such as those envisioning alternative storylines for cult shows and characters.

See also: **Aesthetics, Fans, Intertexuality, Realism**

DIFFERENCE, DIFFÉRANCE

A concept from linguistic philosophy, specifically the writings of Ferdinand de Saussure and Jacques Derrida, which has become a focus for attempts to understand the fundamental capacity of language and writing to mean. For Saussure, difference is that attribute of the language system (**langue**) that allows its elements to be distinguished from one another and so to **signify** at all. At its simplest, the system of differences operates at the phonemic level, allowing a very restricted number of differentiated sounds (forty-four in English) in various combinations to signify a potentially infinite range of meanings. Working to this exemplary model it is possible to claim that difference is the foundation of meaning.

For Derrida, however, this is only the start of the problem, a start signalled by spelling difference 'incorrectly' – 'différance' (in French, this allows the term to signify both 'to differ' and 'to defer'). Derrida criticises what he calls the *metaphysics of presence* as a recurring theme throughout Western philosophy. This is the ideal (metaphysical) situation in which speech (but not writing) is supposed to yield up to the speaker a pure, transparent correspondence between *sound* and *sense*; i.e. between language and consciousness. In the metaphysics of presence, meaning (thought) is *self-present* in speaking (language). Derrida disagrees. For him, the traditional distinction between speech and writing, privileging speech as somehow original or pure, cannot be sustained. Writing, because of its distance (in space and time) from its source, and because of its capacity for dissimulation, has been a traditional problem for Western philosophy since Plato – an impediment to the desire or craving for language to act as the obedient vehicle for thought. For Derrida, writing is not an impure *'supplement'* but is its *precondition*; the very characteristics of writing that led Saussure (and the phenomenologist Edmund Husserl) to set it apart from speech are those that Derrida finds it impossible to leave out of account. However, it is not his project to replace speech as the model of sense-making with writing; his quarry is the *opposition* speech/writing in linguistic philosophy, and the 'metaphysical' tradition which seeks to arbitrate between the two terms in that opposition.

The notion of *différence* is one that Derrida would certainly refuse to call a concept, key or otherwise – his project is not to settle or to define meanings but to *unsettle* them. It encompasses the post-Saussurian idea of *differing*, adds to it the Derridean idea of *deferring* (postponement of what could be present to another time – an 'absent presence' of meaning), and represents these paradoxical ideas (differing suggests non-identity; deferring suggests sameness albeit postponed, perhaps endlessly) in a word whose startling 'misspelling' can be discerned only through writing (since *différance* is pronounced orally the *same* way as the word from which it differs, *différence*).

Derrida's work was especially influential in the 1970s and early 1980s when the Saussurian terminology of signification was becoming well known. After Derrida, it wasn't possible to claim that signifiers referred to signifieds (an absent presence); on the contrary, signifiers refer only to themselves, and meaning is generated by a differential play of signifiers in an endless, self-referential chain, beyond which it is not possible to go for verification. That is to say, there is no 'experience' or 'reality' beyond signification which can act as a test or warrant of its veracity, for all experience and reality is already a representation in signification. Representation, far from being a duplicitous, textual, tainted 'expression' of otherwise pure thought, is all we've got – perception itself is already a representation, and pure consciousness cannot be 'expressed' since it is the differentiating activity of signification that constitutes consciousness. Finally, it isn't possible any more to claim with confidence that individual subjects 'have' an identity (self-presence, self-knowledge), since identity is a product of difference – of the endless play of signifiers in the (absent) system of language.

Derrida co-wrote the script for postmodernism by positing the world as a text. His philosophy of doubt and radical scepticism led to the '**deconstruction**' movement, especially influential in America (*see* **structuralism**).

Interestingly, there's a 'politics of signification' attached to the very notion of difference. Some would argue that Derridean post-structuralism ends up in an idealist, solipsistic, anti-materialist cul-de-sac, where the materialist contention that social existence determines consciousness is short-circuited, giving a new lease of life to an Alice in Wonderland version of critical practice which allows the world to mean whatever the critic decides. On the other hand, some have argued that Derridean *doubt, scepticism and self-reflexivity* are not *radical* philosophical positions at all, because these qualities have been central planks of Western philosophy since Aristotle and Plato. If so, this makes Derridean practice paradoxically a conservative force in intellectual culture, despite its unsettling implications. Certainly it is rationalist at heart, by no means an emotional or 'Romantic' devotion to textual excess.

See also: **Authorship**, **Binary opposition**, **Culture**, **Deconstruction**, **Discourse**, **Individualism**, **Postmodernism**, **Subjectivity**

Further reading: Culler, (1982, 2003); Lucy (2003)

DIGITAL

The Latin word for finger is digit, associated with counting discontinuous numbers. It is this history of counting (rather than the properties of fingers) that has led to the word being used to refer to binary code – zeroes and ones – the 'digital language' of computers. Digital is contrasted with **analogue** (see next entry) as discontinuous values are distinguished from continuous ones. Thus digital data uses discrete values ('on' vs 'off') while analogue forms use continuous gradients (such as the infinite gradations of hue in the colour spectrum).

DIGITAL/ANALOGUE DISTRIBUTION

Digital technology converts **analogue** or continuous information (e.g. film images) into a binary form (e.g. video disc). The digital language into which analogue information is translated consists of very long strings of discrete 'bits' (short for 'binary digits') of information in the form of 1s (an 'on' state) and 0s (an 'off' state). How a strand of 1s and 0s is arranged (whether it is 01 or 10, 001, etc.), will determine how that information will be decoded, or reconstituted into the appearance of the original. As Nicholas Negroponte explains, 'the world is a very analogue place. From a microscopic point of view, it is not digital at all but continuous. Nothing goes suddenly on or off, turns from black to white, or changes from one state to another without going through a transition' (Negroponte, 1995: 15).

In terms of *distribution*, radio, cinema, and television were developed as analogue technologies (using optical filmstock and radio spectrum); broadcasting is progressively converting to digital signals. Analogue signals are transmitted in a continuous *wave*, whereas digital information is distributed as a **code** to be converted by the reception equipment.

As analogue technology is analogous to the original and digital technology is a conversion of the original into binary language, analogue technology was long held by craftspeople (e.g. photographers and sound-recordists) to be more true to the original, therefore offering a better quality sound or image (this caveat is less commonly heard as digital capture technologies have improved). Analogue technology can, however, suffer from interference, where the wave of impulses may be interrupted by competing signals: hence 'snow' or wobbly reception on analogue TV sets. It also suffers degradation through generations of copying. On the other hand, as digital bits are either 'on' or 'off', they can be received perfectly or not at all, and digital information can be infinitely replicated without loss of quality.

There are economic implications to these technological differences. One is that digital distribution allows for interactivity, and therefore creates new marketing opportunities for media and content industries. Another is that digital distribution puts perfect rather than degraded copies at the disposal of pirates. As analogue copies were never as good as the original, consumers were likely to pay for top-quality goods (legitimate first-generation copies). Digital piracy produces copies of a standard that cannot be differentiated from industry produced goods, resulting in new **copyright** concerns.

The analogue/digital dichotomy may assist in thinking about the social implications of technological change. It includes such contrasts as:

Analogue	Digital
one-to-many	many-to-many
mass	interactive
television	computer
media	telecommunications (and convergence)
centralised	dispersed
standardised	customised
public	private
sit-back	sit-forward
'passive' consumer	active user

See also: **Analogue, Digital, User**

Further reading: Ross (2008); Creeber and Martin (2009)

DIGITAL DIVIDE

The digital divide is the stratification of people according to access to interactive computer-based technologies. The 'divide' is the gap between the information rich and the information poor. Communications technologies interconnect people into networks of ideas, information, e-commerce and communities. Those who are excluded are not able to participate to the same degree in the **network society** or be placed in a position of advantage within its economy.

As Castells writes, the 'speed of technological diffusion is selective, both socially and functionally' (Castells, 1996: 34). The digital divide is the result of strategic flows of information that are not bound by nation-state territories. It can be experienced between two neighbourhoods within the same city, between age groups or between language groups. It can even separate different individuals in the same family or household. Most generally, it distinguishes 'the West' and 'the Rest', but not simply in terms of an opposition between 'haves' and 'have nots'. Instead, a technological distinction has emerged where the West is characterised by high uptake of personal computers, whereas 'the Rest' is characterised by high mobile-device usage.

As with other areas of development theory and practice, strategies for overcoming the digital divide can be contentious. For instance, should information dissemination follow development agencies' goals (e.g. the prevention of the spread of HIV/AIDS), or should develop-ment programmes be looking at ways to empower communities to develop their own agendas and strategies through ICT (information and communications technology) use? If so, who within that commu-nity should be responsible for the allocation of resources and the creation of useful programmes?

The digital divide is important to public policy because an 'under-class' of the digitally excluded or under-connected is not only likely to prove electorally recalcitrant when it comes to supporting 'new economy' initiatives, they are also unavailable as consumers for the burgeoning businesses of e-commerce and new interactive media entertainment. Further, the more that information and electronic interactivity move into centre stage, the more that the digital divide will disenfranchise those not connected, contributing to what has been termed the 'democratic deficit' in modernising societies.

Further reading: Norris (2001); Warschauer (2003)

DIGITAL LITERACY

The use of **digital** (computer-enabled) technologies to access, under-stand, produce and to communicate to others (i.e. to publish) textual, audio-visual and narrative materials as an autonomous means of communication, along with the social technologies (hardware, soft-ware, **codes**, social networks) to make this communication possible. Digital literacy is important because it extends the social base of creative productivity and the cultural/economic impact of creative ideas.

Digital literacy is not simply an individual skill but also a feature of digital systems that allow a communicative relationship to be estab-lished in the first place. Thus, digital literacy is impossible without *both* 'producers' (authors, writers, senders) and 'consumers' (audiences, readers, receivers) – who can *both* 'read' and 'write' (or publish) digi-tally generated and conveyed materials. Thus digital literacy is a feature of large-scale, computer-enabled social networking.

Since the 1950s, the communications and entertainment media have grown to unprecedented power and pervasiveness. They have also extended well beyond print media, first to broadcasting and cinema, then to digital (online and mobile) platforms. The asymmetry between few writers and masses of readers has changed radically in the shift from print to digital literacy, where, in principle, *everyone* is an author, designer, publisher, journalist and media producer.

Now, commentators are remarking on the extent to which users and consumers are leading the way in finding innovative uses for interactive media. Teenagers invented SMS (Short Message Service) texting, users built Linux and the open-source movement, fans make YouTube videos and co-create computer games, whole communities play 'massive multi-user games', citizens practice DIY online journalism, bloggers and other amateurs produce billions of pages of new information and ideas on the web, millions of consumers populate social networks like MySpace, Bebo and Facebook with their own creative content, and we all write the Wikipedia. People are making and sharing their own digital stories. Increasingly, technology is migrating out of organisations and even homes; now we're using mobile devices to 'read and write'. Furthermore, these activities are not only a boost to consumption and entertainment, but they are also at the forefront of innovation.

Richard Hoggart (1957) was ahead of his time in seeking to understand the role of media usage in ordinary life, but the educational climate of the day – still influential now – sought to counter the media's supposed **effects** by imposing institutional control (prohibition) and intellectual critique (pessimism). Now that we can see more clearly how the 'uses of literacy' include creation as well as consumption, the challenge for education is to encourage general access, understanding and creation, enabling emergent uses, so that everyone can benefit from digital literacy, and by their uses of it contribute to the growth of knowledge.

Further reading: Hartley (2009a)

DISCOURSE

A collective noun for regularities in the productive social usage of any **semiotic** system: **language** in meaningful use (adjective = discursive). It is widely used across a number of different disciplines and schools of thought.

In linguistics it refers to verbal utterances of greater magnitude than the sentence. *Discourse analysis* is concerned not only with complex utterances by one speaker, but more frequently with the turn-taking interaction between two or more, and with the linguistic rules and conventions that are taken to be in play and governing such discourses in their given context.

The concept of discourse has also developed out of post-**structuralism** and semiotics. Traditionally, and even now in commonsensical language, meaning was ascribed to objects 'out there' in the world, and to the inner identity and the psychologically motivated intentions of individuals. Structuralists took issue with these assumptions, giving causal primacy not to the intention of the speaker but to the capabilities of the system of **signification** through which such organisms as individuals can make sense of the world and their relations with others.

From this perspective, meaning is an effect of signification, and signification as a property not of the world out there or of individual people, but of language's own internal rules – in effect, 'language speaks us'. It follows that both the world out there and individual consciousness are themselves comprehensible only as *products*, not *sources*, of language/signification. The problem with this conclusion is that it is too free-floating and abstract; it gives the impression that, not only in principle but also in practice, the world and the word can mean whatever you like, a *reductio ad absurdum* that jocular empiricists like to refute by kicking the table to demonstrate its objective reality, independent of language. Of course, taken to either extreme, the question of whether discourse is a producer or effect of 'reality' is bound to get silly; but the structuralists had a point: what counts as reality for humans in the ordinary course of human affairs is thoroughly mediated. But 'language' is too abstract a concept to account for the historical, political and cultural elaboration, differentiation and fixing of certain meanings, and their constant reproduction and circulation via established kinds of speech, forms of representation and media technologies, and in particular institutional settings. This is where the concept of discourse is useful.

Once taken up by structuralism, largely through the writings of Michel Foucault (*see* **power**), the concept of discourse proved useful to represent both a very general theoretical notion and numbers of specific discourses.

The general theoretical notion is that while meaning can be generated only from the **langue** or rule-system of language, and while we can apprehend the world only through language systems, the fact remains that the resources of language-in-general are and always have been subjected to the historical developments and conflicts of social relations. In short, although langue may be abstract, meaning never is. Discourses are the product of social, historical and institutional formations, and meanings are produced by these institutionalised discourses. It follows that the potentially infinite senses any language system is capable of producing are always limited and fixed by the structure of social relations which prevails in a given time and place, and which is itself represented through various discourses.

Thus individuals don't simply learn languages as abstract capabilities. On the contrary, everyone is predated by established discourses in which various subjectivities are represented already – for instance, those of **class**, **gender**, **nation**, **ethnicity**, age, family and individuality. It is to this extent that discourses organise practices in such a way as to provide a sense of naturalistic reality for social beings like humans. We establish and experience our own individuality by 'inhabiting' numbers of such discursive subjectivities (some of which confirm each other; others, however, coexist far from peacefully). The theory of discourse proposes that individuality itself is the site, as it were, on which socially produced and historically established discourses are reproduced and regulated.

Once the general theoretical notion of discourse has been achieved, attention turns to *specific discourses* in which socially established sense is encountered and contested. These range from media discourses like television and news, to institutionalised discourses like medicine, literature and science. Discourses are structured and interrelated; some are more prestigious, legitimated and hence 'more obvious' than others, while there are discourses that have an uphill struggle to win any recognition at all. Thus discourses are caught up in **power** relations. It follows that much of the social sense-making we're subjected to – in the media, at school, in conversation – is the working through of **ideological** struggle between contending discourses. Textual analysis can be employed to follow the moves in this struggle, by showing how particular texts take up elements of different discourses and **articulate** them (that is, 'knit them together').

Further reading: Mills (2004)

DIVERSITY

Recognition of difference in politics, culture and heritage. Early discussions of diversity in the media context concentrated on diversity of ownership of media corporations. The idea, backed up by media **regulation** in many countries, is that multiple viewpoints are preferable to a monopoly of ideas. More recently the idea of diversity has been extended to entire cultures: the rise of **multiculturalism**, postcolonial and **diasporic** theory has led to calls for diversity as a fundamental goal of human endeavour, as well as public policy. It has gained strength by association with the notion of bio-diversity more generally – diversity as a resource similar to **cultural capital**. A politics of diversity has been built on this move, generating calls for diversity in areas of semiotic as well as political representation, for example the call for more actors or cover models from non-white ethnic origins. Diversity has become a major plank underpinning **public service broadcasting** policies.

See also: **Ethnicity, Hegemony, Public sphere, Regulation**

Further reading: Siapera (2010)

DIY CULTURE

The form taken by youth activism and media citizenship in and after the 1990s. Associated with rave and free dance parties, **culture jamming**, eco-protest such as anti-road-building campaigns, and DIY media such as *Squall*, a magazine produced by and for squatters (McKay, 1998). By extension DIY culture referred to new possibilities for self-determination down to the individual level, emancipated from territorial and ethnic boundaries; a kind of voluntarist citizenship based on cultural affiliation rather than obligations to a state or territory (Hartley, 1999).

Interactive media changed the by now traditional relation of mass media, where one centralised (corporate or state) institution communicated *to* many anonymous individuals. But the conceptualisation of that relation had itself evolved. **Mass society theory** posited a passive mass that responded behaviourally to stimuli. Marxist analysis wanted an active, struggling mass, but one that was still oppressed, repressed or otherwise overpowered or 'overdetermined' by the **hegemony** of state and commercial institutions. A variant of that position was Michel de Certeau's notion of 'poaching', suggesting that individuals and citizens took or appropriated their own meanings from within the given structures of power and influence, much as pedestrians make their own way, their own patterns, meanings and uses, out of the streets of a city whose structure and direction they cannot alter (Certeau, 1984).

Meanwhile **ethnographies** of **audiences** for media began to develop a notion of community with internal relations of mutuality, solidarity and action for their various subjects, whether these were studied in terms of social class, gender relations, ethnicity or sexual orientation. With interactive media, customisation and feedback, the concept of the **user** displaced that of the audience. Instead of **culture** determining or even dictating identity, via institutions and obligations people had to live with whether they liked it or not, DIY culture described a more interactive relation between centralised institutions and individual people or groups.

Hartley (1999) extended the concept of DIY culture into this context on the basis of the evolving history of citizenship. Noting that citizenship has been extended progressively (though not always and everywhere successfully) from its modern civic and political roots to include social welfare, then **cultural citizenship**, Hartley proposed that the contemporary period of participatory culture, interactive media, and consumer activism can be characterised as 'DIY citizenship'. Instead of accepting their role as passive media audiences or consumers, people could form or join taste constituencies or communities of affiliation, and produce and regulate their own culture.

See also: **Cultural citizenship, Culture jamming, Democratainment**

EDUTAINMENT

On the model of **infotainment** and **democratainment**, 'edutainment' is a hybrid term to describe the use of media **entertainment** techniques in educational services. The term has some pejorative connotations as part of the 'dumbing down' debate, suggesting that the substance of education was being sacrificed for the sake of ratings. But several truths were lost in that rhetoric.

- First, education itself has always been communicative as well as content-rich: the very term 'education' means 'drawing out' in Latin, referring to the Socratic method of teaching by drawing truth out through dialogue (not shovelling it in via examinable 'facts').
- Second, throughout the mass-broadcasting era, entertainment has had an educative function. Movies, popular newspapers and magazines mastered the technique of conveying information that people weren't otherwise interested in – often straightforwardly educative information about the state of the world, wonders of nature, the human condition, costs and benefits of progress, etc. They have adeptly used appealing visual and verbal techniques, circulation-boosting games and competitions, and attractive personalities, to win viewers, readers and listeners, and to persuade them to attend to things they didn't like.
- Third, education is itself a mass medium, and has been at primary level at least since the nineteenth century. With the advent of life-long learning, even tertiary education aspires not merely to mass

but to universal coverage of the population. It has become impossible not to use these techniques, even where they had been resisted previously. The need for education to take on some of entertainment media's techniques is made manifest in the online environment, where educational initiatives such as TED Talks not only vie successfully with entertainment options but also put 'live' classroom practice in the shade. Here as in other walks of life media creativity and ubiquity act as a spur to more general professionalised delivery. Therefore . . .

- Fourth, once the challenge of universal education was accepted, the 'law' of **aberrant decoding** has kicked in. Educators cannot safely assume any shared **code**, or prior knowledge, among student-audiences. Like the universal entertainment media, they need to deliver texts of high **redundancy** (predictable information), with strong plot lines and characterisation, using charismatic presenters, in order to gather that diverse population within the fold, so to teach them.

The existing entertainment media have long been able to show how good they can be at education when they combine a good topic with a good teacher. In the sphere of cultural criticism, a landmark moment was John Berger's *Ways of Seeing* (1972). Berger's series was in part a response to Lord Kenneth Clark's earlier and widely lauded series *Civilisation*. British TV has maintained an excellent record of edutainment: David Attenborough on all things living; John Romer on archaeology; Howard Goodall's *Big Bang* on music; Patrick Moore on astronomy; Delia Smith on cooking. Colin Thomas's *The Dragon Has Two Tongues* (1985) had two presenters, one a Marxist, the other a cultural conservative, who produced literally a different *Wales* from their contending histories, thereby raising historiographical issues.

More recently there has been a spate of comedians fronting documentaries, sometimes in collaboration with Britain's Open University, often to brilliant effect. Thus the figure of the comedian as teacher is now firmly established in the work of such varied personalities as Stephen Fry, Billy Connolly, Michael Palin, Griff Rhys Jones and others. Dawn French made a documentary that 'delves into the strangely uncharted world of women in comedy'.

In the USA Ken Burns' *Civil War* series created an entire genre of similarly presented narrative, including further series by Burns on Americana topics from *Jazz* to *Baseball*. Australia has a thriving export industry in nature and wildlife documentaries. This form of serious, interesting, entertaining information became the staple of entire channels like Discovery or the History Channel.

The media/education interface has already become very fuzzy. Traditional institutions use media and interactive technologies (video, online, and interactive delivery), and entertaining 'software' (charismatic lectures) to service the learning needs of more students than could ever squeeze into their library. Open and business-related learning were both commercially catered and state supported. Publishers converted their backlists into virtual universities; entrepreneurs standardised learning services for profit. In short, 'education' has merged with 'entertainment' in the name of the democratisation and universalisation of knowledge, via the recasting of education from its 'modern' status as national-state institution to its **postmodern** status as customised learning services for sovereign and borderless consumers.

See also: **Visual culture**

Further reading: Hartley (1999)

EFFECTS

The media effects tradition was the only game in town during the early decades of media research, especially in the USA. Based on social psychology and aspiring to scientific status, the effects model sought to show *causal* links between media content and individual behaviour. It investigated the effects of sexual and **violent** content in popular film and television, comics, or popular music on adolescents, women and other supposedly vulnerable groups.

The effects tradition arises from early communications studies, where **communication** was understood as a linear process. Mass media were thought to stick messages into people much as a hypodermic needle squirts drugs into a body. Thus, producers of media **texts** were thought to inject representations and images into viewers (who had no choice but to take them), and these 'stimuli' were expected directly to influence individuals' behaviour, opinions, attitudes or mind-set.

Research using this model was in two stages. First, researchers literally counted images and representations on TV that were considered worrying – 'violent acts' for instance – using **content analysis**. This established the existence of a problem. Then, second, sample 'subjects' were 'exposed' to the 'stimuli' – they were asked to watch a video tape – and their 'behaviour' was recorded, either directly with galvanometers and the like, or inductively via diary reports and questionnaires.

The 'effect' of 'violence' on 'individuals' could then be measured. The researchers then attempted to link their results to social trends.

The problem with a methodology such as this is that it substituted the experimental situation for reality, and regarded **audiences** as isolated individuals, ignoring factors such as **context**, and personal **ideologies** that viewers negotiate when watching media texts. The fact that energetic adolescent boys seemed more uppity when they'd just seen a TV action show was said to demonstrate that television *causes* violence. Such a conclusion would have been much more convincing had researchers shown that the same 'stimuli' had the same 'effect' on a 'controlled' group of people who were not noted for their propensity for aggression – ministers of religion, for instance. But such work was never done. So there was a good deal of wish-fulfilment in 'effects' research.

Challenges to the assumptions of the effects model began in the 1970s with researchers such as Umberto Eco (1972) and Stuart Hall (1973) setting out to investigate whether single texts offered a variety of readings to differing audiences. Media studies recognised the impossibility of carrying out such a task on individuals and instead choose to instigate projects looking at individuals as members of nominated groups defined by for instance, class, race and gender. Writers like Hall, Fiske (1987), Ang (1985) and Morley (1980) claimed that watching TV was a process of negotiation between the text, a given audience, and the ideologies, beliefs and values they bought to the process. From this research it was argued that audiences could no longer be generalised, or thought of as passive recipients of information; rather they were readers, who accepted, rejected, subverted and negotiated all media texts.

Gauntlett (2008: 33ff.) provides a useful summary of the problems of the effects model. Among others, he suggests that the tradition tackles the problem backwards, with researchers looking at media *images* and tying these into recent deviancies, rather than looking at media *audiences* directly, to see how mediated images operate in their lives. Pertinently he notes that the 'basic question of *why* the media should induce people to imitate its content has never been tackled'.

Government regulatory bodies, interest groups, and sociologists all seemed to be exempt from the effects they saw in others among the population. What was it that made these groups invulnerable? The effects model is a pillar of the expert power–knowledge regime sometimes called the psy-complex. The agenda is to reform both media and society, to render the audience more civilised. Audiences won't know how to do this for themselves, so credentialed experts must filter their viewing materials and modify their behaviour. The 'effects tradition' tells us more about the researchers than it does about the audience, because it is a *ruse to power* by those who seek to exercise 'governmental' control over populations.

See also: **Audience, Content analysis, Discourse, Power, Violence**

Further reading: Gauntlett (2005)

ENTERTAINMENT

A regime of universally intelligible mainstream output from the leisure and content industries. Entertainment seems a commonsense term, but as deployed in contemporary media it comprises a complex condensation of individual gratifications, textual forms and industrial organisation (*see* **edutainment**).

Entertainment's production costs are high, so like other cultural or creative industries it is driven towards **audience** maximisation and the reduction of unit costs. The 'ideology' of such a regime is that these commercial imperatives merely supply the demands of the consumer: the form of entertainment reflects what is wanted. While strenuous efforts are indeed made to keep entertainment products both novel and appealing, it is also the case that those products are organised around an industrial mode of production, typically **mass communication** of standardised content to a consumer who has little input into it. Hence entertainment is not so much an escape from the everyday cares of capitalism, but a highly advanced expression of them.

Further reading: Cooper-Chen (2005)

ETHNIC, ETHNICITY

People's ethnicity denotes their national or racial heritage. Everyone has an ethnicity but that of dominant groups tends to be **ex-nominated**, such that the word 'ethnic' seems to apply to 'others', especially non-white minorities in a given population, whose ethnicity is often parleyed into 'cultural' forms, from cuisine to arts and crafts. If you go into your supermarket you may find lentils on the 'ethnic' shelves while you listen to 'ethnic' music on your earphones. But the term is also found in racial politics, especially in relation to immigration in settler societies. Ethnic groups may use it to strive for political recognition; but in its darkest manifestation, ethnic has become a euphemism for genocide – 'ethnic cleansing'.

Ethnicity, like the cognate (and often interchangeable) term **race**, can be construed as *determining* or causing cultural phenomena, as in the populist statement that 'they are like that because it is in their blood' (Gillespie, 1995: 8). When this is coupled with ideas of otherness, subordination, marginality and foreignness, ethnicity can imply that a person's culture and status are fixed and unavoidable; a natural outcome of their ethnicity, rather than a product of social relations, economic situation, and cultural **context**. Where discourses of ethnicity are **articulated** with those of **nation**, ethnic conflict can ensue (*see* **whiteness**).

Stuart Hall among others began to conceptualise ethnicity as a 'project', not a condition, working discursively and institutionally to position everyone. Part of that project can take the form of policy settings that seek to recognise ethnic **diversity** as part of national identity. Settler countries like Canada, Australia, South Africa, the USA and others have various ethnic forums as part of **multicultural** policy. For instance, since 1980 Australia has had SBS, a dedicated national broadcasting network on free-to-air TV and radio. SBS broadcasts 'ethnic' programming sourced from all over the world – in 68 languages – in order to cater for ethnic groups within the overall population.

See also: **Diaspora, Multiculturalism, Nation, Race**

Further reading: Fenton (2003)

ETHNOGRAPHY

Ethnography is a method of field research that evolved in the discipline of anthropology but has developed independently in media and communication studies. It studies a group 'from the inside'. In anthropology this technique has been used as means of understanding non-Western people's customs, **culture** and means of survival. In communications research, ethnography is concerned with understanding media **audiences** and the uses to which ordinary people put their communication technologies.

There are three main types of audience research:

• *Quantitative* research involves undertaking large-scale surveys with a view to tracing a particular trend or pattern amongst participants (Bourdieu, 1984; Bennett *et al.*, 1999). It is designed to produce generalisable results.

- *Qualitative* research uses in-depth or focus-group interviews to identify people's choices and decision-making processes, often contextualised by **class**, **gender** or age group (Morley, 1986; Morrison, 1998).
- *Ethnographic* research relies on long-contact, immersive interaction between researcher and target audience, often using **participant observation**. It arises directly from anthropological approaches. Various non-contact versions of audience ethnography emerged, starting with Ien Ang (1985), who analysed viewers' letters rather than their natural behaviour. More recently, online ethnography attempts to interact online with online communities (Dicks *et al.*, 2005).

Critics of ethnographic research question its **objectivity** and thus generalisability as a social-science technique. Morrison (1998) calls results that cannot be generalised 'inconsequential'. Researchers involved in participant observation may influence the actions of those that they study, thereby affecting the outcomes of the research. Can participants act or speak 'naturally' in the presence of a researcher? May the participants subconsciously perform the role they believe the researcher wants to see or hear? The immersion of a researcher within a nominated group cannot guarantee an unlimited access to the lived realty of that group, only a 'partial truth' (Clifford, 1986).

There are also concerns over the role of the researcher in ethnography. Whilst the necessary data collection associated with this method is acknowledged in ethnographic accounts, little mention is made of the actual the process of writing. As Clifford (1986: 2) argues, ethnography often 'reflects the persistence of an ideology claiming transparency of representation and immediacy of experience'. This suggests the importance of recognising the researcher's own subjectivity and what it is that they bring to the research. The researcher, much like the group under analysis, will also be subject to ideologies and discourses that impact on the conclusions drawn. For an example see Born (2004), where the ethnographer of BBC culture was clearly more in sympathy with the 'creatives' than with the 'suits'.

A development within ethnographic audience research that sought to avoid the issue of objectivity was the study of **fan** cultures, undertaken by researchers who saw themselves as part of the same group as those they studied (Jenkins, 1992, Brooker, 2002). Here, the researcher makes no claims to objectivity, offering instead an insight from within as well as about a particular group.

Another form of non-objective research is 'participant action research', used in development communication, where the researcher joins with the group being studied to pursue a given social objective, for instance poverty alleviation via ICTs (information and communications technologies) (Tacchi *et al.* 2003).

See also: **Audience, Effects, Methodology, Objectivity, Participant observation**

Further reading: Barker (2008); Seiter (2000)

EVOLUTION

Until very recently, evolutionary theory was *not* a 'key concept' in communication, cultural and media studies, except in the limited sense that some archaeologists and anthropologists used evolutionary approaches to analyse artefacts (and therefore **culture**) from very early Palaeolithic settlements. But new developments from literary studies on the one hand and evolutionary economics on the other have begun to bring this important and powerful concept to bear on the cultural and mediated aspects of human life as well as the biological ones. An exemplary work on the literary side is Brian Boyd's (2009) treatment of stories by Homer and Dr Seuss; see also Gottschall and Wilson (2005). Denis Dutton (2009) has tackled art (and opponents of his point of view) from an evolutionary perspective. Brian Arthur (2009) has developed a convincing account of the evolution of technology. Ellen Dissanayake (2000) has attempted to bring cultural and biological perspectives together in the study of art and music. On the economic side, Eric Beinhocker (2006) brought evolutionary theory and **complexity** science to the attention of the business community, in a book that also explores the relationship between storytelling and inductive reasoning, for executive decision-making. The most active work on the evolutionary economics of culture (specifically, the **creative industries**) is being undertaken by Jason Potts (2011).

Evolutionary approaches focus on the evolutionary process itself (*see* **VSR**). Thus, Brian Arthur argues that new technologies follow a 'combinatorial' evolutionary logic, where each new technology is built out of combinations of existing technologies (think of the history of each component in an aero-engine, for instance) in a series of steps that follow the evolutionary logic of variation, selection and retention. By this process, technology is 'autopoietic' or self-creating. Arthur's model of technological evolution is thus compatible with complexity or **network theory**, which asks how things assemble themselves from interacting elements in a patterned but open-ended way. Here it differs from *reductive* science, which (like Saussurian linguistics) seeks the smallest particle or unit as the causal agent. In complexity theory the focus is on the *system* or network (in biology, the *population*; in culture the **semiosphere**) and how this evolves as a whole. Arthur argues that the economy 'emerges – wells up – from its technologies' (2009: 194). It exists always in 'a perpetual openness of change – in perpetual novelty', a situation of 'messy vitality' (ibid.: 211–13).

As for *the economy*, so for *the mind*: Arthur argues that the evolutionary approach involves 'seeing the mind not as a container for its concepts and habitual thought processes but as something that emerges from these' (ibid.: 193).

Brian Boyd, in *On the Origins of Stories* (2009), tackles the question of how 'the mind' can evolve and 'emerge' from its concepts and habitual processes. Boyd argues that the mind is continuingly re-organised through the repeated practice of storytelling, which is a form of play. **Narrative** is both pleasurable and adaptive. Familiarity with stories like *The Odyssey* and its modern successors creates habitual pathways for certain kinds of thought (inductive reasoning; status signalling; competition for attention; productive deception), and also for signalling pro-social values, behaviours, and relationships throughout a community. The latter are modelled in the actions and character of the hero. Admirable qualities are not only 'adaptive' for individual sexual selection (Odysseus signals his prowess in the face of adversity by regaining crown and queen, and his story attracts competitive emulation), but also for maintaining the *social* cohesion that is necessary for *species* survival (e.g. care for others; deferral of gratification; cunning deployment of knowledge).

Evolutionary approaches to culture are at an early stage, but they have exciting potential because they promise the reconciliation of arts and sciences, as well as a 'model' of creative adaptation that applies equally to art, technology, and the economy.

See also: **Cultural science**, **VSR**

Further reading: Konner (2010); Pinker (2003)

EX-NOMINATION

'Un-naming'. Things that are so obvious they don't need to be named; they're naturalised. The term was coined by Barthes (1973).

In relation to **class**, he showed that the bourgeoisie in France at the time was the 'class that does not want to be named'. Although there were political parties in the National Assembly that supported capitalism, none came straight out with it and called themselves 'The Capitalist Party'. This is **ideology** at work. The process worked towards naturalising existing arrangements of **power**.

The idea of **gender** is certainly one area where ex-nomination still seems relevant. As many have argued, men are rarely nominated or named in many **discourses**. In politics, when women enter parliament, it somehow seems only natural for journalists to report their role as wife/mother as well as politician: 'Dilma Rousseff, a 62-year-old grandmother who was jailed in the 1970s for guerrilla activities, was on Sunday elected Brazil's first female president' (AFP, 2010). But men in such circumstances are ex-nominated as men.

Ex-nomination is normal in discussions of **race** and sexuality. Richard Dyer (1997), while white, notes how other people are raced, 'but we are just people', highlighting the naturalising process that comes with ex-nomination. It is not uncommon for people of colour, be they Asian, Black or Aboriginal, to be nominated by race in police and court reports in the news; white defendants are routinely ex-nominated as white. It is also rare to hear people referred to as heterosexual. Indeed, heterosexuality is the 'sexuality that does not want to be named': the study of sexuality is usually concerned with the 'sexual other', 'defined in relation to normative heterosexuality' (Richardson, 1996: 1).

As these examples demonstrate, ex-nomination works to naturalise discursive practices and to normalise certain categories in contrast to others. The ideological implications of this process are that certain privileged positions in culture are able to present themselves as beyond discourse and outside of the act of naming.

See also: **Identity, Representation, Whiteness**

FANS, FANDOM, FANSHIP

Henry Jenkins (2010) defines fandom as 'the social structures and cultural practices created by the most passionately engaged consumers of mass media properties'.

The study of fans, fandom and fanship in media studies was an offshoot of the 'active **audience**' tradition of media research, which itself originated in sociology as the 'uses and gratifications' tradition associated with Elihu Katz, Jay Blumler and others in the late 1950s.

By the 1970s and 80s, the impact of **semiotics** and **cultural studies** added a new dimension to audience activity – the construction of **meanings**, associated with the work of John Fiske (see Fiske, 1992). It was Fiske's first PhD student, Henry Jenkins, who took that idea a stage further, along with other academics/fans such as Constance Penley and Camille Bacon-Smith, producing the book that established fan studies, *Textual Poachers* (1992). In the United Kingdom the chief exponent of fan studies has been Matt Hills (2002).

Fan studies moved 'active audiences' further out of range of both behaviourism and 'dominant **ideology**', 'preferred readings' and the like, by focusing on what fans and fan communities did for themselves, including conventions, costumes, and re-workings of their favourite shows in **DIY** media like 'zines and on what were then called 'song-tapes', now 'vids'. Fan studies also established a new relationship between researchers and audiences. Not only were they themselves fans of what they studied, but also they maintained an active dialogue with fans, whose voices were respected equally with those of scholars. Early fan studies within media and cultural studies tended to focus on television and movie fandom, often sci-fi and fantasy franchises with a cult following: *Star Trek*, *The X-Files*, *Dr Who*, *The Prisoner*, *Star Wars*, *Batman*, *Twilight* or *Harry Potter*. Feminist fan activism also gathered around literary fiction; and horror, anime and manga were studied from an early stage.

Fans as 'active audiences' cross the line between consumers and producers, most clearly when they produce and circulate their own media versions of their favourite shows or characters in the form of slash fiction. This is a spectacular example of deliberately **aberrant decoding**, where characters' sexual orientation was altered to suit the fan's own, often homoerotic, pleasure (e.g. Spock/Kirk scenarios or, more recently, Snape/Potter encounters). Fan fiction (fanfic), slash fiction and vidding (making tribute or slash videos) began as a kind of **subcultural** activity, not least because of **copyright** restrictions on the re-use of original materials. But it entered the mainstream with the spread of the internet, especially when that was video-enabled around 2005. Video-posting sites are a rich resource for fannish expression of all kinds, both within and beyond self-identified communities of fandom.

Fans have also become prominent in yet another turn of the 'active audience' tradition, by becoming critics and activists in the politics of the internet. Not only do they pursue their own interests in relation to identity, sexuality, and textual pleasure, but they also lead and partici-pate in debates and campaigns about **intellectual property**, the commercialisation of internet platforms, and freedom of online expression. As Jenkins (2010) put it:

> Fans have become some of the sharpest critics of Web 2.0, asking a series of important questions about how these companies operate, how they generate value for their participants, and what expectations participants should have around the content they provide and the social networks they entrust to these companies.

The lines that traditionally distinguish producers, consumers, and critics have all been crossed in fandom.

Further reading: Gray *et al.* (2007); Jenkins (2006b)

FLOW

Flow is the textual means by which broadcasters encourage audiences to 'Stay tuned!' The planned sequence of content, and thus the experience of **audiences**, is of continuity, in contrast to the highly bounded forms of single-text encounters that characterised earlier media forms like theatre (the play) or print (the novel).

The concept of flow was popularised in the writings of Welsh cultural theorist Raymond Williams (1974), but it was originally propounded in 1967 by another literary critic working in Wales, Terence Hawkes (1973: 229–41). Hawkes proposed that the 'television experience' included a mixture of **genres** 'in the same unit' of ephemeral time and in the domestic context of reception. He argued that literary-critical 'detailed analysis of a text' was not appropriate to television. Thus for both Hawkes and Williams the importance of the concept was that it demonstrated the limits of the existing disciplinary methods of analysis when applied to popular media forms. Analysis of single shows could not lead to an understanding of *television*. For that it was necessary to relate the organisation of production and distribution (i.e. the 'planned' bit of 'planned flow') to the family home context of viewing, the experience of consumption and the identity or **subjectivity** of audiences. The 'flow' that they were thought to experience cleared the necessary theoretical ground for a turn away from textual analysis to the subsequent flood of audience **ethnographies** in TV studies. However, ethnography did not support the idea of flow. People don't remember flows; they only remember shows.

'Flow' remained prominent in textual cinema studies. Ellis (1982) determined that the 'smallest signifying unit' of television was the *segment* – which led to the notion of TV as 'segmented flow'. Feuer (1983) argued for a 'dialectic' between segmentation and flow. More recently, John Caldwell has mounted a spirited critique of the concept of flow in his book *Televisuality* (Caldwell, 1995: 158–64; 264). Jeffrey Sconce made a sparky connection between 'flow' and the imagined dangers of modernity: 'fantastic conceptions of media presence' (grounded in a 'metaphysics of electricity') 'have often evoked a series of interrelated metaphors of "flow," suggesting analogies between electricity, consciousness and information' (Sconce, 2000: 7). Ellen Seiter (2000: 119) has suggested that in the hands of commercial and advertising 'programmers' the web resembles television – here 'planned flow' consists in the attempt to 'guide the user through a pre-planned sequence of screens and links'.

FRAMING

The tacit assumptions about what is happening and how we see it, that allow an event or encounter to be perceived (as *this* kind rather than another kind), represented (what gets noticed) and communicated (how it is told as a story). Framing is an anthropological term coined by Erving Goffman (1986), to capture how 'definitions of a situation' are built up from a combination of how the events or encounters themselves are organised and how they are subjectively observed by participants. For Goffman, framing is both universal (humans cannot *not* do it) and tacit ('definitions of the situation' arise in the minutiae of a live encounter; they are not consciously imposed). Because framing is tacit, it is very hard to observe and measure.

The term was taken up in media studies with reference to journalism, where a more controversial aspect emerges: the question of whether journalists deliberately frame events in order to communicate a particular (i.e. biased) 'definition of the situation' that seems to emerge naturally from the event rather than from the journalist's rendition of it into a story. Todd Gitlin (1980: 6) used this definition: 'Frames are principles of selection, emphasis and presentation composed of little tacit theories about what exists, what happens, and what matters'. In the hands of news organisations (both partisan and objective), the 'organisation of experience' can shift from innate anthropological process to corporate ideological selection in the twinkling of an (editorial) eye. An implication of this idea is that journalism is 'innately' biased, since journalists cannot help but use framing to perceive, represent and communicate events and encounters. Some critics go further, assuming that journalists consciously impose certain frames on to events (partisan bias).

Is it possible for journalists to use framing but remain unbiased? This raises the question of the extent to which certain types of expertise comprise the professionalisation of human experience and tacit or implicit knowledge, by making them explicit (as a pop-star does with singing, a model with dressing, a chef with cooking, a tailor with sewing, etc.). Is journalism the professionalisation of framing ('definitions of the situation' plus 'people-watching') by making it conscious, explicit, and procedurally codified? If so, can they be trained to correct for its effects on their discursive practices, minimising ideological drag while maximising communicative accuracy?

FRANKFURT SCHOOL

Nowadays 'Frankfurt School' may apply as a general description of work in a certain tradition of critical theory, although it originally applied to a specific institution, now housed at the New School at NYU (not to be confused with the Frankfurt School of Finance and Management in Germany, which is a university of banking). The principal members of the original Frankfurt School encompassed philosophy, sociology, literary criticism, economics, psychology and political science. Max Horkheimer, Theodore W. Adorno, Walter Benjamin, Erich Fromm, Leo Lowenthal, Herbert Marcuse, Franz Neumann and Friedrich Pollock are considered to be the major contributors, with Jurgen Habermas identified as the School's leading second-generation thinker.

The Institute of Social Research was established in Frankfurt in 1923. The historical importance of this time set the scene for the theoretical direction that the Institute (labelled the Frankfurt School in the 1960s) would take. Lenin was to die a year after the group's formation, signalling the advent of Stalinism in Russia and what was to become a centralist and tyrannical turn in the Russian revolution. The Social Democratic Party in Germany, whilst maintaining Marxist rhetoric, pitted itself against more revolutionary socialist groups. By 1930, the deterministic Marxist belief that socialism was an inevitable progression from capitalism appeared less certain as fascism swept through Germany, Italy and Spain. As Held writes, the rise of Hitler signified 'the end of an era and, for all those committed to the struggle against capitalism, a desperate irony' (Held, 1980: 19).

'Critical theory', the umbrella title for the Frankfurt School's contribution to **cultural studies**, emerged out of the theoretical tradition of Marxism and the critical philosophy of Kant. It was also transformed by the emigration of some of their number to the USA in the wake of the anti-semitic fascist ascendancy in Germany. There, they encountered American **popular culture** and media first hand – and were able to theorise their allergic response accordingly. Adorno, and later Marcuse, became celebrity critics of the 'culture industries' – their own critique to some extent entering the very process of mediated commodification that it criticised. The T-shirt slogan 'Adorno was right' still haunts the American campus (Polan, 2009).

Although critical theory does not present a singular theory or worldview, the school was united in its position that fascism was the result of a crisis in capitalism. Their departure from Marxism lay in the belief that capitalism had developed strategies for avoiding crisis and the possibility of demise through proletariat revolution. The working class, which was to serve as the agents of revolution for Marx, was seen by the critical theorists to be caught up in what they saw as capitalism's tendency towards conformity. Technology, mass production techniques, the commodification of artwork and new class configurations were limiting the opportunities for a disruption of the existing social order. The culture industries – or 'distraction factories' as cinema theorist Kracauer called them – were central to the massification of ideas and the resulting cultural uniformity that left little room for productive political action.

The process of investigation for the Frankfurt school theorists had to be radically different from traditional philosophical idealism. If idealism had failed, as they believed, in unifying separate disciplines through rational order, then the task of philosophy must be 'a process of continuous interpretation'. Interpretation for Adorno involved constructing historical truths out of the text of the social world (Pensky, 1997). Like a multidimensional puzzle, everyday articles, modern art and music, streets, films and dress that appeared to be randomly positioned could simultaneously be seen to make up a clear picture. Their encoded messages, Adorno believed, could be misleading and superficial if read apathetically. In order to see the true picture – and to bring about the dissolution of the puzzle itself – the viewer must necessarily take a step back, engage in continual critique, shattering accepted conceptual systems. This was the task of the critical theorist, intended to release conceptual thought from the repressive confines of scientific reason and to point out the gaps and exists on the pathway to a seemingly unavoidable capitalist type of 'progress'.

Adorno called this approach negative dialectics. Negative dialectics is means of confronting **ideologies** as they manifest in social relations.

This requires recognising that we only grasp the meaning of objects by attaching our own conceptual label to them: our history, knowledge, thoughts, and assumptions. 'Identity thinking' is therefore bringing our generalised conceptions to act as a classifying scheme to new experiences in order to comprehend what would otherwise be unmediated intuition. If we are able to acknowledge the insufficiency of this comprehension, then we are able to view the value of the object as part of a historical process. Only through such 'immanent' criticism can we know its limitations, contradictions and place within the world. Therefore, rather than seeing society as simply an object (as it is understood in positivist science), it is a subject-object: it is both subject and object of knowledge. In order to understand society, we must know its processes, and by doing so we can disclose its contradictions. Although the Frankfurt School theorists differed widely in their approaches, their legacy has become that of the power of critique: 'with criticising ideology and thus helping to create awareness of the possibility of a break with the existing structure of domination' (Held, 1980: 357).

Perhaps the most significant contribution of the Frankfurt School was its lasting extension of politics into new areas of culture and everyday life, although literary critics were doing this too. However, in breaking away from established philosophical schools, and yet offering no clear direction or means to overcome the domination they identified, the Frankfurt School in turn attracted critique, for instance for using an unsatisfactory notion of domination. In portraying mass culture as a means to a type of 'thought control', Adorno and Horkheimer in particular overestimate the deliberate, conspiratorial use of technology to shape attitudes.

See also: **Public sphere**

FREQUENCY (OF COMMUNICATION/MEDIA)

Frequency is a familiar term in relation to **broadcasting**, where it typically describes radio frequency (RF), i.e. the frequency of oscillation of electrical current across the radio spectrum, especially low-to-medium-wave frequencies (e.g. AM radio) and high-to-ultra-high frequencies (shortwave radio, VHF-FM, UHF-TV, mobile-phone, super-HF wireless local-area networks (LANs), microwaves). There are frequencies beyond RF, used for submarine communications (lower) and astronomy (higher).

Hartley (2008) applied the concept of frequency to 'public writing', from stone inscriptions up to electronic media and the internet, where the cycle of creation, circulation and consumption of messages indicates the time-period during which a public text remains in public.

Low-frequency cycles (millennia to decades) convey humanity's most portentous and prestigious messages via temples, tombs and monuments (Thiepval, the Statue of Liberty), classic literature (Shakespeare), canonical art (Leonardo), symphonies (Beethoven), definitive works (dictionaries and encyclopaedias), legal and academic attire (wigs and gowns), the wedding dress. Low-frequency communication is associated with high culture, classical or pre-modern society, public office, belief, myth, religion, stable meanings, stone, public space, and nature.

Mid-frequency cycles (annual to monthly) include books, movies, TV-series, albums, the business suit/dress (annual), scholarly publication and seasonal fashion (quarterly), glossy magazines and specialist periodicals (monthly). Mid-frequency communication is associated with intellectual or public culture, modern society, professional office, knowledge, fiction, science, arguable meanings, the page, social space, and power.

High-frequency cycles (the week to the second) include weekly magazines and serial TV programming, via daily newspapers and the nightly TV news, up to rolling-update subscription-TV formats and instantaneous online publishing. High-frequency communication in other forms includes the single (music), the T-shirt (dress). High-frequency communication is associated with **popular culture**, **postmodern** or **global** society, rumour, gossip, commercial occupations, information, volatile meanings, the screen, private space, and identity.

The spectrum from ultra-low frequency (the revered ruin) to ultra-high (online news) is associated with different communicative forms and thence with different socio-cultural functions, suggesting the *frequency* of publications is as important as their content. Historically, there has been a tendency for **journalism** to increase in frequency. Professionally, people trained in one frequency don't understand people trained in another – e.g. journalists (high) can't 'read' academics (mid) or priests (low).

GAMES (COMPUTER/VIDEO)

Games – beginning in the 1970s as 'video' games, progressing to become known as 'computer' games and now just as 'games' – are a relatively recent mass medium of technological recreational fantasy

entertainment. They are played using TV/computer screens and software, and may be located residentially or in retail arcades. Being of Japanese and Korean origin (Nintendo, Sega, Sony), they represent the first mass medium not invented in the West. The earliest home video game is thought to have been *Pong* launched by Atari in 1972. An electronic table-tennis game, its rudimentary design was superseded at the beginning of the following decade by more graphically sophisticated arcade games such as *Space Invaders* and *Pac-man*.

Games began with a one person vs one machine format, but as soon as technology allowed they became fully interactive, with multiple players linked over the internet. Famous at the outset for 'manga'-style graphics, straightforward martial-arts violence, and the promotion of reflexive skills, games have proliferated in type, diversified their user-base beyond boys, and have become as sophisticated as movies in the graphics and spatial architecture department. Indeed, the movie and games industries are **converging** with movie versions of games like *Tomb Raider* or *Dungeons and Dragons*, and games versions of movies.

It is surprising to note the slow take-off of critical inquiry into this medium, although that has changed now that games command higher global receipts than first-run Hollywood movies. Research began in the early 1980s with psychological studies, undertaken to investigate the **effects** of game-playing on children. Here was a continuation of the very same rhetoric that had greeted the popular press in the nineteenth century, Hollywood in its early days, comics and television in the 1950s, 'video-nasties' in the 1970s and the internet in the 1990s. In other words, games provide evidence that new popular media are greeted with anxiety by control cultures.

Other researchers investigated the relationship between games and **gender**. Some chose to examine the representation of women in games (e.g. Provenzo, 1991). Others were more concerned with the gender-specific nature of the games industry. Games were developed by males for males (Cassell and Jenkins, 1998: 2–45). Here again, the anxiety about access and skills acquisition related to technology rather than to games themselves. And the gender divide in games is no longer so starkly one-sided: women and girls both design and play them.

Like the media they study, media researchers suffer from **rearviewmirrorism**, seeking to explain new media using analytical tools designed for previous ones. Thus, cinema theorists used **narrative** analysis to argue that games have elements in common with literature and film. But as Darley (2000: 160) argues, gaming is about puzzle-solving leading to further spectacle, rather than to narrative closure of the traditional kind. Games are structured around action/

space rather than narrative/time, and around use rather than storytelling.

Some comparisons between games and other media have proven more useful. Fuller and Jenkins (1995) argue that the narratives and playing of games are analogous to the emergence of early science-fiction writing in the late nineteenth century. Both create imaginary spaces for intellectual exploration. Jenkins (2000) argues that the experimentation and innovation provided by games is beginning to reveal itself in cinema. For Jenkins, the multi-directional plotting of *Run Lola Run* and the reality/fantasy binaries of *The Matrix* demonstrate the influence of new games media on older forms of entertainment.

While games were a progression from science-fiction and Tolkienesque-fantasy genres, they are also the descendants of pinball (Darley, 2000: 25). Research into video games as *games* and the role of 'gameplaying' is a recent development. Here, the emphasis is on the activity involved in video games rather than simply the content or aesthetics, linking games research to the study of play. Continuing research in this area suggests new ways of understanding the interactivity between individuals and technology, and the role of play in brain development and thus **evolution** (Konner, 2010).

GATEKEEPER

In **journalism** studies, the gatekeeper refers to key decision-making personnel in the choice of which news stories will be published, with what prominence. Originally, the role was seen to be situated between news-gatherers (journalists) and the public: editors kept the gate, opening or closing it for each story as they decided what information was newsworthy. Recent adaptation of the term has seen it applied to managers of the media, as well as newswire services and owners of media channels. Gatekeepers are thus important agenda-setting agents for public debate in deliberative democracy.

The importance of gatekeeper theory rests on understanding under what conditions these personnel make their decisions. While practitioners see their role as professional, analysts argue that various influences on gatekeepers, including personal **ideologies** and values as well as organisational and structural procedures, will in turn influence their decisions.

While the term is usually applied to media involved in the production of news, its relevance extends elsewhere. Film-studio executives, television programme-buyers and radio play-list decision-makers also fulfil a gatekeeper role. New media technologies such as digital broadcasting, subscription-TV and the internet are seen as challenging the gatekeeper role; but in fact may simply be extending it further. Because anyone can publish, it is argued, the gatekeeper role is superfluous. But this may prove to be a utopian assumption. For instance, internet search engines can be seen as digital gatekeepers Halavais, 2009). They are not bound by personal ideologies, yet they are a product of the structural and organisational procedures of the provider who makes them. They may also be subject to legislation that requires them to filter information, thereby causing them to perform a gatekeeping role on behalf of the state. Axel Bruns (2005) argues that the term should be revised from 'gatekeeping' to 'gatewatching' in the era of participatory journalism.

Further, it is clear that there is economic value in gatekeeping: people *want* information checked, evaluated and edited for them by professionals. Despite the huge amount of freely available information on the web, many of the most popular sites are those that edit, organise and manage information on behalf of consumers; frequently, indeed, they belong to brand-name media titles like major newspapers and TV stations.

See also: **Bias**, **News values**

Further reading: Shoemaker and Vos (2009)

GENDER

Generally, in the field of communication, cultural and media studies, gender refers to the *cultural* aspect of sexual differentiation, as opposed to the biological aspect, which is referred to as *sexual* difference. The human species is sexually dimorphic – males and females manifest different body size – although significantly less so in humans than among other primates. This may be important culturally, because *less* dimorphism (among birds) has been shown to indicate a species characterised by monogamy and mutual parental care of the young. Thus it may be, contrary to certain strands of opinion, that the human male is biologically predisposed towards faithfulness and care, like the bonobo, with which our species may also share such traits as altruism, compassion, empathy, kindness, patience, and sensitivity (de Waal, 1995).

Some proportion of the differences between men and women must be ascribed to biological, genetic inheritance. The problem is; no-one knows how much. Furthermore, it can be argued that while **nature** proposes, **culture** disposes – learnt and institutionalised behaviours may over-determine biological propensities: inheritance may be trumped by environment; and cultural transmission may play a more important role than genetics in some situations. Thus it would not be right to argue that all gender role differentiation is cultural, as may sometimes appear from the 'social constructivist' position (in second-wave feminism for instance); nor would it be right to say that gender roles were 'hard-wired in the Pleistocene era', as some versions of evolutionary psychology assert.

However, most of the work in communication, cultural and media studies that focuses on gender is concerned with the socially constructed component. This is because the 'nature/nurture' debate cannot be resolved in the here and now, which is the time-frame of political activism. What can be said with confidence is that it is unwise to impute any 'behaviour' to nature (i.e. to biological, genetic, evolutionary determination), because (a) different cultures around the world, at different times, routinely produce completely opposite (but equally 'natural') gender roles, and (b) attempts to naturalise aspects of gender (as in the claim that 'it's only natural' for men/women to behave in a certain way) is usually a sure sign of **ideology** – or wishful thinking – where an all-too-cultural value is given a biological causation, to win an argument or to protect the status quo. The issues involved escalate very quickly from neutral scientific inquiry (e.g. what are the behavioural consequences of sexual dimorphism for human couples?) to plain nonsense (e.g. 'this explains domestic violence as natural'), because it supplies an *alibi* for unconscionable behaviour and evacuates moral choice from human relations.

Thus, in the here and now, it is appropriate to explore gender as a cultural phenomenon, constructed in the signifying practices of **discourses**, represented in language and media, institutionalised in social structures and organisational forms, and reproduced through conventions of learning. Insofar as gender roles are constructed, they are constructed in language, media representations, processes and ideologies, which thereby offer a massive database for the analysis of the social construction of gender inequalities. Feminist analysts and others have used media texts, relations and processes as a rich resource for unpicking and making explicit the often tacit assumptions about gender that reveal not 'sexual difference' but 'sexism'.

Thus gender is a thoroughly politicised term in the field; to such an extent that some feminist theorists have sought to move away from the idea that gender has a causal connection with identity. Judith Butler (1990, 2004), for instance, has conceptualised gender in terms of performance (rather than essence), with all that that implies about learning – and unlearning – a role and performing it for others; while Donna Haraway's (1990) notion of the **cyborg** is an experiment in imagining a new, technologically motivated identity. Meanwhile, the investigation of gender in the media is an established field of scholarship in its own right, with its own journals (e.g. *Camera Obscura*, *Feminist Media Studies*), its own conferences (e.g. Console-ing Passions), and its own textbooks (e.g. Gauntlett, 2008).

Note: 'Gender' in linguistics refers to the classification systems that certain languages apply to nouns, which may be divided into 'feminine', 'masculine' or 'neuter' types. These have no relation to gender roles in human society (Deutscher, 2006).

See also: **Discourse, Identity politics, Ideology, Representation**

GENRE

Genre is an analytical or meta-discursive term for the categorisation of media **texts** according to shared internal (textual) characteristics. Arising from literary and art criticism, and more recently cinema studies, the term can also be applied to popular fiction, music and television, as well as media not usually thought of in generic terms, such as magazines, dance, or news, all of which display generic tendencies. Genres are recognisable through recurring iconography (the 'look' of a film), repetition of **codes** and **conventions** (stock settings, characters, situations), as well as familiar plot lines, which add up to the difference between, say, westerns, horror movies, musicals and romantic comedies.

Steve Neale (1980: 19) defines genres as 'systems of orientations, expectations and conventions that circulate between industry, text and subject'. For producers (the industry), genre offers a means of creating an identifiable product for sale. If they want to attract an audience for 'rom-com' (romantic comedy) they will think twice about making it look like a western. Directors may gain their reputation – and thereby secure their careers – in a given genre. Audiences meanwhile, especially **fans**, often identify strongly with one genre as opposed to others.

While genre conventions thereby clearly aid the process of media-text circulation, they may also become formulaic (as occurs when an initially innovative horror movie becomes a franchise), which may account for the lower reputation enjoyed by 'genre' films and fiction compared with non-generic forms. Thus 'genre' fiction rarely wins literary prizes, although Hilary Mantel's historical novel *Wolf Hall* won the 2009 Man-Booker Prize. Similarly, a single 'genre film' may confound genre expectations. Neale (1990: 56) argues that 'each new genre film tends to extend [its] repertoire, either by adding a new element or by transgressing one of the old ones'. Such innovations may be good for the individual film's reputation and box-office success; and sometimes breaking with genre conventions may paradoxically revive an entire genre by suggesting a productive new direction.

See also: **Mode of address, Narrative**

Further reading: Frow (2006); Neale (2000)

GLOBALISATION

Globalisation narrowly defined is the extension of cross-border economic ties, leading to greater integration of societies and economies around the world. More broadly, it is used as a proxy term for the market economy or euphemism for capitalism. In relation to television, globalisation of TV-set manufacturing and programming, as well as the global reach of media corporations like TimeWarner, Viacom, Disney, News Corporation, Bertelsmann and Sony, has intensified since the 1980s. Perhaps more to the point, television is one of the key sites for debate and activism in relation to the broader definition of globalisation as 'capitalism'. TV is a convenient metaphor – and scapegoat – for many of the perceived ills of commercial democracies, particularly worries about the effect of popular media on national and cultural identity in different countries.

We would do better to think of 'globalisation' as a *concept* than as a description of historical *process*, because it is not in fact the case that once upon a time economic or social life was city- or **nation**-based and then it began to go global. We are not faced with an evolutionary or developmental change so much as a change in the history of ideas. In other words, we have begun to *conceptualise* the global dimensions of phenomena we had previously thought of (or experienced) only in local or national settings. This way of conceptualising has now gained very wide currency beyond the world of intellectual specialisation, as globalisation has become one of the most dynamic terms in popular media and politics in recent years as well as in more formal academic theorising.

Since the 1980s the world has experienced unprecedented levels of intensity in the international movement of investment and marketing, and also in the global reach of information, knowledge and communications. But even among fully globalised industries, transnational movement is often only one-way. It is easier for US companies than for African and Asian countries to globalise their operations and markets, which means in practice that such Western-originated products and services as pharmaceuticals, infant milk formula and **entertainment** formats find their way into African and Asian homes quite readily, while much of the agricultural, intellectual and cultural produce of those countries is effectively blocked from entry into the USA or European Union. Global movement of people (labour) has also remained much less free than that of capital; again, especially migration to the affluent West from the rest of the world.

Critical analysis of corporate globalisation has focused on analysing these unequal freedoms. Criticism has also dwelt on the feared 'homogenisation' – in practice the Americanisation – of culture in many countries or localities, to the perceived detriment of national identity and local **diversity**. Television has become a potent symbol of these issues in recent years, because TV so clearly interlinks economic and cultural issues. Globalisation is not simply an economic occurrence. Its cultural dimension includes global entertainment, fast food, fashion, and tourism. 'Global' culture can exist alongside local and traditional communities, identities and tastes, encouraging a multiplicity of cultures and providing possibilities for new cultures to emerge.

Meanwhile, no-one can afford not to play. Countries like China, which has a strongly centralised and nationalistic political culture, and a strong fear of both internal chaos and external interference, nevertheless greeted its belated acceptance into the World Trade Organisation in December 2001 as a major milestone of national development. China's own size, dynamism and specificity will inevitably have 'feedback' effects on the globalised economy down the track – influencing as much as it is influenced. The same is true for the other BRICKS countries (Brazil, Russia, India, China, Korea, South Africa). Thus, in addition to the 'vertical' impact of dominant economies (the G7) on the rest, globalisation is having 'horizontal' effects, by means of country-to-country links that may have little to do with previous imperial or **hegemonic** powers.

See also: **Anti-globalisation, Internationalisation**

Further reading: Lemert *et al.* (2010)

HACKER, HACKTIVISM, HACKABILITY

In the 1970s and 1980s, a computer hacker was synonymous with a 'geek' – an enthusiast for programming. Later the term was specialised into the now-familiar sense of one who uses programming skills to gain unauthorised entry to computer systems. These skills may be used for criminal or nationalistic ends. In popular discourse, the security aspect of hacking has predominated; its newsworthiness directly related to the damage done by high-profile penetration of corporate computing systems or interference with sites associated with national identity or security, including 'DoS' (denial of service) attacks.

By the 1990s, the hacker was a **culture-jamming** hero, associated with contemporary protest movements such as anti-globalisation, eco-activism, and countercultural values (Wark, 2004). This gave rise to the notion of hacktivism, defined by Samuel (2004: 2) as 'the nonviolent use of illegal or legally ambiguous digital tools in pursuit of political ends', personified by Julian Assange of Wikileaks.

More recently, Jean Burgess (2007: 89) has made an analytical distinction for new-media affordances between their 'hackability' and 'usability': hackability is 'where a given technology is perceived and presented as open-ended, manipulable and affording complex experimentation with an accompanying level of difficulty', while usability is 'where a technology is perceived and presented as allowing easy access to a pre-determined set of simple operations'. Examples of 'usable' technologies are the Kodak camera, broadcast radio, and the two-knob TV-set; examples of 'hackable' technologies are Flickr, ham radio, and **DIY** content on YouTube. In other words, the distinction pre-dates online, digital media, and to some extent maps over more general distinctions between **modernism** and global **popular culture**.

Further reading: Jordan (2008); Wark (2004)

HEGEMONY

A concept developed by Gramsci (1971) in the 1930s and taken up in **cultural studies**, where it refers principally to the ability in certain historical conditions of the dominant classes to exercise social and cultural leadership, and by these means – rather than by direct coercion of subordinate classes – to maintain their **power** over the economic, political and cultural direction of a **nation**.

The crucial aspect of the notion of hegemony is not that it operates by forcing people against their will or better judgement to concede power to the already-powerful, but that it works by winning consent ✕ to ways of making sense of the world that do in fact make sense, but also happen to fit in with the interests of the hegemonic alliance of classes, or *power bloc*. Hence our active cultural participation in understanding ourselves, our social relations and the world at large, results in complicity in our own political and economic subordination (*see* **power**).

The idea of 'winning consent' extends the concept of hegemony beyond the analysis of class as such. In cultural analysis, the concept is used to show how everyday meanings, representations and activities are organised and made sense of in such a way as to render the interests of a dominant 'bloc' into an apparently natural and unarguable general interest, with a claim on everybody. Thus studies which concentrate on the hegemonic aspect of culture will focus on those forms and institutions which are usually taken to be impartial or neutral; 'representative' of everybody without apparent reference to **class**, **race** or **gender**. Such institutions span both public and private spheres – including the state, the law, the educational system, the media and the family. They are prolific discursive producers of sense, knowledge and **meanings**. Aside from their ostensible function, their cultural importance lies in their role as organisers and producers of individual and social consciousness. Although they are relatively autonomous from one another, peopled by different personnel with different professional skills and ideologies, nevertheless these cultural/knowledge agencies collectively form the site on which hegemony can be established and exercised (*see* **ideological state apparatuses**).

It follows that hegemony operates in the realm of consciousness and **representations**; its success is most likely when the totality of social, cultural and individual experience is capable of being made sense of in terms that are defined, established and put into circulation by the power bloc. In short, hegemony naturalises what is historically a class ideology, and renders it into the form of common sense. The upshot is that power can be exercised not as force but as 'authority'; and 'cultural' aspects of life are de-politicised.

See also: **Bardic function, Class, Consensus, Culture, Ideology, Power**

Further reading: Barker (2008); Howson and Smith (2009)

IDENTIFICATION

A symbolic process that involves appropriating characteristics attributed to another (including the image of a character or celebrity in the media) in order to make sense or construct a sense of the self. This theory of identification has its roots in psychoanalytical psychology, which aimed to understand the symbolic formation of individual identity within the constraints of language.

In media studies, theories of identification most often refer to **representations** and their cultural consequences. In *identifying with* characters, the audience are thought to experience the image as if it was real (Fiske, 1987: 169). This process of identification allows representation to seem part of **nature**, rather than cultural constructions.

Mulvey (1990) has influentially argued that cinema uses **conventions** that invite identification with male characters, while objectifying female ones. Mulvey's argument suggests a subordinate position for women is created via the conventions of the media. But such notions, organised around a psychoanalytic and ahistorical concept of 'the' male gaze, have proven disabling and confining, giving very little scope for challenging and changing the process and terms of identification with media images. Other theorists have attempted to overcome this drawback by positing *levels* of identification (Gaut, 1999: 208); or by positing what Murray Smith (1995: 75) calls 'the structure of sympathy' in which an audience's 'imaginative engagement with characters' is constituted by three elements: recognition, alignment and allegiance.

See also: **Image**, **Mode of address**, **Representation**, **Subjectivity**

IDENTITY POLITICS

Social action organised around cultural identity rather than civic or political citizenship, often associated with the 'new social movements' that gained prominence in and after the 1960s, including the feminist movement, the civil rights movement in the USA, gay and lesbian activism, ethno-nationalisms (e.g. first-people's activism), as well as movements based on disability, youth, and the environment.

Although identity politics is often associated with the political upheavals of the 1960s, it goes back much further; for instance the Suffragette movement of the 1900s was an earlier form of identity politics. Anti-colonial struggles throughout the twentieth century in the British, French and other European empires were also important in the development of identity politics. The civil rights and Black Power movements of the 1960s and the rise of feminism brought such issues to the heart of contemporary public life, and to the top of the political agenda in LBJ's Vietnam-era America. They called attention to the way that the traditional public, political sphere had failed so many even of its own supposed beneficiaries. At this point, attention was called into how 'education, language, lifestyle and representation were imbued with social consequences' (Shattuc, 1997: 2). The shift from 'public man' (Sennett, 1977) to identity politics was succinctly captured in one of feminism's most famous slogans – 'the personal is political'.

The concept of identity is now often viewed as relying on shared characteristics that are cultural rather than natural or biological (*see* **gender**). As a result, political alliances based on an essentialist identity – one fixed in **nature** (ethnic origins and 'blood' or genes) rather than made in **culture** – are often viewed with alarm in radical circles. Spivak's notion of 'strategic essentialism' (Landry and Maclean, 1996) tries to get round the problem. It suggests forgoing the notion of the socially constructed and reclaiming a fixed identity in the context of public debate. For while it may be agreed among theorists that, for instance, sexuality is a culturally constructed signifier, in the political arena itself the rights and privileges awarded to heterosexual and homosexual individuals are markedly different. Here, 'strategic essentialism' supports the notion of a group of individuals coming together under the identity of 'gay' to participate in the struggle for equality.

Similar arguments may be made about ethnic identity (Gray, 2000), and ethno-nationalism, including Indigenous politics. Here, 'identity' means more than 'living as and being accepted by others in that culture'; it means having authenticated bloodlines showing a certain ethnic descent, consequential upon which may be various entitlements and rights, from land to welfare, policed, some have suggested, by DNA testing. Such a development in other domains of identity politics – for example in relation to the sometimes posited 'gay gene' – would be highly controversial, however.

Examples such as this illustrate that identity politics is by no means self-evidently radical or progressive, despite the fact that it is usually associated with marginal groups and with bringing disparate individuals together in the name of social, political, and cultural equality. Another development in identity politics demonstrates its reactionary potential, in the rise of the men's movement (but see Connell, 2005). Some of its rhetoric is explicitly designed to undermine feminist positions; here 'identity' is presented as embattled when challenged *from* a marginal position. Similarly, white supremacists may seek to appropriate policies designed to accommodate multi-ethnic groups, thereby turning those policies on their heads.

Further reading: Gauntlett (2008)

IDEOLOGICAL STATE APPARATUSES

The material or institutional form taken by **ideology**, in specified historical circumstances, in **class** societies. Known as ISAs, and distinguished from RSAs or *repressive state apparatuses*, the two terms were coined by the French Marxist philosopher Louis Althusser (1971).

- *RSAs* are the complex of coercive or regulatory forces available to and directly under the control of the state. They include the penal system, the police, the army, legislatures and government administration. These are distinguished by their legitimated authority to command (whether we like it or not).
- *ISAs*, on the other hand, are various social institutions that arise within civil society (the sphere of the private, as opposed to the state). They too perform regulatory functions, and reproduce ideology 'on behalf of' the state. They include education, the family, religion, the legal system, the party-political system, culture and communication. They are characterised by consent rather than coercion, and by their relative autonomy from the dominant economic class or its representatives in the state.

According to Althusserian theory, the function of ISAs is to reproduce a population's submission to the relations of production – to discipline it into the kind of subjectivity most conducive to the maintenance and continuity of the existing unequal relations of production. They do it by representing class interests as both natural and neutral – this is why they are *ideological* apparatuses, since their efficacy lies in the domain of language, knowledge, and **representation** rather than that of physical force. They literally translate class into other terms. For instance, education is neutral because all are equal in front of the examination. But only certain ideologies – and social groups – pass exams. The legal system is neutral because all are equal in front of the law. But only certain acts are criminalised, and only certain ideological subjects are convicted. The news media are neutral because their representations of the social world are impartial. But only certain ideologies are represented as worthy of impartial treatment, others are not. The party-political *system* is neutral, because within it all positions and opinions can be voiced: except for non-party, extra-parliamentary political voices. Thus, ISAs institutionalise **hegemony**. Although in specific cases the concept of ISAs can be revealing and explanatory, it does also tend towards a paranoiac view of social organisation, where it can too easily appear that *everything* is part of a planned process of subjugation. Handle with care.

IDEOLOGY

Knowledge and ideas characteristic of, produced by, or in the interests of a particular social **class**, over against the ideas characteristic of other classes. By extension, ideology refers to the ideas of groups other than classes – ranging from **gender** (male ideology or patriarchy) to jobs (occupational ideology). Ideology is seen as any knowledge that is posed as natural or generally applicable, particularly when its social origins or sectional interests are **ex-nominated**. In cultural and communication studies, ideology is seen as the practice of reproducing social relations of inequality within the sphere of **signification** and **discourse**.

Ideology as a theoretical concept comes from Marxism. In classic Marxism, the forms, contents and purposes of knowledge, representations and consciousness are part of the material and social activities of production and class antagonism. The activity of production gives rise directly to knowledge of **nature**, and this knowledge of nature is directed towards further and increasing production by bringing all its myriad aspects as closely into line with general natural 'laws' as possible.

It is Marx's contention that knowledge of society springs in the same way, directly from the material 'laws' (as he thought) of class antagonism. But whereas knowledge of nature may, at least in principle, be of benefit to all classes, knowledge of society is produced and reproduced in the interests of those who are for the time being in a position of social supremacy – the ruling class. Thus, for Marx, knowledge of society differs from knowledge of nature by representing *as* natural those social arrangements that are in fact historically contingent. This is the starting point for a theory of ideology. The fundamental premises on which the Marxist concept of ideology is based are expressed in two of Marx's most celebrated contentions:

The mode of production of material life conditions the social, political and intellectual life process in general. It is not the consciousness of men that determines their being, but, on the contrary, their social being that determines their consciousness.

The individuals composing the ruling class possess among other things consciousness, and therefore think. Insofar, therefore, as they rule as a class and determine the extent and compass of an epoch, it is self-evident that they do this in its whole range, hence among other things rule also as thinkers, as producers of ideas, and regulate the production and distribution of the ideas of their age: thus their ideas are the ruling ideas of the epoch.

(Marx, 1845: 176, 389)

If the ideas of the ruling class are the ruling ideas of an epoch, then 'bourgeois ideology', for instance, should not be understood simply as what individual members of that class think, but as the prevailing ways of making sense that are established throughout bourgeois society. These ways of making sense may be produced and distributed not by the ruling class directly, but by relatively autonomous and apparently fragmented groups, ranging from intellectuals and teachers to media professionals and hairdressers.

The contention that social being determines consciousness gives rise to the Marxist notion of *false consciousness*. In case of the ruling class itself, false consciousness occurs when that class imagines that its powers in society are determined by the laws of God or nature, as in the feudal doctrine of the divine right of kings or, in bourgeois philosophy, the doctrine of individualism and the conception of society as a social contract. False consciousness for subordinate classes occurs when they make sense of their social and individual circumstances in terms supplied by the prevailing ideology, rather than in terms of their own class interests in opposition to the dominant classes. In this context, ideology is seen as the production and distribution of ideas in the interests of the ruling classes.

For Marx, not all knowledge of society is necessarily ideological. In particular, the science of historical materialism (Marxism) itself could not be seen as an ideology, given the notion of ideology as an illusory knowledge. The understanding gained in the struggle to change both society and nature is partial and limited and can be mistaken but, for Marxists, the objective existence of natural and historical laws is not open to question, nor is the belief that materialist science provides the means to bring those laws into knowledge. Thus Marxists, including the Communist Parties of the Soviet Union and China, long persisted in describing Marxist theory as a science.

The concept of ideology has proved very influential in the study of communication and culture. So much so, in fact, that it has become somewhat over-extended in use. In particular, in some popularised versions of Marxism, ideology has been reduced to a mere reflection of the economic base. As a result, ideology is often confined to the superstructure, where it is defined in terms of 'bodies' of thought, beliefs, ideas, and so on. This move reduces it from a conceptualisation of social relations and practices to a set of empirical things.

Just as language is hard to analyse if you look at words rather than the laws which produce words, so the reduction of ideology to ideas does not explain their production or forms. Thus the concept needed to be re-theorised, and this led to the notion of *ideology in general*. This notion is associated especially with Althusser (1971), for whom ideology is the mechanism which turns individuals into subjects, but is also implicit in Volosinov (1973). It implies that all knowledge, whether scientific or otherwise, is produced within language, and that language is never a transparent medium through which truth can be observed. Hence all language is seen as ideological, and truth as a product not a motivator of language. It follows from this that no specific discourse (including Marxism itself) is exempt from ideology. Instead, there are at any one time numbers of contending ideological discourses in play within an overall social formation, and that what is at stake in the way they are produced, deployed, regulated, institutionalised and resisted is not only knowledge but also power.

However, at the level of specific ideologies, it is clear that ideology isn't a unitary medium that we inhabit like fishes in the medium of the sea. Even within what is often called *dominant ideology* there are contending and conflicting positions – as between say different educational philosophies and policies. And ideology is always encountered in institutional forms and local circumstances which ensure that there is never a complete fit between dominant class interests and dominant ideology. Further, however naturalised and successful dominant ideologies might seem, they are always in contention with resistances to them from 'below', either in the form of coherent alternatives (feminism, Marxism) or as practical accommodations/rejections (*see* **subcultures**).

The concept of ideology has become central in the study of the media in particular and communication in general. It is useful in insisting that 'natural' meanings, inherent in an event or object, should be treated with extreme scepticism, and also that the mediated meanings into which events and objects are constructed are always socially oriented – aligned with class, gender, race or other interests. Further, ideology is not a set of things but an active practice, either working on the changing circumstances of social activity to reproduce familiar and regulated senses, or struggling to resist established and naturalised sense thus to transform the means of sense-making into new, alternative or oppositional forms, which will generate meanings aligned to different social interests.

Further reading: Barker (2008); Hawkes (2003)

IMAGE

The objectification of self-knowledge for communicative purposes. At an individual level, one's 'image' is made up of the cues by means of which others make sense of the **performance** of the self. These include visual attributes (looks, clothes), and intentionally communicative acts (speech, interaction with others), but also behavioural characteristics that project an image beyond the control of the self: a 'tearaway', 'self-confident' image, etc.

At a cultural level, image is the alienation of personal attributes for semiotic purposes. The 'image' of various groups in the media, especially those taken to be vulnerable or open to victimisation, has been much studied. This is because it is widely feared that such alienated images of the self are projected back into real selves by the media, with material effects on behaviour and self-esteem.

The media image of women, ethnic minorities, and various groups organised around marginal tastes, lifestyles, subcultures or regions, have all been studied, often by an investigator who represents the group so portrayed. Examples include 'images' of: women as projected by Hollywood and fashion; black, Aboriginal or migrant people projected in news; gays and lesbians in popular culture; regions such as Northern Ireland or Palestine (for which 'calm footage' is all too rare). Such images are thought to have cultural and political, not just individual consequences. Some analyses are sophisticated, for instance Annette Kuhn's *The Power of the Image* (1990), based on cinema theory and feminism. Others are more demotic, hotly contested within popular media themselves, including those by advocate organisations and activists, for a sample of which, see any issue of *Adbusters* (Lasn, 2000).

Commercial organisations themselves have entered image-politics. For instance, Anita Roddick, founder of the Bodyshop, purveyor of beauty and cleansing products, maintained a high-profile politico-advertising campaign against 'impossible' images of women (i.e. super-models). Olivier Toscani, inspiration and photographer for Benetton clothes, made a career and a brand name by using Benetton advertisements themselves to subvert stereotypical images.

The term 'image' has figured prominently in Western philosophy, ever since Plato proposed that humans don't perceive truth directly, but only in an indirect, distorted 'image'. Humans cannot see themselves as they are, Plato argued. Knowledge is perceived in distorted, indirect form, as if it were projected, like the shadows of dancers grotesquely capering on the wall of a cave in the light of the campfire. Such 'shadow in the cave' images of a reality that is located somewhere elsewhere and beyond experience is all that humans can hope for, thought Plato. Thence, a conviction took hold of Western thinking that 'images' were opposed to reality, coterminous with illusion.

The natural pessimism of intellectuals was force-fed with a strong diet of self-loathing during the Christian era, when 'image' tended to become associated with 'graven' or 'corporeal' – that is, with the trumpery and seductions of the flesh, attended by the temptations that contemplative monastic writers had to conquer. Thinking about 'images' became focused in on the visual, the fleshly, and the seductive, and on expressions of loathing for all that (and for women, who unwittingly but literally embodied it). Images drove the poor monks mad by luring then away from contemplation of the divine. Hence, and curiously, Western traditions insisted that the most corporeal and self-evident *things* (bodies) are 'illusory', while transcendent, metaphysical, irrecoverable phantasms (ideas) were regarded as real.

Contemporary media and communication studies, to say nothing of politics, have inherited some of this confusion, regarding 'image' as unreal, illusory, seductive, feminised. Anything that devotes time to producing and maintaining its image in a professional way is automatically suspect – the very language is inherited from misogynist loathing of flesh – an image is 'tarted up', etc. Less fatally, 'image' is now a staple of art history and cinema studies. This is a worry for film and television studies, for the fixation with images, as largely visual phenomena, neglects the complex interplay between sight, sound and sequence that screen media exploit. As a result, otherwise astute analyses may appear to have been undertaken by people who are not clinically but culturally deaf.

Despite the pejorative attitude of the philosophical and metaphysical tradition, an image *industry* is now well established, from PR and marketing specialists, spin doctors and pollsters, to fashion advisers and stylists. No-one lasts long in public life, whether they are politicians, entertainers, athletes or even philosophers and bishops, without attention to their 'image'. Thus a new market has arisen, and a new class of professionals, in 'image management'.

See also: **Celebrity, Identification, Ideology, Representation**

Further reading: Dyer (1993)

IMPARTIALITY

The doctrine of not taking sides in the reporting of public affairs in the broadcast media (not including newspapers or subscription-TV). Impartiality is the practical and pragmatic exercise of an accommodation between broadcasters and parliamentary political parties (especially governmental parties). It is a strategy whereby reporters are supposed to take account of:

- a full *range* of views and opinions;
- the relative *weight* of opinion (this means that established or orthodox views get priority over challenges to them);
- *changes* that occur in the range and weight of opinion over time.

Traditionally, impartiality had to be exercised *within* news bulletins. That is, if you quote a Conservative view you must quote a liberal view in the same timeslot. Since the advent of Channel 4 in the 1980s, the notion of impartiality *between* shows gained acceptance. Here the idea is that if the subject demands it you can give just one position in a single programme, knowing that others will give the opposing view at another time. This development resulted largely from pressure from broadcasters themselves. Some wanted to establish 'positioned journalism' with its own point of view, while others objected to having to stop a good story in its tracks while 'the two sides' slugged it out.

Impartiality is often distinguished from two other concepts, namely *balance* and *neutrality*. It is supposed to overcome their shortcomings. Balance is the allocation of equal time to opposing viewpoints, where what is said is less important than the time it is said in. Neutrality is the indiscriminate accessing of any and every viewpoint without any principle of selection. This is deemed unsatisfactory because parliamentary politicians don't take kindly to air-time being given to groups or parties dedicated to the overthrow of parliamentary politics. Thus communist, nationalist and socialist parties operating outside the parliamentary framework are routinely denied access, without broadcasters having to admit that they're failing to be impartial – they're just not neutral. As a result, the doctrine of impartiality can be seen as a major prop to the parliamentary (two-party) *system*. In the United

Kingdom at least, impartiality is a statutory requirement laid on broad-casters by Parliament.

See also **Bias**, **Ideology**, **News values**, **Objectivity**

INDEPENDENCE

A concept of scale and opposition, with no intrinsic features. However, two types of independence are worth attention, because they signify opposing values. The term 'independent film' has served to signify freedom *from* commercial constraints. But 'independent tele-vision' (in the United Kingdom) signifies freedom *for* commercial interests. This means that 'independent' can describe 'radical, opposi-tional, experimental or innovative outsiders and avant garde practices'; or it can describe 'global commercial blockbusters, formats and fran-chises'.

In relation to the first type (which may include other forms than cinema), types of independence differ. They may be organised around different mobilising discourses: community, avant-garde, agitprop (i.e. *agitation and propaganda*), art, connoisseurship, alternative sources of finance, regional production centres, non-English-speaking produc-tion houses, etc. In each case the mobilising **discourse** produces specific sets of practices, working more or less self-consciously against the grain of mainstream entertainment. Such independence may imply:

- different, alternative or oppositional processes of *production* (for instance, working against traditional divisions and hierarchies of labour; non-capitalist finance);
- different *aesthetics* (experimentation at the level of image, narration and structure, promoting attention to meaning-construction, rather than to 'show-and-tell' plots with 'tennis-match dialogue');
- a *self-reflexive* concern with the practitioner's role as well as with subject matter or financial returns;
- different relations with *audiences* (getting away from 'bums on seats' towards active engagement with audiences as spectators or as participants);
- serving a defined audience '*constituency*' rather than the 'mass' (e.g. women, workers, a region or community, people involved in political, social or environmental action).

Increasingly, even in this context, 'independent' is a branding tool, serving to differentiate certain styles of product in the marketplace. Hence, the very notion of 'independent film' has become a contentious term in the contemporary cinematic landscape, especially in the USA. The financial, professional and semiotic independence of independent film has been compromised by Hollywood studio involvement. By 1998 many independent distribution companies had become subsidiaries of various Hollywood studios. This has led to a 'crossover' effect with mainstream cinema production. The 'Indiewood' phenomenon unites the stylistic endeavours of independent film with the more commercial focus of Hollywood, leading to a model of independent film which places less emphasis on its mode of production, instead allowing it to be viewed as a form of product differentiation from mainstream Hollywood. Chris Holmlund argues that 'indie' film predominantly signifies a product based on aesthetic difference, whereby the label independent 'suggests social engagement and/or aesthetic experimentation – a distinctive visual look, an unusual narrative pattern, a self reflexive style' (Holmlund and Wyatt, 2005: 2).

In relation to the second type, the term independent is used to describe private-enterprise funding-sources rather than the taxpayer-funding associated with public-service broadcasters like the BBC. In this context, the term is a simple euphemism for 'capitalist' or 'commercial' in the British broadcasting scene, where the main commercial channels in both television and radio (ITV and ILR) are dubbed independent, presumably of *state* ownership. In the same media ecology, however, the British 'independent film sector' (which in any case is now supported largely by commercial TV Channel 4), uses the term to help secure public funds from bodies like the Arts Council, British Film Institute and local councils for low-budget film production. Hence the same term has been found useful at the opposite extremes of the same film world.

INDIVIDUAL

A synonym for person. The word is derived from a medieval conceptualisation of the nature of the Christian God – three persons but *indivisible*. People were 'individual' because they had indivisible souls. By extension it became an adjective for that which cannot be divided further, like an atom. Here it solidified into a gender-neutral noun for persons, and entered science as a convenient label for the 'unit' of most social-scientific research, which is based on 'methodological **individualism**'. But just as the physical sciences had to rethink the notion of the atom as the smallest unit of matter when they began to split it into ever-tinier particles, so the social sciences have had to concede that individuals are not universal or uniform; the realisation that 'individuals' are no such thing has been called the 'cultural turn' in the sciences.

INDIVIDUALISM (METHODOLOGICAL)

The mainspring of capitalist philosophy; the doctrine that individuals are the starting-point and source of human action. That is, each person 'owns' his or her capacities, especially their capacity for action and labour, and is not in debt to society or to a feudal overlord for these capacities. Hence individuals are free to sell their labour power for whatever wages can be commanded in the marketplace, and are not obliged to consider anyone else in the process. This 'freedom' of the individual, then, is what underlies the operation of the 'free' market economy. The only inhibitors of individual freedom in this model are competition (where what can be had for labour power is limited by what others charge) and contract (where each individual's social relations take the form of commodity exchanges: for example, labour for wages with mutually binding conditions).

Individualism is rarely discussed in studies of communication, but the assumptions of 'methodological individualism' are implicit in a great variety of theorising on the subject. The most common occurrence is for the notion of the free individual, who is essentially complete and taken to be the source of action and meaning, to form the 'unit' of study. So, according to this notion, communication takes place when individuals exchange messages (the contract model); or audiences are made up of aggregates of individuals (abstracted from discursive, economic and political relations except in so far as these can be rendered as variables within an individual); or social forces are understood as deriving from individual actions. Media are said to have their **effect** on individuals, which are construed much as billiard-balls, apt to go wherever they are sent by some external force.

The alternative perspective to individualism certainly doesn't deny the existence or action of individual people; nor is it 'collectivism'. However, it does maintain that their existence and action is the product and not the source of social relations and signifying systems. As a result, the concept of individualism has been displaced in, for instance, structuralist, semiotic, Marxist and feminist writings by the concept of **subjectivity** (positioning in language). And in evolutionary approaches, it is being challenged by the contrasting concept of *externalism*. This posits that individual actions, choices, and even identities are formed in, conducted through, and result from *social relations and networks*. That is, our brains operate in linked interaction through complex systems like language, culture, and copied behaviour; the individual is not the source of causation but both agent and outcome of a complex dynamic open system.

Further reading: Hodgson (2007)

INFORMATION SOCIETY/ECONOMY

In the 1980s Daniel Bell described society as post-industrial, distinctive for its service-based economy, rather than manufacturing. Since then, the services sector of the economy has been transformed by dynamic growth in information and communication technologies (ICTs), to such an extent that the impact of information has spilled out of businesses to transform society as a whole. Thus, the contemporary period has been dubbed the information society.

The possession of *information capital* is surpassing labour as the means to wealth creation. In this respect, the information society is not just a reliance on information; it is the magnitude of its use and its centrality to the processes of the market and everyday life. Machinery, industry and wage-labour predated the industrial age, but were exploited in the nineteenth century to the point where they came to transform the way that people lived and viewed their lives. So it is now with information.

The information society has been heralded by some as representing a new-found freedom. An information society contains an informed population, capable of self-expression and political and cultural participation through new technologies (Leadbeater, 1999). But the information age has also brought with it a new set of anxieties. The ability to use information technologies in surveillance is seen by some as a means to social control and power, and an end to privacy (*see* **panopticon**).

After describing the features of the information society, Manuel Castells decided that the term was too vague, as knowledge and information are essential to all societies. What is new 'is a new set of information technologies' (Castells, 2000: 414). He preferred his own concept of the **network society**.

See also: **Knowledge economy**, **Network society**, **New economy**

Further reading: Hassn (2008); Webster (2004)

INFOTAINMENT

A term used to describe the blending of factual reportage with the conventions usually associated with fictional or variety entertainment. In everyday usage, infotainment refers to particular types of television programming. Examples of this would include 'tabloid' current affairs programmes, as well as instructional or **lifestyle** formats such as cooking, gardening and home improvement shows, and **reality TV**. Here, the term comes to represent the means by which television is able to impart information in an entertaining way.

In critical discourse, the concept is often used to lament the loss of 'traditional' news values. Those who criticise infotainment often have a preference for modernist forms of communication, privileging reason over emotion, public over private, and information over entertainment. But the entertainment characteristics that inform contemporary journalism were to be found in its earliest incarnations. Sex, scandal, disaster and celebrity have been intrinsic to modern journalism since the Enlightenment (Hartley, 1996), so the shift to infotainment should not necessarily be considered as a recent one.

Broadcast news on television cannot avoid the need to entertain and appeal to viewers. Capturing audiences is as much a priority for factual programming as it is for fictional/entertainment genres, so it is hardly surprising that over time news has borrowed characteristics from non-news formats. **Narrative**, spectacle, personality presenters, non-**diegetic** soundtrack and personalised address are all now central to the broadcasting of news in entertaining ways. The term infotainment then could be said to recognise the porous nature of television and its **genres** rather than a decline in the absolute values associated with **journalism**.

At the heart of criticisms levelled at the move to infotainment is the perceived damage to civil society where citizens' right to rational (political) discourse has been replaced by an influx of private (trivial) affairs. To agree with this is to ignore the major movements that have been able to gain visibility as a result. The environment, and issues regarding youth, sexuality and ethnicity are all contemporary political issues that have arisen outside of the traditional public sphere. Infotainment, with its evocation of style, celebrity, gossip, and informality, provides a new space within which new paradigms of politics can be discussed, represented and made meaningful.

Infotainment is also necessary in a medium where **aberrant decoding** is the norm, because viewers have to be encouraged to attend to things they don't like or know about when their commitment to watching at all may not be high. In this context, infotainment may not be dumbing down people who'd otherwise be reading the *Financial Times*, but taking information to places it would not otherwise reach, and thus be seen as both educational and tactful.

See also: **News values**

Further reading: Thussu (2007)

INFRASTRUCTURE

The physical platforms upon which systems, facilities and networks are run are known as *infrastructure*. Infrastructure is essential to the information communications technologies as it enables **connectivity** and provides services via **applications**. Roads, footpaths and buildings are infrastructure. In telecommunications, the required infrastructure is the copper or fibre-optic telephone line or cable, or the satellite through which information is distributed. **Privatisation** has brought with it issues of access to infrastructure, whereby private companies are capable of controlling the use of infrastructure previously considered a public resource available to all. Infrastructure is commonly linked with two other terms, connectivity, and content, where infrastructure is understood as the bedrock investment; connectivity as the next phase (ICTs in business); and content follows (social network markets).

INNOVATION

New economy R&D; the process by which emergent ideas are implemented. The first step in the creation of new tools, products or creative works is an idea. In traditional manufacturing industries, ideas are said to circulate at a low rate, inhibited by routine, tradition and existing methods of reproduction, using well-known patterns. Production, in the industrial economy, is governed by the technology at hand and innovation restricted to experts directly employed by the firm. In innovative fields (media, software development, biotechnology, music production for example), so the argument goes, ideas circulate between people rapidly, both inside and beyond the firm, increasingly including creative inputs from consumers, for instance in the improvement of computer games by players. In this scenario, science and discovery create the new technologies, pushing products to new levels. The discussion of ideas, contributions from others, the eventual development of an idea into something new, and the uptake and extension of that idea as part of the process, are central to the success of these industries.

In policy and business discourses, innovation is distinguished from creativity: creativity produces new ideas, innovation is their implementation. Therefore, creativity is a precondition for innovation, but innovation − the evaluation and assessment of the creative idea and then its realisation in a practical context − is what will make the difference in competitive product and service development, and therefore profitability. For innovation to occur, it may entail stepping outside of routine or structure, and it can therefore be the result of dissent or a process of risky experimentation. Often it is simply the ability to use old ideas as the raw materials for something new.

In the **knowledge economy**, where companies rely on information to improve their products and create new ones, innovation becomes the central component for wealth-creation and growth. Once the idea has been hit upon, it will then be necessary to locate the required resources, possibly a team to work on the development and knowledge of factors that might inhibit the production of the work. Entrepreneurs bring the idea to fruition. Innovation therefore requires a range of appropriate conditions, skills and knowledge in order to occur. Fostering the right conditions for innovation has become a chief concern within the science, business and arts industries of the knowledge economy.

See also: **Creative industries**, **Information society**, **Knowledge economy**

Further reading: Leadbeater (2008)

INTELLECTUAL PROPERTY

Ownership of intangible information. Intellectual property (IP) is a legal framework that enables information to be privately owned, and thence allows the owner to restrict its use or to determine who uses it. Intellectual property takes various forms, including patents, which are less significant in the cultural and media domain than **copyright**, which covers creative intellectual property.

Although intellectual property is a legal concept, its boundaries are far from clear. The tension between private ownership of information and its fair use and circulation in the public domain is constantly being negotiated in law and regulation, and tested out in practice, especially in the key domain of **bioscience** (Boyle, 1996).

A related issue is the extent to which anxiety over the capacity for piracy inherent in digital media has lead to the development of encryption technologies and a rise in contractual agreements in order to ensure that intellectual property is protected. Where it was once hoped that digital technology would allow for greater freedom in the exchange of information and services, there is the possibility that our rights in digital arenas will become more tightly constrained than those in the analogue world. For instance, although paperback books can be borrowed or swapped without monetary exchange (this can come under the definition of 'fair use' or 'acceptable use' laws), certain e-books may only be accessible upon payment or once an agreement has been entered into. Users can find it difficult (or a broach of license conditions) to transfer music files from one device to another.

As Donald Richards (2008: 268) has pointed out, intellectual property has a tendency to create monopoly power for rights-holders, to restrict the effects of technological advances, and thereby to reduce social welfare (rights-holders raise prices and restrict the growth of knowledge). IP rights are also an ineffective incentive to **innovation**. These are paradoxical developments, because the tendency towards monopoly is normally regulated by governments, and yet IP rights are enforced through state-sponsored legislation; and IP enforcement is routinely justified on the grounds that it encourages innovation, but it stops anyone outside the firm from innovating.

See also: **Biotechnology, Biopower, Content industries, Copyright**

INTERACTION DESIGN

With the rise of computer communication, an entire professional group or 'creative class' (Florida, 2002) has arisen around the interface between computers and humans, and between computers and organisations. The innovation encapsulated in 'interaction design' is that it associates human–computer interaction with aesthetic rather than scientific disciplines, shifting the field of study from its background in engineering, computer and cognitive science towards a future in the arts and design, and improving the status of practitioners from information-technology 'technicians' to art-college educated 'designers'. Some see this shift as a tension. However, the same journey has been taken by other technical skills in the past, notably design (graphic, product, industrial, etc.) and architecture. Thus 'interaction design' is by no means alone in rebranding technological competence *as art*, a direction whose pull has seemed irresistible since the Renaissance, when anonymous artisanal painters first emerged as named or 'authorial' artists like Giotto or Leonardo da Vinci.

The abstract idea of 'design' is now used to organise large investments, as an industry sector' involving both economic and cultural values. 'Designer' now applies to myriad occupations distributed throughout the economy. It is the default descriptor of the information age, just as the 'engineer' was the master-metaphor for the industrial era. Designers are but the latest group of expert service-providers who make explicit and professionalise previously tacit knowledge based in ordinary practices. The 'knowledge economy' works by taking tacit knowledge (e.g. cookery) and making it explicit (the recipe), replicable (published) and entrepreneurial (celebrity chefs) (Leadbeater, 1999).

A critical problem arises when the industrial-era distinction between producer and consumer is reinstated during this process, by setting expert designers apart from the ordinary user:

Producer	Consumer
Supply	Demand
Expert	Amateur
Provider	Client
Corporation	Customer
Organisation	Individual
Causal action	Behavioural effect
Television	Audience
Designer	User

Such a division is not so easy to justify in the knowledge economy, or in the context of creative innovation. For although trained expertise is clearly vital, equally important is the productive role of users and consumer co-creators (OECD, 2007), many of whom will bring their own expertise to a problem which can be solved collaboratively rather than competitively. This is the process of 'mass creativity' that Charles Leadbeater (2008) has dubbed 'we-think'.

The tension between producers and consumers is made more complex by *technologies* that are at once the product of scientific expertise and universally available for anyone to use. But professional self-preservation seems to dictate that designers continue to stand between users and technologies. Interaction design is being re-imagined as a commercial service profession, 'helping people participate' in their interactions with computers, and thence with each other, for a fee; but not encouraging interaction design to become a generally distributed capability among the wider population. Thus, inadvertently, interaction design is turning into a profession and a discipline only at the cost of reproducing a **mass-communication** model of the relations between producers and consumers, just at the moment when the technological potential of digital and online media will allow it to be superseded.

See also: **Interactivity**

INTERACTIVITY

Interactivity signifies the development of the relationship between person and computer, and with others via the computer. Our ability to have a two-way communicative process with technology means that we are not 'destined to become a race of babysitters for computers' (Bagrit, 1965: 1). Instead we are 'navigators', 'users', 'surfers', in control of where the technology takes us at any given moment, even though the evolutionary process of technology itself (Arthur, 2009) is beyond individual control (just as surfers can ride waves without controlling them or even grasping their nature, genesis, and complexity). We can be constructive through our choices, and our own invention.

Marshall McLuhan (1964: 349) wrote that 'automation is not an extension of the mechanical principles of fragmentation and separation of operations. It is rather the invasion of the mechanical world by the instantaneous character of electricity'. The 'instant inclusive embrace' of automated technology meant that the consumer also became the producer, 'fusing' information and learning. The progression from the mechanical to the automated has brought with it new possibilities for participation, and our ability to make choices: technology becomes a means to empowerment. The excitement surrounding the emancipationist potential of interactive media has been curbed by more cautious theorists who remind us that the interactive uses of new technologies are not driven by democratic ideals on the whole, but by commercial imperatives, and that although these can coincide they don't have to. As the development of the technology has been largely left to the market, citizen feedback can be limited to online shopping options, interactive game shows and discussion resembling talk-back radio (Calabrese and Borchert, 1996).

See also: **Cyberdemocracy, Cybernetics, Cyborg, Interaction design, User**

INTERNATIONALISATION

Activities that occur between nation-states are *inter*-national. International-*isation* suggests an increasing occurrence of such activities, but unlike **globalisation**, it does not imply that the nation-states are losing their control or their influence over flows of information and financial capital. Rather, the existence and autonomy of nation-states seems assured by the fact that international processes are only made possible by the complicity and consent of national governments.

The difference between globalisation and internationalisation is important because while business processes and audience experiences may be globalising, legal, regulatory and taxation regimes remain firmly national, as do individual countries' periodic propensity for protectionism, restricting international flows of anything from cultural products to migrant workers. Hence quite a few *international agencies* have emerged to deal with the problems arising from this asymmetry. Some of the latter are associated with the prosecution of first-world agendas (e.g. WIPO, the World Bank, IMF, OECD, G20), while others are associated with developing-world agendas (UNESCO, UNCTAD, UNDP, etc.).

The social theorist Paul Hirst has disputed that globalisation is taking place. For him, 'globalisation' assumes that economic adjustments 'are not thought to be the subject of policy by public bodies or authorities, but are a consequence of "unorganised" or "spontaneous" market forces'. Hirst argues that, on the contrary, 'the world-wide international economy has been determined in its structure and the distribution of power within it by the major nation states' (1996: 2–3). Thus internationalisation is an alternative model of geopolitical power relations, criticising the concept of globalisation. Paul Krugman in his book *Pop Internationalism* also warns against overstating the advent of globalisation, by pointing to historical international relations that demonstrate globalisation to be nothing new. Prior to the First World War, for instance, Britain's overseas investments exceeded its domestic stock capital; 'a record no major country has ever come close to matching since' (1997: 207).

For David Held, the problems associated with globalisation, such as environmental and economic interdependency, cannot be solved at the level of nation-states. Recognising that little has changed in international political structures and processes does not offer new ways forward (Held, 2002). It also downplays the popular uptake of international and global traffic, which national governments certainly seem minded to manage as best they can, but which they clearly don't control. In other words, official agencies are surfing global waves too.

See also: **Anti-globalisation, Globalisation, New economy**

INTERPELLATION

A term from the writings of the French Marxist political philosopher Louis Althusser (1971), sometimes translated as 'appellation'. It refers to what he takes to be the process by which **ideology** 'hails' individuals as its subject. Individuals are said to be interpellated by the discursive, linguistic, symbolic order in which they live, for example by gender-discourses (Butler, 1990). Thus, for Althusserians, ideology is general and inescapable, as well as being a material product of **ideological state apparatuses**. Interpellation is the very mechanism by which people are subjected to ideology, via the textual operation of 'audience positioning'.

Both the notion of interpellation and that of 'ideology in general' have been criticised since the early 1970s, when they were most influential, as being too essentialist and abstract. It doesn't take us very far in understanding specific ideological operations, because everyone is immersed in language – and thus being 'hailed' – all the time.

However, interpellation can be useful as a concept when applied to specific **discourses**. For example, Laclau (1977) writes of a struggle between discourses in pre-Second World War Germany, where the discourse of 'old Prussianism' interpellated a 'nationalist and authoritarian' subject, while 'in Nazi discourse . . . the interpellated subject was a racial one' (pp. 116–42). In this kind of usage, interpellation has something in common with the concepts of **mode of address**, orientation and preferred reading, with the added conceptual advantage that it presumes the *politics* of discourse.

See also: **Mode of address, Subjectivity**

INTERTEXTUALITY

Semiotic relations among **texts** (i.e. internal textual features, not relations between texts and producers or users). Many literary works allude to, quote, copy, or mock other literary works, and bear within themselves marks or traces of the semiotic universe in which they move, from generic **conventions** down to topical phrases and words. Because texts are communicative, what they are made of must always come from, connect with, and relate back to the system of sense-making of which each one is a product and differentiated part. You have to use words that others have used. Humpty Dumpty's idea, in Lewis Carroll's *Alice Through the Looking Glass*: 'When *I* use a word . . . it means just what I choose it to mean – neither more nor less', is rightly understood as Alice-in-Wonderland nonsensicality. This is because *all* texts are constitutionally intertextual.

Although they are much more complex than the individual **signs** from which they are made, media texts (like news items, advertisements, music-videos, and full-scale fictional forms) nevertheless display the same *negative* characteristic that Saussure identified in concepts, which he defined: 'not positively, in terms of their content, but negatively by contrast with other items in the same system. What characterises each most exactly is being whatever the others are not' (Saussure, 1974: 117). From this insight, semiotic and **structuralist** theories have argued that intertextuality is inescapable at the most fundamental level.

While naturalistic and realistic content strives very hard to appear transparent, conveying directly some trace of the extra-textual reality that the text seeks to signify, other forms, especially comedy, parody, satire and spoof, rely very heavily on intertextuality. Indeed, as Jonathan Gray (2006) points out, intertextuality is the basic proposition of hit comedy shows like *The Simpsons*, which uses parody to talk back to naturalistic genres like sitcoms, advertising and the news. The appeal of *The Simpsons* includes the fact that it celebrates rather than suppresses the intertextuality of popular culture, thereby both flattering and extending its media-savvy audience's extensive media literacy.

See also: **Genre, Representation, Signification**

Further reading: Fiske (1987); Orr (2003)

JOURNALISM

Non-fictional writing about current events, for pay and publication. Journalism is an occupational category and practice; usually distinguished from the output of that practice, which is *news*, although some definitions of journalism designate it as the collective noun for 'newspapers and magazines' as a whole. Journalism has been a growth industry and hot topic in communication, cultural and media studies in recent years, for two opposing reasons.

First, the occupation itself is rapidly professionalising, in the Western world especially, so that now it is rare for a someone seeking employment in the mainstream press and news media not to have at least an undergraduate degree in journalism or a cognate subject. As a result of this growth in teaching programmes, the field of journalism *studies* has also grown very rapidly, with many new books, journals, conferences and websites devoted to it and, therefore, much new academic debate about and research into journalism as a profession. *Professional* journalism research is largely devoted to empirical studies of the industry and its practices, from a social-scientific perspective that is interested, for example, in the sociology and psychology of news organisations, the political science of communication as part of the democratic process, and (more rarely) the behaviour of news consumers (Allen, 2010; Wahl-Jorgensen and Hanitzsch, 2009; Löffelholz *et al.*, 2008; Lumby and Probyn, 2004).

Second, and simultaneously, journalism itself is in the middle of a major, historic crisis. Three things are happening at once:

- technological disruption, as the affordances of social networking, interactive, participatory online media have become ever more extensively available;
- a controversy about what counts as journalism and who practices it, that centres on perceived differences – and persistent low-level warfare – between paid journalists (working in newsrooms for recognised proprietors and mastheads) and 'amateurs' (the blogosphere; citizen journalists; wiki journalism like Wikinews or WikiLeaks; participatory media like OhmyNews, etc.);
- the lack of growth in employment openings for traditional journalists (despite the increase in journalism graduates and technological opportunities), and as a result of declining profitability in analogue media, a radical alteration of the way the press and broadcast news industries are organised internally.

In the midst of this turbulence, whereby journalism is becoming more embattled as it becomes more professional, and where professional advocates represent a decreasing share of total practitioners, it is perhaps hardly surprising to find the field of journalism studies at loggerheads with some of its disciplinary neighbours, especially **cultural studies**, which investigates the field of news media but seems to pay scant regard to journalists. The evident gap between journalism and popular culture is real, but it is also a link. The respective fields of study are linked too, because they are at either end of the same information supply chain. At one end is the writer (producer) and at the other the reader (consumer). Journalism studies in the USA, United Kingdom and other countries like Australia have tended to focus on the occupation of the news reporter and the history, personalities and procedures of the industry, often with little interest in the readership beyond its scale. Cultural studies, conversely, has had more to say about the *cultural form* of journalism, investigated from the point of view of the reader or audience, giving no special status to journalists themselves. Furthermore, it is out of the humanities-based fields of cultural and media studies that most scholarly attention has been devoted to the new, non-canonical versions of journalism (Bruns, 2005; Flew, 2008). The often strained relations between scholars of journalism and culture may simply be 'referred pain' – an expression of a real but indirectly experienced conflict of interest between producers and consumers of news in modern societies (*see* **consumption/production**). However, since that very distinction is now under attrition, perhaps it is time for journalism studies and cultural studies to recognise their commonality in the larger historical and technological context.

See also: **News values**, **Objectivity**

KINESICS

The **semiotics** of movement, especially human movement and gesture. Movement, both of the body and by locomotion, is not merely functional but is also **coded**, meaningful and communicative. What is conveyed when you wave your arms about may differ considerably from the 'same' message uttered with arms folded. Walking is highly communicative, bringing posture, speed, direction, etc. to bear on meaning. It is further semioticised via such 'media' as the fashion catwalk. Dance is the aestheticisation of kinesic codes, and some versions of modern dance can be regarded as a mode of analysis thereof. Kinesics was introduced into psychological approaches to non-verbal and interpersonal communication by Birdwhistell (1970).

More recently, interest in kinesics has been revived through automation for animation, often using a process called motion-capture or moco, where an actor or performer wears sensors that allow their motion (but not their appearance) to be captured for digital modelling. Thus the performance is purely kinesic.

KNOWLEDGE

Skills, expertise, theoretical and practical understanding, within the knowing subject; the body or corpus of what is known on a topic inter-subjectively, or in repositories such as the internet, or in discovery processes like science; in philosophy, information generally accepted as justified, true, and believed; in science, the contestable outcome of a social practice of empirical observation, measurement, and theorising. Knowledge is an important topic in communication, cultural and media studies because, although it is known by individuals, it is fundamentally a social and communicative phenomenon.

Knowledge is not just a 'thing' (like a fact). It is part of a social process of production, circulation and use, an idea captured in Francis Bacon's famous phrase 'knowledge is power'. In order to be used it must be communicated to others through **representations**, **language** and technologies like writing, printing, or screen media. At each stage of this process there is opportunity for error, delusion or deceit, resulting in a persistent suspicion of such media – especially **new media** – as if they themselves are responsible for tainting knowledge or making people forget how to produce it for themselves (this was Plato's objection to writing). Knowledge can thus become the prize among contending systems of representation, as in the Renaissance when rational, scientific method based on print began to challenge revealed, divine knowledge conveyed by ecclesiastical authority and expressed in oral (liturgical) modes. The 'iconoclasm' (breaking of icons) of the Reformation was seen by the militant Protestants who smashed statues in cathedrals across Northern Europe as the literal destruction of false knowledge, to be replaced by truth, which was to be found in The Book. This is but one example of many where the means of transmission have taken the fall for carrying messages that emergent ideologies disputed.

In recent times the idea that knowledge is not confined to consciousness – the human brain – has developed in the biosciences, where genetics requires that something like knowledge is transmitted through DNA or the immune system, for instance, without any reference to the human mind as such. Hence it is now possible to see knowledge as a function of *complex systems*, with three criteria for it to count as usefully available (although not conscious) knowledge:

- The system needs to be *adaptive* and *retentive* – dynamic and self-organising, with feedback loops or *learning* mechanisms, i.e. it produces and uses knowledge to sustain itself as a system;

- The knowledge it produces must in some way *represent* the environment beyond the system (the outside world; other systems) and be *usable* to deal with that external environment – it must be both *realist* and *selective*;
- The system has to be able to *access* information quickly enough for it to be useful – a *retrieval* mechanism to convert 'object' (knowledge) into *action* (*Wikipedia*: Knowledge; Traill, 2005–8).

Knowledge as a property of complex systems underlies the emergence of the concept of the **knowledge economy**, where the economy itself is seen as an open, dynamic, complex system (or system of systems). This idea has had a transformative impact on economics as a discipline, moving beyond the notion of 'allocation of scarce resources' to reconstitute the 'object of study' of economic as *the growth of knowledge*. In turn this is important for communication, cultural and media studies because the social process of generating, selecting, implementing, retaining and destroying knowledge fully overlaps with culture, communication, media and creativity. Thus, creative imagination is the driver of ideas, which – in the form of **intellectual property** – are the engine of innovation in post-industrial economies.

Here a distinction between 'tacit' and 'explicit' knowledge needs to be recognised. Traditionally understood, intellectual knowledge was contained in (and often confined to) one of the recognised disciplines or branches of formal scientific inquiry or their equivalent in the social sciences and humanities. Within each disciplinary specialism, new knowledge could be tested against existing bodies thereof, using established methodology and techniques of inquiry. This is explicit knowledge. Tacit knowledge or 'know-how' is traditionally of lower status, being regarded as technical, the province of artisans and mechanics, even 'old wives' tales', not that of scientists and intellectuals.

But in the **new economy**, knowledge has become much more volatile, inter-disciplinary, and exposed to the workings of commerce, entrepreneurship, and large-scale exploitation. Scientific, intellectual and tacit knowledge are much more inter-dependent; for instance in the information technology area, where technical skills, intellectual innovation and commercial investment are inseparable. Although this is seen as a defining characteristic of the knowledge economy, it has to be acknowledged that it is nothing new. Indeed, entire new sciences, such as avionics and rocketry, were established by imaginative-entrepreneurial trial and error, outside of the formal scientific institutions of knowledge, and only once they had been proven to work did they gain acceptance.

Knowledge in the new economy has to be distinctive. It has to be easy to replicate, but hard to imitate (Leadbeater and Oakley, 2001: 19). Further, it has to be put into an entrepreneurial context, to mobilise capital resources, and find a market. Such knowledge differs from the kind of 'public good' knowledge exemplified by the traditional sciences and disciplines. But it may still sustain public, even utopian, ambitions. Charles Leadbeater, for instance, argues that the new economy is about creating value, human and social as well as financial: 'Political empowerment and economic opportunity stem from the same root: the spread of knowledge' (Leadbeater, 1999: 222).

See also: **Information society, Knowledge economy**

KNOWLEDGE ECONOMY

Charles Leadbeater (1999) uses chocolate cake recipes as a metaphor to describe the workings of the knowledge economy. A chocolate cake itself is what economists would describe as a rival good: If I eat it you will not be able to eat it. A chocolate cake recipe, on the other hand, is a non-rival good. Many people can use the recipe without it being depleted. In the knowledge economy it is the recipe that is valuable. It can be transferred to others and reproduced and copied by chocolate cake eaters around the world. The production of the cake is therefore not limited to one recipe owner, who would then have to spend significant time and resource producing many cakes. The cake belongs to many producers, with consumers becoming creators themselves in the baking process. As Leadbeater writes,

> knowledge can make a lasting impact on well-being: a recipe stays with you long after cake has been eaten. The more an economy promotes the production and spread of knowledge, rather than just the exchange of goods and services, the better off we become.
>
> (Leadbeater, 1999: 33).

The knowledge economy is a significant new development in economic activity. The Organisation for Economic Co-operation and Development (OECD), estimated that half of member countries' national output to be 'knowledge based' by the mid-1990s. In a knowledge economy the use of information and ideas power growth rather than tangible assets (*see* **intangibles**). Giddens (2000) compared the market-to-book ratio (the difference between its material assets and saleable value) of Microsoft with General Motors (GM). For Microsoft the market-to-book ratio was 13, whereas for GM it was only 1.6 . . . and GM went on to eventual bankruptcy. Assets such as property and equipment can no longer be relied upon to assess the value of a company. Instead, in the knowledge economy, value lies in the expertise, ideas and innovative qualities of the workforce.

For Manuel Castells the defining characteristic of the knowledge economy is not the *generation* but the *application* of **knowledge** in a way that feeds back to generate new knowledge – a virtuous cycle of knowledge creation (Castells, 2000). Information sharing in the knowledge economy is accumulative. Computer software is a **code** that can be distributed to many in order for them to create using the software's information, or structure. It is not used up or consumed, but reproduced, added to and utilised in the production of new innovations.

As a knowledge economy relies upon a knowledge base, developing strategies to foster an entrepreneurial, 'smart' society are becoming prevalent in policy arenas. Education is central to the cultivation of a knowledge economy, providing people with the skills to become creators and to use information shrewdly in business practice. Information and information technologies are also important in the development and distribution of knowledge as are appropriate legal frameworks to ensure **intellectual property** protection.

See also: **Globalisation**, **Information society**, **Network society**, **New economy**

LABOUR, PRECARIOUS LABOUR

The 'labour theory of value' is a Marxist concept, derived from the classical economics of Adam Smith and others, in which the price of goods is related to the amount of labour required to produce them. Marx differed from his predecessors by assuming the *exploitative* nature of capitalism, which he thought must follow from the difference between *labour power* (the available potential of workers to perform labour, given their own capacities and strengths), *actual labour* (production of value), and *surplus labour* (the difference between the cost of hiring workers for their labour power and the price obtained for the product of that labour). This difference takes the form of profit. Thus Marx saw profit as the appropriation *by* capitalists *of* the value of labour power *from* workers: a kind of socialised theft, kept in place by *class* monopolisation of the means of production (capital, resources), a coercive *state* dedicated to preserving in the political domain the asymmetry of power between capitalists and proletariats generated in the economic domain, and a **hegemonic** superstructure of **culture** and **ideology** to provide the grubby reality with a nice frockcoat.

While this model may have had some explanatory – or dramatic – power in the context of the nineteenth-century factory system of mechanical industrialisation, it has found less favour subsequently, in both economic theory, which went over to the mathematical modelling of marginal utility in neoclassical economics (Marshall, 1961; Schumpeter, 1976), and in post-industrial economic systems, where value is seen to be created not directly by labour but through the application of **knowledge**.

However, a vestige of Marxist theories of labour has survived into contemporary communication, cultural and media studies in the form of the concept of 'precarious labour', which is used as a critical concept to draw attention to the downside of otherwise welcome developments in the **new economy**, based on ICT (information and communications technology), knowledge and creativity – developments such as participatory culture, consumer co-creation, shared or crowd-sourced knowledge, the open source movement, developments like social networking and the Wikipedia, and consumer input into the development of new media forms such as computer games.

Thus, 'precarity' is used as part of **anti-globalisation**, anti-neoliberal discourses, to critique the impact of **globalisation** (in this case of the labour market, where low-paid jobs are exported to developing countries) IT-based automation (where manufacturing workers are made redundant), consumer services (where the low-pay labour force is typically feminised and casualised, and populated by migrant or unregistered labour), creative industries and consumer co-creation (where 'free labour' is extracted from both artists and consumers).

Critics draw attention to the tendency in these sectors for work to be casual, outsourced, part-time, feminised, de-unionised, unprotected by insurance, pension rights, etc., and frequently altogether unpaid, as when workers are on call 24/7 or where corporations profit from the participatory creative inputs of consumers, e.g. online social-networking sites. A prominent literature has emerged in cultural studies to prosecute this line of argument.

Further reading: Deuze (2007); Deuze and Banks (2009); Florida (2002); Ross (2009)

LANGUAGE

Speech – usually taken to refer to the whole body of words (vocabulary) and ways of combining them (grammar) that is used by a nation or people, or a speech community. The ordinary usage of the term tends to assume that language is:

- a specific language, like Welsh, Nyungar or English;
- a nomenclature – an instrument or tool for naming objects that exist out there in the world;
- an instrument for expressing thoughts that exist inside the head ('inner speech').

None of these usages has survived intact in the study of communication. First, language is studied as a *general capacity*, not as an aggregate of individual languages. Second, the relations among thoughts, words and external objects have been the focus of much theorising, the result of which, at the very least, is to put in question any idea that words simply name objects or express thoughts. Such an idea assumes language to be a mere reflection of something else that can be known externally to language. The objection to such an assumption is that it denies any active force to language, reducing it to a mere instrument or tool, like a hammer. Thus commonsensical ideas about language as an expressive nomenclature fail to take into account the extent to which both thoughts and objects can be known only through their representation in some form of language.

Just as atomic physics started by isolating individual atoms but ended up by identifying much smaller particles and forces, so linguistics has identified language as comprising structures and rules operating between elements within words. In Saussurian linguistics, the most basic is the **phoneme**, or unit of recognisably distinct sound that figures in a particular language. Different languages have different phonemes (e.g. there's no /j/in Welsh; no /ll/, /ch/, /rh/ in English). But all languages operate with a finite number of phonemes which can then be combined to form words. So language is no longer seen as a 'body of words', but rather as a generative structure or **langue** which is capable of producing **signs**. Beyond phonemic analysis, linguistics has developed around the study of **semantics** and syntax (rules of combination).

Linguistics has traditionally centred on speech. **Semiotics**, on the other hand, has taken on the Saussurian model of language and used it to analyse all kinds of **signification** other than speech – writing, architecture, television, cinema, food, fashion and furniture, for instance; in short, any system that can be used to signify. There is no doubt that sign-systems like dress codes do signify (that is, the way their elements can be selected and combined does serve to communicate **meanings**), but whether they do it *as* language or *like* language remains a matter for debate.

Within communication and cultural studies there is widespread agreement that whether they are studied as languages or as language-like, signifying systems of all kinds share certain characteristics. These are:

- meaning is not a result of the intrinsic properties of individual signs or words, but of the systematic relations between the different elements;
- language is not an empirical thing but a social capacity;
- individuals are not the source of language but its product – language thinks itself out, as it were, in individuals.

Language always escapes the individual and even the social will: it's the paradigm example of an evolving, open, adaptive, complex network-system. Some of the more important concepts and terms associated with the study of language are included under separate entries.

See also: **Code, Diachronic, Discourse, Language (functions of), Langue, Paradigm, Parole, Phonemic/phonetic, Phonology, Pragmatics, Semantics, Semiosphere, Semiotics, Signification, Structuralism, Synchronic, Syntagm**

LANGUAGE, FUNCTIONS OF

The purposes which **language** can be made to serve in different situations. Although we may regard language primarily as a means of making statements that are true or false (the *referential function*), or as an instrument for the communication of ideas (the *ideational function*), this is only part of the total picture. Thus, while the referential or ideational function may be *seen* as prominent in news reporting, science writing, courtroom testimony, and so on, several other functions have come to be identified as important in everyday language use.

One well-known and continuingly useful account of language function is supplied by Roman Jakobson (1960; Hébert, 2006), who identified six functions of language:

- Referential (the thing 'spoken of')
- Phatic

- Regulatory (or 'Conative')
- Emotive
- Aesthetic (or 'Poetic')
- Metalinguistic

We commonly use language not just for articulating ideas but for making and sustaining contact, often using quite ritualised formulae which are almost devoid of content. This use is known as the **phatic** *function* of language. It is frequently misunderstood and dismissed as 'meaningless babble', 'chat' or 'gossip', for instance when commentators criticise instant messaging or online social-networking sites like Twitter. But instead of belittling such functionality, observers would be wise to note from them how important phatic communication is to the human animal.

Language is also used to affect the actions and dispositions of others by commands, requests, instructions, and other more subtle acts of verbal persuasion. The language of advertising and of political campaigns relies heavily on this function, which is known as the *regulatory* or *conative function*. In the case of the regulatory function the focus of the language is on the actions and dispositions of the addressee. In contrast to this, language may be used to express the feelings and dispositions of the speaker irrespective of whether an audience is present at all. This is known as the *emotive function* – language used (sometimes involuntarily or unwittingly to the speaker) for the expression of feelings. Language may also be used as a source of intrinsic pleasure. The general name for this kind of activity is the **aesthetic** or poetic function. More or less self-conscious playing with language operates in differing linguistic domains, involving not only sound-play, as in rhyme and alliteration (nowadays more dispersed via popular song than by poetry as such), but also punning, ambiguity, grammatical rule-breaking, language games and contests, and so on. Advertising and – at its best – teaching, also employ language as much in its aesthetic function as in its conative.

Another important, if sometimes overlooked, function is the use of language to explore and reflect upon *itself*, known as the *metalinguistic function*. A surprising amount of everyday discourse turns out to be metalinguistic – from the television interviewer's 'Is what you're saying then Prime Minister . . .?' to someone in an argument complaining 'That doesn't make sense'. Grammar books and dictionaries, of course, rely heavily on the metalinguistic function, as does a book like this, especially at moments when it supplies definitions of terms.

The notion of function is important principally because it helps to emphasise the way in which language is much more than a tool for thinking with or a vehicle for conveying information. In this way, functional perspectives tend to stress a range of other pressures upon language, and other possibilities for its use, than the need to express some kind of 'propositional content' in a strict logical form that may be measured for its truth value. *Speech act theory* focuses specifically on stipulating a range of actions which discrete utterances are capable of performing.

LANGUE

In Saussurian linguistics, the abstract system of **signs** and **codes** underlying individual acts of speaking. The role of langue may be seen as analogous to that of the musical score that underlies individual performances of a tune, or the rules of chess that make possible an unlimited variety of actual games. A musical score is independent of any one performance, and chess may be played with many different sequences of moves, on many sizes of board, with different kinds of pieces, and yet remain chess as long as the basic rules of the game are observed. In the same way, for English or Swahili or Gujarati, there is a common storehouse of basic, necessary conventions or rules which speakers of that language follow when framing their utterances. It is these conventions that constitute the langue for that language; and it is by following such shared conventions that intelligibility is guaranteed between speakers of that language. In this sense, langue is very much a social product shared between members of a social body as a whole and out of the control of any one individual.

The term was developed initially in the work of the Swiss linguist Ferdinand de Saussure. For him, contrasting langue with **parole** was an important methodological step in isolating the object of linguistic enquiry by focusing on the institution (langue) rather than the event (parole). The distinction is similarly formulated in much modern linguistics, whether as *competence* vs performance in the work of Noam Chomsky, or *potential* linguistic behaviour vs actual linguistic behaviour in the work of the systemic functionalist, Michael Halliday. In **structuralism** and in **semiotics** the notion of langue was extended to embrace other kinds of the sign than the purely linguistic one. Thus, patterns of kinship, the social organisation of furniture, food, and fashion have all been considered as examples of underlying systems.

See also: **Code**, **Parole**, **Syntagm**

LIFESTYLE

The **aestheticisation** of the practice of living. As a term in cultural and media studies, lifestyle crops up in two contexts, both of which designate a kind of middle-of-the-road version of **DIY culture** or **subculture**.

- The first relates to identity. Here 'lifestyle' may be added to the list of affinities covered in **identity politics**, as another marker of **difference**: class, race, ethnicity, sexual orientation, age, lifestyle, etc. This sort of lifestyle may relate to urban subcultures, or to **fanship**, music, sport, and the like.
- The second relates to the **content industries**. Here 'lifestyle' refers to a genre of TV programming and of general interest magazines, devoted to non-news journalism about household matters (home improvement, gardening, pets), bodily enhancement (fitness, health, beauty), or consumerism (shopping, travel, fashion).

Lifestyle is the fastest growing sector of **journalism**, out-performing news, and establishing whole new market sectors, for instance (to speak only of print media) the 'lad mags' which led the boom in lifestyle magazines aimed at both men and women in the 1990s and beyond. There is a globalised subscription TV channel called Lifestyle, which targets women viewers. Googling 'lifestyle' yields hundreds of millions of internet pages.

LITERACY

The social institution and practice of writing; by extension communication by any technological means other than speech, e.g. print and digital literacy. Literacy is not and never has been a *personal* attribute or ideologically inert individual skill. Neither is it a mere technology, though it does require a means of production, both physical (a tool to write with and a material to write on) and social (a recognised notation or alphabet and a way of transmitting the knowledge required to manipulate it). As a social institution, literacy is subject to similar kinds of forces to do with its distribution and regulation as are other kinds of institution. As a mode of communication, it is socially networked rather than individually acquired.

Its early history is usually characterised by strict controls as to who had access to it (priesthoods and economic or administrative officials) and what it was used for (sacred and state business). Modern societies are heavily committed to 'universal' literacy, and use it as an autonomous means of communication quite different from that of speech. This has led many observers to seek to account for the peculiarities of modem culture by reference to 'literate consciousness'. Prominent among them was Marshall McLuhan (1962). More recently, literacy has become the focus of important debates about the ideological function of education since, it is argued, literacy is a vehicle for the dissemination of values (as well as skills) that may be effective in reproducing hegemonic order. At the extremes, competence in codified and formalised literacy can be over-rewarded through the examination system, while other means of knowing and communication, such as creative imagination and oral performance, can be defined as disruptive and − if 'diagnosed' as attention deficit hyperactivity disorder (ADHD) − medicated rather than rewarded (Robinson, 2010).

Without having to claim that writing 'caused' the forms of consciousness and through them the social organisation of twentieth-century society, it is still possible to study the extent to which literacy carries with it more value than just an innocent skill. It is ideologically and politically charged − it can be used as a means of social control or regulation, but also as a progressive weapon in the struggle for emancipation. Above all, however, a literate workforce is a precondition for industrialised production, and the reproduction of a literate workforce requires large-scale state intervention in disseminating the appropriate level, type and content of literacy for this purpose. Hence, the era of mass industrialisation is also marked by the introduction of universal schooling, specifically to inculcate print-literacy in the industrial workforce.

Literacy has come to be associated with alphabetic writing, and not applied to the decipherment of audio-visual media like television or online affordances. One reason for this is that throughout the broadcast era 'media literacy' was confined for most people to the ability to *read only*. You could watch television, but it was much harder to 'write' with it. Furthermore, the introduction of *'media literacy'* education in schools and universities was often premised on the attempt to limit or control people's 'exposure' to media and the movies by teaching audiences to be more critical of what they watched, rather than seeking to teach them how to make their own TV. Now, new media technologies have brought prices of digital cameras down to that of a good pen, and computer software enables new possibilities for editing and exhibition, which means that it is within reach of anyone with access to digital technology to be a publisher and producer as well as a consumer. It is not too far-fetched to say that, as in the Renaissance period when written literacy began to proliferate, the gap between those who can read only and those who can both read and write is closing. Digital literacy as a widely dispersed mode of two-way communication is at hand.

See also: **Orality**

Further reading: Hartley (2009a)

LOCALISATION

Exploitation of the geographical niche. Following **globalisation** and new-media technologies, it may seem that the place in which an industry or creative production is made should be decreasingly relevant as world markets become increasingly connected at a level beyond state jurisdiction and national regulation. However, regions and cities are still known for what it is that they do well. Fashion is most intense in Paris, designer shoes are made in Italy, watches in Switzerland, films in Hollywood, audio equipment in Japan, and Indigenous art in Australia. Local niches are 'hubs' of creativity in a global system that stimulates differentiation rather than homogeneity in different regions.

The increased productivity made possible through industry **clusters** means that specialised local production can prevail. In fact, as Porter has pointed out, globalisation can make locational advantage more important than it has been in the past, as barriers to trade and investment are progressively dismantled through international trade agreements. With new communication technologies, firms are less dependent on the physical features and resources of a place and can 'choose the best location for productivity and dynamism' (Porter, 1998: xii; Florida, 2002). Krugman had a similar thing in mind when he stated that Los Angeles is no longer attached to the physical land that it occupies, but has 'cut loose from its geographical moorings' (Krugman, 1997: 209). People go to LA because the film companies are there. Restaurants, retail and tourism, and new media from television to games and software designers, follow the film people. So LA still has a *local* economy, but one based on its status as a world leader in **creative industries**, rather than its proximity to oilfields, or even incentives like low taxes – in a contact-intensive industry you can't afford *not* to be there. The next big city down the coast, San Diego, is not in the least like LA, because it has its own local economy, based in part on a naval base and proximity to Mexico.

If the cities of today function as self-perpetuating networks, then local culture is also likely to be strengthened and to develop alongside global culture. In **broadcasting**, the public projects of mass information dissemination through government television and radio are no longer the primary source of information in a multichannel, multimedia environment. A renewed interest in the local has emerged as the technological justifications for nation-wide broadcasting are eroded. Digital television technologies will soon make local TV as cheap to gather and distribute as local radio.

In recognition of this, city councils and local and regional governments are increasingly looking to enhance and promote the **lifestyle** of their locality. With a dual agenda of social/neighbourhood regeneration and competitiveness within the global economy these policy approaches have a specific focus on place rather than the nation as a whole. The mobilisation and coordination of funding bodies, arts, heritage and tourism agencies as well as private and third-sector groups is central to this trend. By providing opportunities for creative workers, creating programmes for skills development and advancing cultural industries with a wide appeal, cities (and some towns) are attempting to stand out in the global landscape.

See also: **Clusters, Creative industries, New economy**

MASS COMMUNICATION

Mass communication is the practice and product of providing leisure entertainment and information to an unknown audience by means of corporately financed, industrially produced, state-regulated, high-technology, privately consumed commodities, in the modern print, screen, audio and broadcast media – newspapers, magazines, cinema, television, radio and advertising; sometimes including book publishing (especially popular fiction) and music (the pop industry). The term 'mass' locates this concept in the industrial era, during which time cognate notions such as 'mass society' and 'the masses' coloured what it meant, associating the term with centralised control and often population-wide reception of often propagandistic messages, whether on behalf of the state or commerce.

Caution should be exercised with respect to the term itself. The word 'mass' may encourage the unthinking replication of **mass society theory**, while the word 'communication' in this context masks the social and industrial nature of the media, promoting a tendency to think of them as interpersonal communication. Since mass communication is neither mass nor communication as normally understood, the term should be seen as something akin to a proper name, denoting the field of media sociology (McQuail, 2005).

Mass communication is not a concept that can be defined, but a commonsense category that is used to lump a number of different phenomena together in a non-analytic way. Attempts to define it, however, are plentiful. They fail either because they are forced to be too restrictive, in which case the definition doesn't do justice to all that we commonly think of as mass communication – it is hard to encompass the diversity of what constitutes print, cinema, radio and television within one definition. Or else they fail because they are forced to become too over-extended, in which case the definition ends up applying equally well to things that are not usefully understood as mass communication – like education, religion, or even speech itself. Fortunately, the term is fading in scholarly prominence because online and digital media are not organised as 'mass communication' at all, but as customised and differentiated systems and networks.

Further reading: McQuail (2005)

MASS SOCIETY, MASS SOCIETY THEORY

An early twentieth-century model of the social organisation of industrial/capitalist societies which characterised them as comprising a vast work-force of atomised, isolated individuals without traditional bonds of locality or kinship, who were alienated from their labour by its repetitive, unskilled tendencies and by their subjection to the vagaries of the wage relationship (the *cash nexus*) and the fluctuations of the market. Such individuals were, it was thought, entirely at the mercy of totalitarian ideologies and propaganda and undue influence by the mass media (comprising, in this period, the press, cinema and radio). Mass society theory was an understandable response to the economics and politics of the 1930s, and was neatly summed up in Charles Chaplin's film *Modern Times* (1936). But it has hung on in a commonsense version which is associated largely with cultural and literary critics, for whom industrialisation and modern society in general remain a regrettable aberration from values and habits which these writers imagine used to prevail before the invention of machines, democracy and the like.

Mass society theory has been active in a wide range of media studies, where it tends to produce apocalyptic visions of what television and cinema are *doing to* the masses (but never, oddly enough, to the critic). Any time you speculate on what '**effect**' the media have on (other) people, especially if your thoughts turn to notions such as dependency, aggression, narcotisation, brutalisation and desensitisation, then you are thinking 'mass society theory'. Don't! Go and watch television, and ask yourself why these things are able to afflict others if they aren't happening to you.

See also: **Audience**, **Effects**

Further reading: Carey (1992)

MEANING

The import of any **signification**; meaning is intended, expressed or conveyed by a speaker, and inferred or decoded by a recipient (and these may not be causally connected). In linguistics this is the object of study of **semantics**. In some branches of philosophy (e.g. positivism), meaning results from verification and is a species of *truth*; in others, following Wittgenstein, meaning is an outcome of the *use* of language by speakers. In **semiotics**, meaning is the product of the relations among signs. Meaning is not 'immanent' but relational and contextual. It should not be assumed to reside *in* anything, be it **text**, utterance, programme, activity or behaviour, even though such acts and objects may be understood as meaningful.

Over the years the supposed *location* of the *source* of meaning has drifted down the producer–commodity–consumer chain (Hartley, 2008):

- In *pre-modern* (medieval) textual theories, meaning was divine, fixed in texts such as the Bible by God. Authorial intention was therefore unarguable: texts meant what their rather formidable '*producer*' said they did. All you had to do was work out what the Author 'meant'. Priests – 'authorities' – were on hand to do that for you.
- In **modern** times, textual theory located meaning in the *text*. Texts meant what they said. This was the heyday of modernist literary criticism, including the New Critics and Leavisites. You got at meaning yourself by using the technique of 'practical criticism' invented by I. A. Richards, which meant 'close critical reading' of the text, without reference to contextual features, including knowing who wrote it and when, or what other critics had said about it.

- In **postmodern** times, meaning was located in the **audience** or *reader*. Given the anonymous popular sovereignty of contemporary democracy, this was an egalitarian approach to meaning. It required large-scale sampling and ethnographic methods to get at what a text meant, because it meant what sufficient millions of people said it did.

It might be wise to hang on to all three of these links in meaning's 'value chain' – they all have some influence over the production, circulation and reproduction of meaningfulness.

Meaning has been proposed by Marshall Sahlins (1976) as a common 'third term' – added to material goods (economy) and social relations (politics) – to unify the anthropological study of culture. Meaning *in* economic and political arrangements thus becomes the proper subject of anthropology; and meaning becomes the product *of* culture. Working from this premise, Sahlins produced the notion of 'semiotic affluence' to match the then prevalent idea of the (economically) 'affluent society'. He proposed the notion of Stone Age affluence – it was rich in meanings.

Meaning is also the object of study in linguistics: see especially **pragmatics** and **semantics**.

Further reading: Barker (2008)

MEDIA POLICY

'Media policy' may refer to the protocols adopted by an organisation to regulate the dealings of its personnel with the media; or it may refer to the regime of regulation governing media ownership and control. It is in this latter sense that you are most likely to encounter the term. Media policy is a prominent branch of cultural policy studies (Lewis and Miller, 2003).

Media policy in any one country has tended to go through historical phases. Early policies were likely to favour the development of media industries (state subsidies for infrastructure and tax breaks for producers), and to protect the interests of state security. Later, especially after the Second World War in Europe and its colonies, media policy shifted to the concept of 'public service'; while in the Communist bloc it was tied to the interests of the ruling Party. After the Thatcher/Regan era of deregulation (and after the fall of communism), media policies turned to privatisation, although many countries continued to enforce rules restricting monopoly or foreign ownership of dominant media platforms. More recently, after the extension of the internet, media policy has turned to questions of access (digital inclusion), child protection (**censorship**), **intellectual property** rights management, and questions of national sovereignty.

In specific countries media policy may be guided by local traditions, influenced by constitutional, political, or religious interests. Thus, in the USA, the First Amendment (freedom of speech) is a major force in media policy. In China, conversely, central control over the 'culture industries' (newspapers, TV, etc.) has a direct impact on media content, as do the religion-inspired policies of states like Saudi Arabia and Iran.

MEDIASPHERE

The mediasphere is a term coined by Hartley (1996, 2008; Hartley and McKee, 2000), following Yuri Lotman's designation of the **semiosphere** (Lotman, 1990). The semiosphere is the whole cultural universe of a given culture, including all its speech, communication, and textual systems like literature and myth. The mediasphere is a smaller 'sphere', within the semiosphere, that includes all the output of the published media, both fictional and factual, on all **platforms**. The mediasphere, in turn, encloses the **public sphere**, and the 'public sphericules' that seem to have proliferated within that. The idea is that the public sphere is not separate from but enclosed within a wider sphere of cultural meaning, which is itself *mediated* as it is communicated back and forth from the cultural to the public domain. The idea of the mediasphere also allows for 'downward causation', where the overall systemic structure needs to be in place for communication at the micro-level to occur. Hence it is an alternate model to Saussurian linguistics, which seeks to account for meaning by isolating the 'smallest signifying unit' (i.e. the **signifier**). The mediasphere draws attention to the macro level, seeking to explain the mechanisms through which incommensurate and mutually untranslatable systems communicate with each other, and change (while remaining the 'same' system).

MEDIUM, MEDIA

A medium (plural = media) is simply any material through which something else may be transmitted. Painters use what they call 'medium', which is a clear transparent liquid that 'transmits' pigments. A psychic medium is one who purports to transmit messages between the world of the living and that of the dead (Sconce, 2000). Media of communication are therefore any means by which messages may be transmitted. Given the promiscuousness of human **semiosis**, just about anything can transmit a message, from a length of string with cans at either end, a length of wall with turrets at either end, to the internet.

By common usage, the term has narrowed to focus on the 'mass' media, rather than on telecommunications. '*The* media' were the **content industries** devoted to reaching very large popular audiences and readerships in different media: print (newspapers, magazines, popular publishing); screen (cinema, TV); and aural (recorded music, radio). During the twentieth century, these 'mass' media were characterised by their one-to-many centralised address, standardised content, high capital costs and technological innovation, and an tendency towards repertoire and **genre**. Despite their desire for ratings and reach, the 'mass' media had a take it or leave it attitude to audiences, i.e. audiences chose from among a repertoire of finished products; they didn't participate in content creation directly.

The media are still giant industries, and still display tendencies towards monopoly and vertical integration, exemplified by organisations like News Corp, which not only owns entire media industries in television, print and cinema, but also owns some of the sporting clubs and competitions whose matches draw viewers and readers to those media outlets. But since the 1990s, with **convergence** among the content media, telecommunications and interactive computing, the situation has changed radically. New media like computer games are interactive between users and manufacturers, with a proportion of content actually coming from consumers, who are as much partners as clients of media content providers. In other words the one-to-many model of media has been superseded, and now 'content' has integrated with telecommunications and computer interactivity, allowing 'many-to-many' communication, including private individual to private individual, exemplified by social network media like Facebook, YouTube, Twitter, etc.

The implications of this change for journalism, television, and the 'mass' media are still being thought through, although the virtually limitless archiving capacity of the internet, combined with the global scale of its potential reach, is already being exploited with sites for every specialist interest under the sun. Journalists are transforming into *editors* (manipulators of existing information) rather than *gatherers* (*see* **redaction**). Television has evolved into various post-broadcast forms, including 'media' that use webcams to transmit private life into cyberspace, there to become public spectacle.

METAPHOR

A **rhetorical** term where one thing stands for another. Metaphors become embedded in languages to such an extent that some linguists, e.g. Roman Jakobson (1960), have argued that they are one of the fundamental mechanisms for meaning-creation (the other is **metonym**). Humans make sense of the world, of themselves, and of their interactions, by extending to unknown or new phenomena the characteristics of known ones, thus capturing new experience in terms of something already known. The embeddedness of metaphor is intriguing, since it is unclear how far metaphors of space (especially higher and lower), for instance, condition people's thinking about each other's status. Symbolic and social life is completely suffused with metaphor: there's really no such thing as 'plain English'. The choices made to produce almost any *lexical string depend on embedded metaphor* – indeed, 'lexical *string*' is a metaphor; 'depend' is a metaphor (Latin '*hang from*'); 'em*bed*ded' is a metaphor; '*metaphor*' is a metaphor (Greek '*I carry across*' from *meta*, 'with, across, after' + *pherō*, 'I bear, carry').

Visual metaphors abound in cinema and TV, especially in the way that concrete visualisations stand for abstract ideas: there are both novel and clichéd ways to convey 'normality', 'threat', 'the city', 'prostitution', 'bad guy', etc. In television, visual metaphors are used to cue viewers as to the social standing of sitcom or soap opera characters or families – the style and decoration of fridges on the set, for instance. There was at one time a vogue for *spice racks* as a set dressing for sitcoms and serials; they served for a while was an almost infallible visual metaphor for 'middle-class family', presumably on the theory that no working-class family would be seen dead with one.

See also: **Metonym**

METHODOLOGY, METHOD

Academic disciplines are constituted by their methodology – the ways and means they use to find things out. Methodology is not the same as method; it is a meta-discursive term denoting the study of, or explicit concern with, methods of investigation in research of any kind, or the body of methods used in any one branch. The methodological tool cupboard of communication, cultural and media studies is capacious, because these are interdisciplinary fields. They have borrowed methods from sociology, anthropology and other social sciences with a history of serious concern for methodology, as well as from literary and textual analysis, in which formal method training has traditionally played a less prominent role.

Methods are usually rule-bound modes of investigation, taking care to outline their function and field of enquiry. Before a method is chosen it is important to establish what knowledge we are attempting to access and for what purpose. This is where methodology as the 'science' of method is useful, hovering behind such choices as a check not only on how well what is proposed fits in with established rules and procedures, but also on whether the right method for the job has been chosen.

Methods fall broadly into two categories – empirical and theoretical. Theoretical methodologies within communication and cultural studies include Marxism, psychoanalysis, **semiotics**, textual analysis, feminist and **queer theory**, as well as theoretical work done in contributory or neighbouring disciplines, from science to sociology. These types of methodologies are less interested in providing an individual method; rather they are concerned with the possibilities of understanding how we make sense of the world. They can be understood as 'macro' approaches, largely devoted to conceptualising and investigating the social-constructedness of culture, meaning, relations, identity, and thence various power inequalities operating in modern complex society.

Empirical methods operate at the 'micro' level, and are concerned with studying actually existing recoverable artefacts. These may include quantitative data – the numbers and statistics that may result from content analysis, censuses and surveys. Or the data may be qualitative, e.g. that collected via participant observation or ethnographic methods. Both quantitative and qualitative data may be suitable for *generalisation*.

But equally, individual texts are irreducibly empirical – you can prod them. So the practice of 'close textual reading', as done by cultural analysts, is itself an empirical method. However it is directed not towards generalisable samples, but *particularistic* readings.

There are frequent squabbles between 'empiricists' and 'textualists', because although both are interested in an empirical object of study, the method chosen in each case is very different. However, quantitative, qualitative, ethnographic and 'textual' methods are all necessary in the overall methodology of cultural, communication and media studies.

See also: **Audiences, Content analysis, Effects, Ethnography, Participant observation**

Further reading: White and Schwoch (2006)

METONYM

A figure from **rhetoric**, where a part stands for the whole. 'Silk' stands for 'lawyer'. Metonym works the other way round too: whole stands for part: 'The USA' might refer to the government of that country, or its basketball team, or a presidential opinion – all of these are metonymic uses of the term 'USA'. Metonymy may be used to identify a significant function: e.g. 'hand' for labourer, 'squeeze' for partner, 'head' for cattle. Along with **metaphor**, metonym was thought by the linguist Roman Jakobson to be a fundamental mode of meaning creation. Where metaphor works though choice substitution ('ice' for 'diamonds'), metonym works along the chain of **signification** (the **syntagm** as opposed to the **paradigm**). Jakobson thought that realistic novels were metonymic – part of life standing for its entirety. News is metonymic on the same principle, whereas drama may be metaphoric.

Further reading: Chandler (2007)

MODE OF ADDRESS

This concept refers to those processes that take place within a text to establish a relationship between the addresser (e.g. author) and the addressee (e.g. audience). It refers to how both media texts and media organisations cast their imagined reader. While it originates from the study of face-to-face communication, mode of address can also refer to textual features beyond verbal language.

Mode of address has a social aspect. In everyday communication, the way the same story is related will often alter when told to a friend, a parent, in a statement to a police officer, or via an office email.

In the textual context, mode of address is reliant on the **genre** in which it appears. It will alter between, for example, news and current affairs and game shows. One very obvious example is that in *factual* systems, like news, weather forecasts, sports reporting and documentary, the presenter looks at the camera (at *you*); in *fictional* stories characters never do – their gaze stays within the **diegetic** world (except in avant-garde films such as those of Jean-Luc Godard).

There is also a technical aspect to mode of address, where the medium itself imposes constraints on how its audience or spectator is positioned. A good example is perspective painting in art – an invention of the fifteenth century designed to solve the problem of how to render the spatial relations between objects *within* a painting, which had the peculiar (but now quite naturalised) effect of positioning the spectator *outside* of the text, at a single viewing point.

While there are differences in the processes involved, mode of address allows media texts to invent an essentially fictional image of their preferred audience. This is the foundation of psychographic consumer profiling. Therefore, Althusser's theory of **interpellation** is relevant. Interpellation refers to how subjects are 'hailed' by the discourse of a text. Consider the example of sports reporting. Here, interpellation works through the **ideology** of nation (or city, etc.). The commentator's mode of address assumes or even requires (hails) a partisan *national subject*. To understand the force of interpellation, then, you only have to watch sports coverage from someone else's nation or city – they're clearly not addressing you at all, and what's more they're getting excited about things that don't matter; it's all too obviously ideology. The Althusserian position is that *all* media discourse is ideological in this way, because no matter what it is about, it must employ a mode of address that interpellates a subject.

Consideration of mode of address need not be limited to individual texts. Entire television stations will utilise different modes of address in order to differentiate themselves and make unique the types of programming they offer. This feature can be noted most obviously in a station's own promotional advertising. The same can be said of newspapers, where what differs between one title and another is not the content (they cover the same stories) but the mode of address – one aims for women, one for lads, another for business leaders and so on. So the difference between the 'quality' and 'tabloid' press is at least in part a difference in mode of address, creating a special relationship between addresser and addressee through discursive strategies.

See also: **Ideology, Interpellation, Genre**

Further reading: Chandler (2007); www.aber.ac.uk/media/Documents/S4B/ sem08b.html

MODERN, MODERNITY, MODERNISM

Modern is a comparative term, traditionally paired with its conceptual opposite, 'ancient', which served to distinguish the moderns from their Classical, barbarian or mythological predecessors. It became significant only when that contrast was itself productive, i.e. from the European Renaissance onwards. Thus, we have not always been modern. In many ways we are not yet. Modernity may therefore be thought of as a period. Modern*ism* is a (later) ideological attitude towards this period.

Like all historical phenomena, modernity developed unevenly. It 'began' at rather different times over about half a millennium, depending on what you were looking at:

- *Economic* modernity began in the 1400s in the city-republics of Italy, with the invention of banking, joint-stock companies, international trade and therefore of capitalism.
- *Technological* modernity may be traced even further back to 'early modern' inventions that were made in medieval times, but without which modernity could not have taken the course that it did. These included the plough, compass, gunpowder and printing in Europe from the 1200s to 1450s. Technologies of exploration, mapping and navigation, associated with a range of maritime nations from the 1400s to 1600s – Genoa, Portugal, Spain, the Dutch, England – were also 'modern' applications of medieval technologies.
- *Literary* modernity began with psychologically realistic secular drama presented to an unknown audience for profit (Shakespeare); the novel (Cervantes); realism (both journalistic and literary); these developments occurred by the turn of the seventeenth century.
- *Scientific* modernity began with the scientific revolution of the seventeenth century, associated with Galileo and Francis Bacon, and with the Royal Society, founded in 1662.
- *Philosophical* modernity began with the Renaissance in Italy, and fruited in the Enlightenment, centred on the eighteenth-century philosophers of France.
- *Political* modernity began with the transfer of sovereignty from monarch to people. After an interrupted English experiment (1645–60), it was inaugurated successfully, i.e. continuingly, in the American (1776) and French (1789) Revolutions.
- *Industrial* modernity began with the Industrial Revolution, associated with the 'steam age' and manufacturing pioneered in England from about 1780 to 1830.
- *Cultural* modernity came of age in the nineteenth century, when all these influences were fused and generalised internationally, with the great metropolitan cities, rapid communication systems, industrial workforces, popular entertainments, and the beginnings of media, tourism, department stores, and mechanised warfare. Here was where New York began to outshine its European antecedents.

Modernism as an artistic or literary movement was associated with the intellectual and artistic reaction to the last named of the developments noted above; it was influential at the turn to the twentieth century. There was also, perhaps more importantly, a 'small-m modernism' that turned the historical amalgam of modernity (as above) into a kind of manifesto. This was modernism as the pursuit of modern ideals – reason, truth, progress, science, secularism, popular sovereignty, open society, technology, communication. Such an **ideology** of modernism may be contrasted with the *condition* of modernity by its partisanship, which has tended to become more pronounced the more it felt itself threatened. Threats to modernism of this sort came from three directions:

- Premodern thought – magical systems, traditional authority, private realities.
- Modernity's own 'dark side' – the horrors that reason and science could unleash, from the Holocaust to Hiroshima, Apartheid to colonialism, exploitation by market, gender, race, class, etc.
- **Postmodernism** – 'high' modernists saw 'postmodern' developments as undermining truth and reason in the name of relativism and irrealism, displacing the hope of progress in the rush for identity, which was seen as retribalising modern societies.

See also: **Culture wars, Meaning, Postmodern**

Further reading: Childs (2008)

MULTI-ACCENTUALITY

A property of **signs**, consisting in the capacity every sign has to signify more than one meaning, depending on the circumstances of its use. The term was coined by Volosinov (1973) as part of an argument which sought to show how the meaning of signs is fixed not by the abstract system of language (langue), but by the dialogic interaction of social relations within which the potential for meaning is fixed.

In principle multi-accentuality is a property of all signs, but in practice most signs are not constantly the object of active struggle. However, the concept remains useful in accounting for such phenomena as *anti-languages* or languages of resistance such as those of slaves in the West Indies in the eighteenth and nineteenth centuries, which are characterised by complete inversions of existing signs and their values (thus 'black' is inverted to become the sign for 'good', 'powerful', 'sacred', and so on). Feminism too has demonstrated that apparently inert signs ('he', 'man', 'mankind') are ideologically loaded and represent social power relations. They are multi-accentual, depending on who uses them.

MULTICULTURALISM

According equal status to the **diversity** of **ethnic** and **national** populations and their **cultures** present in a given society, as an objective of public policy. The advent of multiculturalism as a governmental programme marks a deliberate departure in the way that nation-states have historically chosen to depict themselves. Rather than projecting an image of the nation as a unified, ethnically and culturally homogenous group, multiculturalism recognises that contemporary society is made up of distinct and diverse groups. The official policies of multiculturalism aim to manage cultural diversity through welfare, culture (including media) and social-justice initiatives. The intention is to move away from 'assimilation' of migrants or Indigenous people, towards wider social acceptance of **difference** as something legitimate and valuable, for example in terms of national competitiveness in a globalised world.

Multiculturalism emerged in the latter half of the twentieth primarily as a response to political demands from ethnic minorities. Migration took on new significance for settler countries. It was no longer simply a means towards rapid population growth, but something culturally significant requiring government recognition and assistance.

Canada was the first country to establish multiculturalism as official state policy, to accommodate the separatist pressure from Francophone Canadians, especially in Quebec. It was later extended to include Inuit culture, eventually resulting in the establishment of the Indigenous territory Nunavut in 1999.

In the 1970s Australia declared itself multicultural, replacing its previous 'White Australia' policy. Considerable infrastructure was erected to support the new policy, including the SBS or Special Broadcasting Service, which is a national network of both radio and television dedicated to free-to-air broadcasting of materials in languages other than English, and English-language programming that promotes multicultural aims. SBS television, run on a shoestring compared to established public broadcasters (in Australia the ABC), is a wonder of world television.

Early works on multiculturalism advocated 'toleration' as a means to living peacefully in a society made up of disparate groups (Walzer,

1997). These have been replaced by demands for public affirmation and respect for difference, as toleration can have the negative implication of 'conceding the validity of society's disapproval and relying on its self-restraint' (Parekh, 2000: 1).

Some people of colour have rejected multiculturalism as cosmetic and even part of entertainment culture, arguing that it hasn't had sufficient effect on the living conditions of people living in non-white neighbourhoods. As Joan Morgan put it in the American context, multiculturalism *can* come over as another 'brand' of white consumerism:

> What white American racism offers to people of color, under the guise of multiculturalism, is an invitation to a dinner where we are expected to lay out a cultural smorgasbord while white America shows up with a very big fork.
>
> (Morgan, 1994: 34)

Multiculturalism has also come under attack from host communities, especially in populist politics and talkback radio, in the wake of radical Islam, although there are obviously two sides to that story. Some observers fear that multiculturalism is steadily being abandoned by Western societies.

See also: **Ethnicity, Diaspora, Nation**

MULTIMEDIA

The term multimedia was originally used to describe audio-visual presentations consisting of slide presentations synchronised to sound (Wise, 2000); the very same mode of exhibition as magic lantern shows of the nineteenth century. The literal definition of the term, as the processing and presentation of communication by more than one medium (audio *and* visual), still holds true, but has been extended and complicated in contemporary use. It is now most widely used to refer to communication that is mediated by computer technologies and that utilises a repertoire of graphics, text, sound, animation or video. This includes websites, video games, digital television, electronic books and CD-ROM. The boundaries of multimedia's definition are far-reaching and unspecified in literature on the subject. A common characteristic, however, is the appearance of cohesion, or 'seamlessness'. The integration of images, text, audio and video within multimedia is often made possible by digital technology, although it may also involve analogue media. Multimedia has liberated the way in which ideas are presented. The sci-fi dream of being able to layer sensory experiences in the recreation of real or imagined worlds – complete with taste, sound, touch and visual images – may not be yet fully realised, but it appears to be getting closer owing to multimedia developments.

See also: **Digital/analogue distribution, New media**

MYTH

Myth is generally understood to be a form of pre-modern **narrative** that is shared among members of a traditional community or culture. For Roland Barthes (1973), myth also refers to the appropriation of signs for the purposes of **ideology**, by making the cultural and constructed seem unarguable, a force of nature. Thus, in **structuralism** and **semiotics**, myth is not confined to traditional society.

Structuralism was influenced by the work of the anthropologist Claude Levi-Strauss, who argued that myths are unique to specific cultures and are used as a means of explaining the workings of the world: they are inductive thinking machines. The contradictions inherent in human existence and the continuities found in nature were thought through by the use of **binary opposition** (producing discontinuity in a continuous field), and story (causal sequence), to arrive at a form of 'practical reasoning (Sahlins, 1976) that explained but also **naturalised** the world. Structuralist analysis sought to apply these ideas to contemporary sense-making practices.

Where Barthes argued that myth was the 'second order' of **signification** (1973: 117), Fiske and Hartley (1978) posited a third order, which they called *mythology*, comprising strings of second-order signs, rendered into ideological narratives, as for instance in news coverage.

See also: **Narrative, Semiotics**

Further reading: Barker (2008); Lotman (1990)

NARRATIVE

Narrative is the art of sequential storytelling. It has two facets. The first is the *chain* or plot. Plot tends to move between an opening equilibrium that is disrupted, precipitating the action that goes through the usual tribulations, towards a new or restored equilibrium. The second facet involves *choice* or presentation – the way the story is realised or told, which may be via an 'omniscient' narrator outside of the story, or via a character within it (sometimes first-person), or it may be told through documents such as letters (real or fictional). Narrative is now strongly associated with prose, especially long-form fiction such as novels, but historically it can apply to other forms, including both narrative drama and narrative poetry. Thus, the devices and surprises *chosen* for a given narrative performance is often the focus of textual analysis.

Narratives may be analysed to reveal the work of **ideology** and **discourse** in both plot and presentation; chain and choice. In the former, narrative is driven by a series of questions and answers – often crises and conflicts faced by characters and their resolution in battle or marriage (or their semiotic equivalents) – in the movement between opening and closing equilibrium. Which character or discourse underpins these questions is often referred to as the 'point of view' that leads to a 'preferred reading' of the text. The resolution of these questions may involve the re-establishment of dominant cultural beliefs.

Thus, critics of news media point out that news stories are often populated with a cast of heroes, villains, fools and victims, stock characters who are 'played' for a day by some hapless unsuspecting politician or member of the public, including racial and gender stereotypes. In the presentation of such narrative, what types of individuals are chosen as heroes, victims, villains, or innocents may reproduce common cultural assumptions – quite possibly going back to Homer (Boyd, 2009).

Despite its sequential nature, narrative can be found in still images such as photographs and display advertisements, where the viewer is invited to make sense of the image in terms of a story – what happened before the image was captured and what will happen after. Thus it is clear that much of the work of narrative is done by the addressee as well as the addresser.

See also: **Discourse, Genre, Myth, Representation, Structuralism**

Further reading: Bordwell and Thompson (2006)

NATION

An 'imagined community', typically but not always linked by bounded territory, ethnic and cultural descent (sometimes including a common language), and self-determining political sovereignty (including the institutional apparatus of law, taxation and security). However, none of these positive attributes of nationhood determines how the *concept* is used in **discourse**, where, semiotically, it is a relational term; like any sign, one nation consists in being what the others are not.

Although in English 'the nation' originally signified all the *people* in Britain, 'nation' is more often used to mean *nation-state* – a sovereign polity with its own government, boundaries, defence forces, etc., and symbolic markers of nationhood such as a flag, an anthem, local currency, head of state, membership of the United Nations, and so on. However, there are many nations that are not also nation-states. Some states encompass more than one nation (e.g. Wales, Scotland and Northern Ireland in the United Kingdom). Then there are nations which exceed current national frontiers (e.g. China) or those incorpo-rated in several other states (e.g. Kurdistan). And there are some nations without a state or any territory at all (Palestine, for instance).

If territory doesn't define a nation, then neither does race or ethnicity, and nor does language or culture. Most modern nations are multiracial, multilingual and **multicultural** to some degree, if not always in official policy, and getting more so. So the dictionary or commonsense definition of a nation as being a large number of people of common ethnic descent, language and history, inhabiting a terri-tory bounded by defined limits, is seriously at odds with the facts.

In fact when nations are regarded as ethnic, coupling them to the state – putting nineteenth-century liberalism's innocent looking hyphen in the term 'nation-state' – can have disastrous consequences. A nation may be ethnic, but state ought not to be. 'Ethnic cleansing' is the latest technique for trying to make a state and a nation cotermi-nous. 'Balkanisation' is a term for the process of dissolution of a state into (often warring) statelets based on ethnicity. Rwanda in 1994 showed what can happen when a *state* apparatus is used to impose *ethnic* national ends. Many nation-states produce less bloody but nevertheless real internal tensions by coupling the nation to the state. For instance, despite the Indigenous nations living within it, and a very diverse multicultural population, Australia's official national icons, myths and heroes are relentlessly white and Anglo-Celtic.

This may explain why important critics such as Paul Gilroy believe that 'nation' is an irredeemable term, and that nationalism is always racist (Gilroy, 1987, 1993). In the context of Black activism, and the dispersal of African and Afro-Caribbean people right around the nations bordering the Atlantic Ocean from South America to Scotland, such a view has force. Even so, there are nationalisms that work from socialist and non-essentialist principles – in Wales for instance. And some postcolonial or decolonising countries have produced non-racist nationalisms that could be a model for others – Singapore for one. Indigenous ethno-nationalisms are 'mixed' in this context: they are emancipatory movements, but rely on ethnic descent to identify those in need of emancipation, and are not normally 'independence movements' as such. They seek recognition of ethnic nationhood within a larger nation-state. Perhaps they point the way towards nationalisms that can recognise race without succumbing to racism.

Clearly 'nation' refers not to the external world of 'facts' but to a symbolic referent – an 'imagined community' (Anderson, 1991), which is maintained by a wide variety of discursive institutions, ranging from national literatures and languages to national curricula in education. There are of course national inflections in all areas of economic, political, cultural and discursive life; but certain institutions play a more prominent and routine role in creating and sustaining an evolving referent for the concept and its subjects. Among the more important of these are the media.

Participation in the nation is 'imagined' because no-one can know more than an infinitesimal number of the other citizens of their nation, but it is a 'community' because everyone has complete confidence in the simultaneous co-existence of all the others. This sense of community is built and sustained by the quotidian rhythms of print and electronic media output, along with periodic national ceremonies which are themselves communicated through the media (Madianou, 2005).

With increased migration and mobility, these symbolic markers of a nation can be the only common 'heritage' it has. Certainly, such markers are ever more prevalent in the media, a common motif in advertisements, continuity and the like to propose a euphoric unity among groups which otherwise display few common traits. Here, the nation has been appropriated as a 'user-friendly' metaphor through which *multinational* firms mobilise not citizens but consumers. However, it is more than ever vital to make such markers ethnically inclusive.

See also: **Branding, Internationalisation**

Further reading: Anderson (1991)

NATURALISING

The process of representing the cultural and historical as natural.

Naturalising is a distinctive feature of ideological discourses. The ideological productivity of naturalisation is that circumstances and meanings that are socially, historically, economically and culturally determined (and hence open to change) are 'experienced' as natural – that is, inevitable, timeless, universal, genetic (and hence unarguable).

Naturalisation is the prize in modern cultural and signifying struggles; class or male supremacy, for example, is expressed as natural, and conversely resistance to that supremacy is represented as unnatural. So alternative discourses have to contend both with the naturalised discourses that continuously encourage us to understand social relations in ways that reproduce class and gender inequalities, and with the difficulty of establishing *as* natural (or as not unnatural) their alternative discourses and representations. Naturalising, then, is a force in the maintenance of hegemony.

See also: **Hegemony, Ex-nomination**

NATURALISM

A term which is often used as a synonym for **realism**. It first became influential in the theatre, where it referred to those **modernist** plays, especially Ibsen's, which tried to do away with **signs** and replace them with the objects that such signs had stood for. Thus, a play set in a living-room would be staged with a living-room on the stage – aspidistras, chintz curtains and all. Speeches would be written not as staged speeches, but as if they were 'actually happening'. Actors would not represent their characters, but become them; this became codified as 'method' acting. Of course, everyone on stage has to pretend the audience isn't there, since audiences aren't generally to be found in people's living-rooms. So this kind of theatre is voyeuristic from the point of view of the audience, a point of view known as the 'fourth wall', since that is the perspective the audience uses to view the play.

Clearly naturalism was a gift for cinema, and even more for the domesticated medium of television, where the camera and crew replace the audience in the setting, so you don't even have a sense of 'being in the theatre' to put alongside 'being in that person's living-room'. The ideological productivity of the naturalist conventions is considerable, because the 'reality' of the objects and interaction represented allows the representation itself to appear as innocent, self-effacing. Our attention is devoted to looking 'through' the screen and into the setting, so that any sense we might make of the drama appears to arise directly from the scene depicted, and not from its representation. It may come across more imperatively than something clearly constructed or 'handled' according to recognised conventions might do.

NATURE

The material world as a whole together with its determining forces; the inherent or essential qualities of an object which determine its form, substance and behaviour. Because it is a multi-discursive concept which defies attempts to give it a precise referent, the term should be used with care in analytical work. At the very least the nature of an object, or the material world of nature, or the word nature itself, should not be taken as self-evident with respect to any qualities, properties or characteristics whatever: these natures are the object of study, not the premise.

Nature is often contrasted with **culture**; the non-human as opposed to the human. However, this non-human nature is often taken to be an inherent or essential quality of the human itself – as in 'human nature'. In such usages the concept appears ultimately to be a secularisation of the category of God – a non-human agency which is beyond our control but which determines our characteristics and behaviour. In this kind of usage, nature is an ideological category.

The other main way in which nature is used in analytical discourses is as the material properties of an object. Hence the nature of something is contrasted with whatever conceptions of it might be available (the nature of the planet earth is contrasted with conceptions of it as flat). Hence nature in this sense is the proper object of study for science: the attempt to reveal or discover by analysis the 'true' nature (determining properties) of an object of study.

Further reading: Eagleton (2000)

NETWORK SOCIETY

In the late twentieth century, a historic shift occurred in the configurations of social organisation. Statism and capitalism – around which existing social principles were ordered – were both fundamentally redefined through the development of information technologies. Manuel Castells (1996, 2000) named this new social landscape the 'network society'.

Networks are interconnected, dynamic, rule-governed systems that exchange data selectively and intentionally. They dissolve centralised power and institutionalised hierarchy. Access to a network requires the ability to decipher, to understand the technology and its rules. In the network society, economic and political transactions are conducted by organisations that are arranged as information networks. Globalised (and largely digitised) markets shift capital strategically around the world at a rapid speed. Nation-states strive to become network states, maintaining influence not by 'splendid isolation' but through partnerships (the European Union, the United Nations, trade agreements, etc.). Individuals act and identities are established in social networks. Technology is vital: the internet is itself a decentralised communications network, supporting the network society.

Information technologies are at the centre of the network society. Microelectronics, communication technologies and genetic engineering signify a shift to a new technological paradigm characterised by connectivity and information. Whereas the technologies of the industrial age were created to accelerate the manufacturing of material goods, the technologies of the network society are used in the production and distribution of knowledge and information. **Biotechnology** and **nanotechnology** represent the extension of this cycle. These technologies manipulate the organic, coordinating the information of life at the molecular level.

Within the new paradigm, information technologies are used to create increasing returns within the network. Network pioneer Bob Metcalf realised that networks increase exponentially with each new addition. Thus, with telephone services, each new person with access to the phone-line significantly increases the possible pairings between all callers. Thus networks become more productive the more 'nodes' they carry; and this applies to digitally mediated social networks too (Barabási, 2003).

However, the network is selective and strategic by nature. An individual's or a group's place within a network will have consequences for their ability to generate wealth and to communicate effectively with others within the network. Individuals, localities and nation-states are susceptible to exclusion from the network, becoming disenfranchised. For Castells, choosing or being forced to live *outside* the network is associated with fundamentalism. Rejection of the network may motivate Al Qua'ida terrorism; which may therefore be said to be a product of its extension across the world.

See also: **Information society**, **Globalisation**, **Network theory**

Further reading: van Dijk (2006)

NETWORK THEORY

Network theory underpins the sociological concept of **network society** from the perspective of computer science, with mathematical models of the properties, behaviour, growth and dynamics (change) of networks. An important figure in the context of the growth of information networks like the World Wide Web is Albert-László Barabási, whose book *Linked* (2003) was designed to promote network thinking, in particular about scale-free networks and power-law distribution. Scale-free networks are those where the 'nodes' within the network can vary in the number of connections they have with other nodes, from very few to very many, according to a power-law distribution, which is better-known as the 'long tail' curve made famous by Chris Anderson (2006). Those nodes with very many connections are called 'hubs'.

In the first place this structure of hubs and nodes serves to protect the network as a whole from failure, because the probability of highly connected hubs being affected is low (in comparison with the risk to the high number of less-connected nodes), so the connectivity of the network as a whole is robust and able to tolerate local failures. This is of course one reason why the internet was invented in the first place, to provide increased security of information systems by distributing command and control functions across a network structure, rather than maintaining a centralised model which would suffer catastrophic failure if the single, central command 'hub' were to be destroyed.

When applied to social networks, the scale-free, power-law, long-tail attributes of networks explain various phenomena, such as 'small world' networks, where people who are not physically neighbours can nevertheless connect with myriad others via a small number of steps. It also provides a new model, in contrast to the structured opposition of previous, class-based models of social relations, of the relatedness of 'ordinary' people and those who enjoy power and prominence in society, such as politicians and celebrities. All these figures are nodes within a very large, complex social network structure (which also displays clusters, systems-within-systems, and dynamic change). Where 'ordinary' people are simply long-tail 'nodes' with very few connections (with their social group, community, workplace, etc.), celebrities and public figures typically have *myriad* connections. They are 'hubs', serving to link the network as a whole. They are responsible for the 'small world' phenomenon by allowing individual nodes to link with distant others (Figure 3).

Their importance to any network is signalled by the attention they

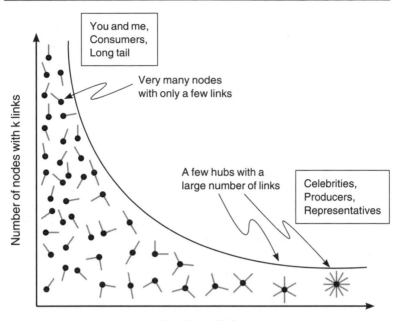

Figure 3 Power-law distribution. (Modified from Barabási, 2003: 71. Used with permission.)

receive simply for having lots of connections. This especially applies to celebrities who may not have an official or institutional position to justify their connectedness, which seems to arise purely from their social-network appeal to other 'nodes' on the network, in what has been dubbed the 'economics of attention' (Lanham, 2006). Such figures include, for instance, Paris Hilton (not least on YouTube), Stephen Fry (especially on Twitter), and teen stars like Miley Cyrus or Justin Bieber, whose star-bursts are often intense, but brief.

This indicates another feature of power-law curves, which is their 'winner-takes-all' characteristic. The amount of attention (and often financial reward) gained by those at the top of the 'hub' axis seems to be out of all proportion to those at the end of the long tail (although it's the same curve). What's more, mathematically at least, the 'winner' appears to be chosen by random probability rather than intrinsic properties. Thus people with half a dozen connections and people with half a billion may seem to occupy different worlds, but they don't, and in principle at least a kind of 'equality of opportunity' is in play, because from the point of view of the system *any* node can increase their number of connections and find their way to the 'head' end rather than the 'tail' of the long tail. Combining network theory with competitive individualism offers a new approach to the economics of attention.

Further reading: Newman *et al.* (2006)

NEW ECONOMY

An economy whose growth depends on the capitalisation and commercialisation of information and knowledge, delivering ICT- (information and communications technology) enhanced services. Manufacturing is still necessary, but much of this activity has been redistributed or outsourced to developing or emergent nations (*see* **globalisation**), or adapted to new technologies, in order to increase efficiency. In this way, the new economy consists of the knowledge and service industries. Skills, personality, knowledge, intelligence, information and the technology to mobilise such qualities are at the centre of the new economy. For some the new economy brings with it increasing risk, requiring new attention to the cultivation of social capital and trust (Giddens, 2000; Leadbeater, 1999).

The difference between 'new' and 'old' services can be seen in the tourism industry, where profitability was once concentrated in the provision and price of basic services like transport, hotels, etc. Now, however, tourism relies on the added value of the 'experience economy' or 'extreme' tourism, where people pay a premium not to travel cheaply but for an 'authentic' experience of the otherness of cultures, the thrill of risky activities, or even the 'dark tourism' of places touched by war and disaster. The value is in the knowledge-transfer from producer to consumer, not in the airfare.

See also: **Globalisation**, **Information society**, **Knowledge economy**, **Network society**

NEW MEDIA

A time-based, context-dependent, relative term, since what counts as 'new' depends on when you are making the observation. Obviously, *all* **media** were new at some point. However, the term 'new media' has become attached as a kind of proper name to the fruits of **convergence**, where *telecommunications* (networked, many-to-many or peer-to-peer communication), *computing* (ubiquitous ICT (information and communications technology), very-large-scale data, interactive software), and *media* (cinema, broadcasting, the press, publishing) began to overlap and integrate as part of the process of **globalisation** (Flew, 2008). New media industries are therefore those that exploit and benefit from online, digital networks and social network markets. They are marked by **interactivity** or participation; they are 'spreadable' media (Jenkins, 2009), and they are increasingly integrated with other aspects of life, especially via mobile devices and 'ubiquitous' computing.

Further reading: Creeber and Martin (2009)

NEWS, NEWS VALUES

News is a **media** form, distinguished from others by its textual-generic features (recent, factual, internally unconnected stories), mode of production (news-gathering and distribution), **mode of address** (to the citizen, voter, or public, rather than directly to the consumer), its institutional form (news organisations) and professional practices (**journalism**). Like other media forms (movies, music, photography) it is found across different media **platforms**, including the press (newspapers, magazines), radio and TV (broadcast news, subscription news networks like CNN, BBC World) and online (OhmyNews, Google News, www.guardian.co.uk).

News values are professional codes used in the selection, construction and presentation of news by these means. News values do not necessarily relate to individual journalists, who themselves are subject to personal values, beliefs and attitudes. Professionals generally justify the selection of stories not by reference to news values at all, but by reference, first, to the story itself – it has to be inherently newsworthy; and second, to the demands of the audience – i.e. the story is serving the public interest or satisfying their curiosity. Rather, the concept relates to the informal, often tacit, institutional and professional 'code' adopted by news organisations. Within these environments, news values work to unify varying ideological stances amongst journalists and **gatekeepers**.

Lots of things are true, recent, and interesting, but they don't end up in the news. Conversely, some things make headlines that turn out to be none of the above. This is why critical attention turned to news values. What institutional, ideological and systematic factors influence the choice and prominence of stories in the news? The following categories may be helpful, as long as it is recognised that news values are about news *stories* and not events themselves:

- News values prioritise stories about events that are recent, sudden, unambiguous, predictable, relevant and close (to the relevant culture, class or location).
- Priority is given to stories about the economy, government politics, industry and business, foreign affairs, domestic affairs either of conflict or human interest, disasters and sport.
- Priority is given to elite nations (USA, United Kingdom, Europe, etc.) and elite people (decision-makers, celebrities).
- News values often involve appeals to dominant **ideologies** and **discourses**. What is cultural and/or historical will be represented as natural and consensual.
- News stories need to appeal to readers/viewers so they must be commonsensical, entertaining and dramatic (like fiction), and visual.

(*See also:* http://mediaresearchhub.ssrc.org/icdc-content-folder/news-values)

In a handbook of 'independent journalism', ironically published by the US Department of State (i.e. as *propaganda* for the *free press*), Deborah Potter (2008) offers these news values: timeliness (recency), impact (affects lots of people; or has emotional charge), proximity (affects people 'here'), controversy (gets people upset), prominence (celebrity mishaps), currency (everyone's talking about it), and oddity (man bites dog).

See also: **Bias, Gatekeeper, Infotainment, Objectivity**

Further reading: Hartley (1982); O'Neill and Harcup (2009)

NOISE

A concept from information theory, noise refers to any interference that is experienced during the transfer of information between a sender and a receiver. Aside from its literal meaning, the concept refers to those outside influences that may alter or disrupt the original meaning of the information being sent. Noise can be either mechanical or semantic. The former includes, for example, static interference on radio and television, or pre-digital crackle over the phone. Semantic noise refers to confusion over the meaning of the message.

This can be caused by language and cultural differences as well the use of jargon or slang that may not be familiar to the receiver. While not central to contemporary media studies, the term is nevertheless useful for communication practices such as public relations. Here, noise refers to a broad range of interference to optimum communication such as lobby and interest groups, as well as competing discourse.

OBJECTIVITY

Objectivity is an invention of American journalism in the period around the turn of the twentieth century, when the idea of the 'informed citizen' gained prominence, along with the presumption that the press was the chief means for providing citizens with the information needed to make rational calculations and informed judgements about the issues, controversies and problems of the day (Schudson, 2001; Schudson and Anderson, 2009).

This notion of objectivity was taken over by television broadcast news in the heyday of Network TV, where news was seen as a flagship form of programming whose value lay in the profile, branding and reputation it accorded to the host TV station (rather than in its populist appeal). Thus CBS in particular, with Ed Murrow's show *See It Now*, and news anchors Walter Cronkite and Dan Rather, established a serious reputation for objective reporting.

Objectivity has never been a defining feature of the press in Europe, especially the United Kingdom, where a partisan model of the press has remained in place, even among the so-called 'newspapers of record' (the 'quality' press), which routinely support one side of politics over another. In continental Europe, many countries retain a subscription method of newspaper sales, which results in newspapers being tied to particular parties and their supporters. Such papers may well strive towards fair, impartial or objective reporting of *events*, but they maintain an editorial line in relation to *opinion*. The situation is different for broadcast media, especially in the context of public-service broadcasting regimes such as that which operates in the United Kingdom and other European countries (and their former colonies). There, broadcasters are required by legislation to maintain **impartiality**.

The demand for objectivity was partly driven by *spectrum scarcity* – it is more important where there are fewer choices of outlet. After the advent of subscription (cable) TV, and immeasurably more so after the wide extension of digital online media, there were plenty of outlets from which to choose. Objectivity was less crucial *within* a given channel or masthead. The first prominent TV station to convert this observation into a business plan was Fox News, which pioneered partisan TV-news on American television. It borrowed formats, rhetoric, personnel – and audiences – from talkback radio and the 'shock jocks', whose influence was based not on objectivity but on populism, i.e. news reported in congruence with the world-view of target audience psychographics.

Internet news is the most varied of all forms, and here objectivity can be so elusive that it may become a viable business plan. Thus the *Guardian.co.uk* website is the United Kingdom's biggest online 'newspaper', attracting nearly 40 million unique users, two-thirds not resident in the United Kingdom (January 2010: www.observer. com/2007/guardian-reclaims-america). This follows a deliberate strategy to attract international readers, especially refugees from Fox News in the USA, who are hungry for objectivity.

See also: **Bias, Impartiality, Journalism, News values**

ORALITY

That which characterises speech; by extension a culture characterised by the primacy of speech over other communication technologies, like writing. Usually opposed to **literacy**, orality refers to those aspects of a culture's way of life that are attributable to its investment in the resources of spoken language. These may include formal ways of organising thought (**myth**) or knowledge (magic); or they may be associated with rhetorical and other systems for fixing and transmitting sense.

The idea that oral cultures are fundamentally different from literate ones at the level of social and individual consciousness is associated with Marshall McLuhan, and may be followed up in Ong (1982). The analysis of oral systems of thought has occupied social anthropologists for years, and is perhaps best approached via the work of Lévi-Strauss (Leach, 1976, 1982), whose structural method revolutionised Western thinking about 'primitive' myths, analysing them as a form of reasoning appropriate to oral societies.

Despite its official promotion and pervasive presence in industrial societies, literacy nevertheless has to coexist with an abiding orality in certain crucial cultural spheres – perhaps the most obvious of which is the early socialisation of infants.

See also: **Digital literacy, Literacy, Rhetoric**

ORDINARY (CULTURE)

Ordinary culture, people and life, as opposed to high culture, the arts and literary learning, drawing attention to culture in the anthropological sense as 'whole way of life', and implicitly rejecting the Arnoldian idea of culture as the 'best that has been thought or said'. The study of ordinariness, everyday life, and cultural practices embedded in banal environments, including domestic spaces, the schoolyard, shopping malls and workplaces, can be traced directly from an essay by Welsh writer and critic Raymond Williams (1958b), 'Culture is Ordinary'. This became celebrated as one of the opening moves of contemporary cultural studies, and was a signature move in Williams' own work throughout his influential career.

Interestingly, the very essay that inaugurated the study of ordinariness was singular and far from ordinary in its literary quality, intellectual reach and cultural reference. Clearly Williams was not arguing for ordinariness as a site of a watered down, family-safe notion of culture – on the contrary he sought, and modelled, a culture in ordinariness that could give any 'teashop' snobbery or literary canon a run for its money, and take seriously the capabilities of the ordinary population, as English radicals have been doing since at least the Levellers and Tom Paine.

'Ordinary culture' can be linked to cultural anthropology, although unlike the latter it focuses on the analyst's own culture and language, and on contemporary rather than traditional life. It is also congruent with the sociology of 'everyday life' inaugurated by the Marxist thinker Henri Lefebvre and elaborated by Michel de Certeau (1984).

ORIENTALISM

An image of 'the Orient', projected by Eurocentric observers over the Near East (Ottoman Turkey), Middle East (from Israel to Iran), and Far East (especially China and Japan) in Western literature, philosophy and art. The term was coined by Edward Said (1979, 1985), a Palestinian intellectual living in the USA. Orientalism is to be found in both historical and academic accounts, arising from former imperial powers like Britain and France, and more recently the USA.

It was not a direct form of intentional racism; rather it arose from the desire of writers, artists and travellers to understand **difference**. To represent it, however, Said argued that they projected on to the 'other' what was regarded as exotic, mysterious and desirable in the 'home' culture. Orientalism is thus a discourse that reveals more about those who imagined 'the East' than it does about the people and cultures of those regions. According to Said and **postcolonial** writers, despite often benign intentions, its material effects were racist. The imperialising and hegemonic powers, which intervened in these countries politically and commercially for several centuries up until the present time, treated local populations according to the Orientalist images in their heads, rather than as those populations wanted to represent themselves.

Orientalism produces a **binary opposition** that places the West as the 'subject' of modern, enlightened thought, and the Orient as the mysterious and often dangerous 'object' – the Other. Like all such oppositions, this one relies on a series of cultural constructions that **naturalise** and displace cruder biological essentialism, as well as overlaying and as it were providing an alibi for uninspected racial, religious and cultural prejudices. The concept of Orientalism is useful for analysing media constructions. *Indiana Jones and the Temple of Doom*, among many others, provides an example (it's not being picked out for any particular culpability, but just because it is typical). The Western hero is represented as noble, brave, strong, sexual and of consummate ability. In contrast, Oriental characters in the movie are either helpless victims awaiting the arrival of the hero (especially if female), or villains who enslave their own people (if male).

Said (1985) argued that contemporary versions of Orientalism re-code Arab and Islamic cultures. Certainly this concern seems apparent in the reporting on events such as the Gulf War as well as the USA's post-September 11 2001 'War Against Terrorism'. Here, the generalisation and grouping together of religious and national cultures that are collectively perceived as a threat to world order requires critical consideration.

In recent times, many scholars have criticised Said for the very faults he found in the Western imagination (Irwin, 2208; Varisco, 2007). There has been a period of revisionism where Islamic scholars themselves (e.g. Warraq, 2007) have pointed out how a very different image of the East was carefully brought to the attention of Western readers by Islamic writers, and how Western culture itself was far from uniform in its approach to 'the East'. In short, Said's concept was too binary, even though it was responsible for a welcome burst of self-reflexive criticism among Western literary critics.

See also: **Discourse, Ideology, Race, Representation**

PANOPTICON

'Panopticon' refers to a 'central inspection' system for prison design, pioneered in the US Penitentiary system in 1790, and promoted by the English philosopher Jeremy Bentham, who used it to argue vigorously against the system of convict transportation to New South Wales, notably in a pamphlet called *Panopticon versus New South Wales* of 1802. In this he argued for the superiority of the penitentiary prison with a 'central inspection' design, over the corruption, sloth, prodigality, drunkenness, improvidence, depravity, incendiarism (arson) and lack of spirituality that he discerned in New South Wales. In the event, no panopticons were built in the British Empire, while convict transportation to Australia continued to 1868. Perhaps no more would have been heard about it, except that the idea was picked up by Michel Foucault (1995) as part of his genealogical analysis of discipline, punishment and incarceration systems in the modern era. Since then, the idea of the panopticon has been used very freely and metaphorically to signify a 'surveillance society' in which populations (not just prisoners but all citizens) are encouraged to discipline their behaviour under the surveillance of the state, for instance through CCTV cameras in public places. 'Surveillance studies' is now a sub-discipline in its own right. Meanwhile, New South Wales has recovered, somewhat.

Further reading: Bentham (1802); Levin *et al.* (2002); Wood (2007)

PARADIGM

In **semiotics**, a paradigm is the notional set of **signs** from which a particular sign is chosen to be included in a syntagmatic combination. Paradigmatic selection involves *choice* among potential signs (pick a word, or a dish), where **syntagms** are the resultant *chains* of sequence (a sentence, or a meal).

Paradigmatic analysis is useful in examination of **representations**, in particular for ascertaining what signs have been chosen in place of others. Words, images, colours, etc. are chosen from a potential set. Sometimes such choices are highly significant, for instance the decision about whether to use the term 'soldier', 'terrorist', 'freedom fighter', or 'armed man' in a news story (Hartley, 1982).

The concept of paradigm is useful also in film studies where the sets of signs to be considered include characters and settings, as well as technical elements such as camera–angle and lighting. Considering the paradigmatic selection within a text may reveal particular discursive strategies and ideologies at work (*see* **commutation test**).

See also: **Paradigm shift**, **Representation**, **Syntagm**

PARADIGM SHIFT

The effect of a 'scientific revolution' on the conduct of science. The term 'paradigm shift' was popularised by the historian of science Thomas Kuhn in his book *The Structure of Scientific Revolutions* (1962). It is about the dynamism of scientific thinking, marked by periods of conformity (normal science) interrupted by rapid change (revolution), which installs a general change in thinking and approach (paradigm shift). The term 'paradigm' here refers to widely held assumptions among scientists about how to do science; a mental model of a discipline shared among its practitioners. Kuhn's point was that over time, anomalies accrue that do not fit the currently accepted model, and these are either not observed, ignored or suppressed in the course of 'normal science', until a 'scientific revolution' is caused to precipitate a 'paradigm shift' towards a new definition of the situation, which in its turn becomes 'normal science'. Examples of a paradigm shift might include: the acceptance in biology of the Darwinian theory of evolution; in physics of relativity; in mathematics of probability, chaos theory and complexity; in geology of plate tectonics; in medicine of the *Helicobacter pylori* bacterium as a cause of ulcers.

PAROLE

In Saussurian linguistics, the actual performance of speech, as distinct from the rules that generate the possibility of speaking meaningfully. The term was used by Saussure (1974) to separate out those variable and accidental aspects of speech that were to be excluded from the focus of linguistic inquiry. Parole therefore needs to be understood in relation to its contrasting term, **langue**. Parole refers to individual instances of speaking; langue to the abstract system that underlies it. Although what people actually do when speaking may be of interest to the physiologist or the behavioural psychologist, for Saussure it could not form the basis of linguistic study, because it was subject to too much random fluctuation. Instead, he argued that linguistics should focus on the underlying sets of rules and **conventions** that make parole possible and guarantee its intelligibility notwithstanding variation of utterance.

There is nonetheless a close and complementary relationship between langue and parole. Parole may be seen as a continual implementation of the underlying system constituted in the langue; but conversely the continual practice of speaking adorns and adjusts the langue, moulding it gradually into a different form (*see* **diachronic**). No one individual can control or shape the langue; but generations of speakers can and do alter it from one historically specific state to another. Thus language is evolutionary (Pinker, 2003; Deutscher, 2006), and while the rules (langue) change slowly, the practice (parole) throws up constant random variations and adaptations to new circumstances that may over time generate new rules.

Like many of the terms originally developed in Saussure's lectures between 1906 and 1911, langue and parole achieved new currency during the 1960s and 1970s with the emergence of **semiotics** as the study of cultural **sign** systems. The promise was that a particular film or fashion ensemble could be seen as an individual instance of parole, generated by a underlying system of 'film language' (Christian Metz) or 'the fashion system' (Roland Barthes). It is clear that systems of rules do govern the 'parole' of many non-linguistic systems. What was never resolved was the question of whether such systems function *as* a language, or *like* a language: Does the same langue underlie all meaningful performances? Can we analyse art, say, as the 'parole' of *linguistic* rules, or does it have its own set?

See also: **Code, Langue**

PARTICIPANT OBSERVATION

A method used in the social sciences to study the lived practices of a community or group in a 'natural' environment, i.e. outside a laboratory or experimental context. Participant observation is a form of **ethnography** that has been used in media studies as a means of understanding how selected audiences make sense of and utilise media texts in their daily routines. Research of this kind seeks to garner a greater understanding of individuals through the submersion of the researcher into the lives of their research subjects.

See also: **Audience, Ethnography, Fandom, Methodology**

PERFORMANCE, PERFORMATIVITY

The semiotics of self. The concept of performance has gained ground in recent cultural analysis; it encompasses both institutionalised, professional performances (drama, ritual), and a non-psychologistic approach to individual people's self-presentation and interaction. It also seems to suffuse American **popular culture** and everyday encounters – it is an aspect of everyday life that is shifting from tacit knowledge to professionalised commodification.

The appeal of performance as a general analytic category is twofold. First, its very generality: the term has been applied not only to what actors and other professionals do but also to the 'performance' of unrehearsed cultural practices in everyday life, the actions of audiences, spectators and readers not least among them. Although performances in **ordinary culture** will differ markedly from big-deal theatrical or media performances, there are sufficient connections to make comparison worthwhile. You can analyse the differences between fictional and public performance (**celebrity** and politics); between acting conventions (naturalistic and ritualistic); between media (cinema and television); between periods (soap opera and Shakespeare) and so on.

Second, the concept of performance directs the analyst's attention away from the internal psychological state or behaviour of a given player, towards formal, rule-governed actions that are appropriate to the given performative genre. If you start looking at ordinary encounters in this way, from doctor–patient interviews to telephone calls, it is clear that there are performative protocols in play that require skill and creativity in the manipulation of space, movement, voice, timing, turn-taking, gesture, costume, and the rest of the repertoire of enactment.

Performativity was given a theoretical boost by feminist philosopher Judith Butler (1990, 2004), who used the term to develop an account of **gender** not based on essential identity. She wrote that gender identity is the outcome of 'the tacit collective agreement to perform, produce, and sustain discrete and polar genders as cultural fictions' (1990: 179). In other words, everyone, more or less, is in drag; and the reason we don't see the performance as such is because people are habituated to their roles, and are punished for deviating from the script of this culture-wide costume drama.

Further reading: Davies (2008); Goffman (1986)

PHATIC COMMUNICATION

Communication designed to open or maintain contact between addresser and addressee. Its classic form in speech is the greeting:

Hello; G'day! Phatic communication was identified by Roman Jakobson as one of the six **functions of language**.

Phatic communication is used 'ideologically' by broadcasting organisations. News anchors will say 'Good evening' to a camera, but (hopefully) be heard as establishing communication with each viewer. The more populist and entertainment-oriented the show, the more it will distend phatic communication. Game-show hosts will engage in phatic communication with both contestants and viewers, at least in the non-competitive, fun versions of such shows. Their warm and friendly linguistic performance slides into corporate marketing, because the TV channel itself is associated with the openness and other-orientation characteristic of phatic communication.

Phatic communication is often derided as meaningless babble when it is used in online environments, perhaps because it looks odd in textual (rather than spoken) form. Compared with *The Seven Pillars of Wisdom*, such language-use as 'lol' or Facebook's prompt 'What's on your mind?' may indeed seem impoverished, but without contact-maintaining traffic the online environment would not be able to function at all. Further, it can serve to remind us that the bulk of most media usage, speech included, is phatic rather than something more 'worthy' but less communicative.

See also: **Language, functions of**

PHONEMIC/PHONETIC

A conceptual distinction between two kinds of elements in a **signi-fying** system – one capable of generating meaning, the other not. The terms are borrowed from linguistics, but are applicable to any sign system. In linguistics, a **phoneme** is one of a limited number of sounds (in English there are about forty of them) that are *recognised* as part of the system of such sounds. Verbal utterance is based on the selection and combination of strings of these phonemes in a rule-governed order. *Phonetic*, on the other hand, describes the sounds *actually made* by a speaker. The point about this is twofold:

- Each speaker will use her or his physiological, regional, contextual and other resources to produce *a unique* version of the generally recognised phoneme. No one sounds a letter or word in quite the same way as anyone else, but everyone in a speech community will recognise the phoneme it represents, when used by a native speaker.

- All languages recognise, as 'the same' phoneme, some sounds that are actually (phonetically) different. For instance, the 'k' sound in the spoken words 'kin' and 'ink' *sound* 'the same' to the speaker and the hearer. But they are *actually* different sounds, produced in slightly different parts of the mouth. Try it. In another language, such phonemic differences may be significant and yield differences in meaning, but not in English.

The conceptual point about this is again twofold:

- If we paid attention to the sounds we all *actually* make rather than the ones that are *recognised by the language* there's little chance of us being able to make sense of anything – there are too many differences.
- The power of language (as opposed to actuality) is so great that it's difficult for us even to perceive anything outside its recognised elements: you may flatly disagree that the 'k' sounds differ – but an oscilloscope would spot it.

There's no mystery about this property of language. Following Saussure, we can say that phonemes are abstract, they belong to **langue**, whereas phonetics are concrete, they belong to **parole**.

See also: **Difference, Langue, Parole, Phonology**

PHONOLOGY

The branch of linguistics devoted to studying meaningful sound patterns of a **language**. The human vocal organs are capable of producing an extremely rich array of different sounds. Each language, however, draws for communicative effect upon only a small portion of this total range. Phonology examines which particular units of possible sound constitute the basic meaningful set for any one language. It does so in the first instance by building up contrasting pairs of sound on the principle that for any one language certain sounds will cause changes in the meaning of words, whereas other sounds will not. In English if we change the initial sound of /pig/from /p/to /b/we end up changing one word into another – changing *pig* to *big*. By using this test, known as the minimal pairs test (*see also* **commutation test**), it is possible to discover which sound substitutions cause a difference in meaning. Each change in meaning isolates a new element of the basic sound structure of the language, each element being known as a phoneme (*see* **phonemic/phonetic**). The total inventory of phonemes built up with this method *is language-specific*. Phonological analysis is to be distinguished from **phonetic** analysis where the emphasis is on the description and classification of speech sounds independently of meaning.

PLATFORMS (MEDIA)

The term platform has gained in prominence as media have converged and integrated. It refers to the technological base upon which content can be circulated – possibly the same content across different platforms. As with many terms in media studies, it arose in industry discourses and in response to practical developments, so it can refer to different kinds of platform. For instance, **analogue** platforms like publishing and the press, radio and TV, cinema and cartoons, can be contrasted with online platforms, in which the brands and content associated with one are distributed on the other, as is common among newspaper mastheads. In this instance, the internet as a whole is a platform. But in other contexts, different web applications can be seen as separate media platforms in their own right. For instance, business commentators may wish to compare which 'social media platform' is most popular, among Twitter, Facebook, YouTube and blogs. In this case there is no reference to analogue platforms at all; the social network market is treated as an entirely online phenomenon.

Because so many platforms are now available to carry creative content or traffic, media scholars like Henry Jenkins (2006a) have started to write about 'transmedia storytelling' to capture the phenomenon of distributing a story across many media platforms, including mobile phones and social media sites, as well as in the traditional platforms of TV or cinema. Thus we have multiplatform media content.

See also: **Convergence, Digital, New media**

Further reading: Creeber and Martin (2009); Flew (2008); Jenkins (2006a)

PLEBISCITE

In politics, a plebiscite is a poll of the general electorate to determine a yes/no question. Plebiscitary television is a form of **reality TV** where part of the entertainment appeal of the format is participation in voting. It originated with *The Eurovision Song Contest* and now pervades TV talent shows. Its usage has spread much further than variety shows, as plebiscites are held to determine what anything means, from recent news events to history's most important figures (philosophers, scientists), or to discover a community's best-loved music or children's book. Plebiscitary industries have emerged to conduct and coordinate plebiscites, often as part of the marketing effort of producer organisations, but frequently drifting across into the public domain too.

Plebiscites are not much admired among media critics, for whom they are merely an instance of 'demotic' television (Turner, 2010), but they are nevertheless a response by traditional broadcasters to the challenge of consumer activism and passionate choice, and a potential tool for the reform of 'consumer democracy' in the creative industries.

Further reading: Hartley (2008)

PLENTY, PHILOSOPHY OF

Cultural studies, according to Hartley (2003), is a philosophy of plenty, developed to account not for scarcity (in the way that neoclassical economics does) but for abundance, especially semiotic abundance, in contemporary cultures, where the organisation and distribution of choice and expansion of difference have become a cultural problem.

POLITICAL ECONOMY

This term has a long history, being the derivative of that branch of eighteenth-century moral philosophy concerned with the just distribution of wealth; a pursuit that eventually evolved into economics, which was called 'political economy' by founding figures such as Adam Smith and, through him, Karl Marx. An early attempt at a 'political economy' of the aesthetic or media domain (i.e. semiotic rather than economic wealth) was undertaken by the art critic John Ruskin, who wrote several essays and books in the 1850s–60s with the term 'political economy' in their title, including *The Political Economy of Art* (1857), which broke up the subject into four headings – the discovery, application, accumulation, and distribution of artistic *genius*.

For Ruskin, political economy is a civic duty, comparable with household management, incumbent upon all those with the vote, at a time when the franchise was steadily being extended beyond the propertied classes. Ruskin was active in promoting an **aesthetic** idea of value in this context, reminding working people of their duty to value genius, as well as money. In this he differed from Marx, writing in the same period, whose approach to political economy was not to teach it to everyone but to turn it into a science, which eventually took the form of Marxism.

The version of political economy that has become familiar in media and communication studies was derived from Marxism, not from Ruskin's civics. Writers associated with the political economy approach include, in the USA, Herbert Schiller, Bob McChesney, Toby Miller, Janet Wasco, Vincent Mosco and others; in the United Kingdom, Graham Murdock, Nicholas Garnham, James Curran and Jim McGuigan. The political economy approach focuses on the ownership and control of media corporations as the explanation for media forms, content, and **effects**. According to this approach, media need to serve the interests of their owners and advertisers, and it is this that explains the *mode of production*, where highly capitalised firms, supported by the state, pursue strategies of audience-maximisation, in order to maximise profits.

For the proponents of such an approach, it was no surprise to find popular media forms suffused with sex, violence and bad language, because this was needed to attract 'eyeballs' for advertisers. Thus the political economy approach was often accompanied by a socially conservative and pejorative view of content, very different from a literary or anthropological approach that saw contemporary media as the continuation for a popular dramatic tradition going back to Shakespeare (Hawkes, 1973).

The political economy approach relies on a Marxist 'base/superstructure' model of media. It entails two very dubious assumptions. The first is that more or less all corporately originated media *content* is an **ideological** reflection of the interests of the owners and controllers of media. The second is that media have more or less direct (and always negative) effects on audiences' beliefs, values, attitudes, and political choices. These assumptions were often unstated or even held unwittingly by theorists who were interested only in the production rather than consumption end of media communications. Both have been thoroughly criticised, not least by Stuart Hall's branch of cultural studies (Hall, 1973). They tried hard to elaborate a model of media that retained the Marxist presumption of economic determination while at the same time allowing 'relative autonomy' to the experience of consumption, which thereby became a site of struggle, where dominant meanings might be negotiated or resisted (Fiske, 1987).

In practice, however, the problem has never been resolved. Instead it has led to a generation-long stand-off between the 'political economy' branch of media and communication, which remains interested in the relationship between the production process and social power, and the 'culturalists', who remain interested in the experience and meaning of mediated culture for the population at large. It may be that the top-down political economy approach is more favoured among those with a sociological training; the bottom-up culturalist approach to those with humanities training. Certainly, the bifurcation between the Marxists (theorists) and the Ruskinites (teachers) has persisted for a century and a half.

Further reading: Barker (2008); McChesney (2008)

POLYSEMY, POLYSEMIC

'Many-meanings': a property of **signs**, whose meanings are context-dependent and therefore multiple. This concept recognises that **meaning** is not reproduced by referral to a sign's internal properties or essence, but rather is achieved through the difference of one sign from others. Furthermore, the polysemic nature of the sign confirms that there is no natural relation between its components, the signifier and the signified, but rather that this relationship is arbitrary. To take the example of a 'black dress' as a sign, depending on the **context** in which it appears it may signify eveningwear, mourning, or widowhood.

Barthes' (1973) notion of 'anchorage' argues that strategies are employed in all texts to 'anchor' the 'preferred meaning'; or in other cases to suggest that one meaning is more apposite than others. In advertising, images may be anchored by text; and in film or TV, genre **conventions** may serve to limit polysemy. Barthes claimed that anchorage is necessarily an ideological imperative through which the polysemic nature of the sign is controlled. Writers such as Fiske (1987), on the other hand, understand polysemy as part of the pleasure, and indeed one of the required features of media that strive to reach a mass and diverse audience.

See also: **Aberrant decoding, Multi-accentuality, Semiotics, Sign**

POPULAR, POPULAR CULTURE

There are three different usages of popular culture that are of relevance to communication, cultural and media studies:

- *Anthropological*: the culture of **ordinary** people, everyday life and vernacular pursuits;
- *Textual*: the products and (social) practices of the media and entertainment industries;
- *Evaluative*: the opposite of 'high' culture.

'Popular' is often synonymous with 'good' in ordinary conversation, but this is an inversion of its earlier pejorative connotations. In its original form, 'popular' was used to distinguish the mass of the people (not 'people in general') from the titled, wealthy or educated classes. Not surprisingly, since most writers on the subject were either members or clients of the latter three classes, the synonyms for 'popular' were: gross, base, vile, riffraff, common, low, vulgar, plebeian, cheap (*OED*).

From these inauspicious beginnings the term has to some extent been 'decolonised', principally through its usage in democratic politics in and since the nineteenth century. However, it still retains sufficient traces of its history to be a multi-accentual term: the popularity of something may be taken as an indication of positive or negative value. Thus the concept is not exempt from politics, which has in fact dogged its usage within the sphere of cultural analysis. The popularity (ubiquitousness) of the mass media in particular has resulted in a recurring ambiguity in both academic and public debate about whether the products of the media are good because they're popular (democratic), or bad because they're popular (demotic).

The ambiguity is not simply a matter of the personal prejudices of the critic. It is implicit in the position of those people and products that can be described as popular. The ambiguity has two aspects. First, there is ambiguity about the extent to which popular culture is *imposed on* people in general (by media corporations or state agencies as in **political economy**), or *derived from* their own experiences, tastes, habits, and so on. Second, there is ambiguity about the extent to which popular culture is merely an expression of a powerless and subordinate class position, or an autonomous and potentially liberating source of alternative ways of seeing and doing that can be opposed to dominant or official culture.

These ambiguities have an important bearing on the study of *popular culture*, since they make it very hard to specify an easily agreed object of study. What 'counts' as popular culture depends to some extent on whether you're interested in what meanings are produced *by* or *for* 'the people', and whether you take these meanings as evidence of 'what the public wants' or of 'what the public gets'. Further, the study of popular culture requires some attention to cultures other than popular – especially what is known as *high culture*. Discussion centred on differences between popular and high culture has traditionally focused on matters of taste and artistic merit. For instance, there is an implicit valuation in distinctions such as those between 'serious' and 'pop' music, which are frequently institutionalised in the form of taste-specific radio networks; or between creative genius (high culture) and commercial exploitation (popular). At stake in the attempt to specify popular culture is the status of these naturalised evaluations, for they may be explained as an means whereby class-based relations of supremacy and subordination may be 'lived' as natural differences.

The recognition of a relation between class and culture has led on to further issues. First, attention has broadened beyond its original focus on such obviously cultural artefacts as texts, to include practices, lifestyles and 'lived culture' – especially in the **ethnographic** study of **subcultures**. Second, there has been a rediscovery of 'cultural politics', often associated with the work of Gramsci (1971) and his concepts of **hegemony** and the 'national-popular'. Finally, attention to **class** has led on to consideration of the complex relations that exist between this and, especially, **gender** and **ethnic** relations.

See also: **Class, Cultural studies, Culture, Ideology, Subculture**

Further reading: Storey (2003)

PORNOGRAPHY

Creative work in textual or screen media intended or used to stimulate sexual desire, usually as part of a commercial transaction (the Greek origin-word meant 'writing about prostitutes'). Porn is a thorny problem for the media field, because it provokes normative and censorious responses among analysts and critics, as well as in the **mediasphere** more generally, so the traditional dispassionate divide between scholar and activist may be eroded, for instance in 'anti-pornography feminism' (e.g. Boyle, 2010), or, conversely 'advocacy' scholarship (e.g. Strosser, 2000). Further, porn is notoriously difficult to research in terms of its production, circulation and use (but see McKee *et al.* 2008). Hence, many studies focus on its textual form, in ways that frequently erase the First-Amendment distinction between saying and doing, by presuming that depiction and action are the same (but see Kipnis, 1999).

Porn as a sector of the media industry is credited with innovations that have helped to establish or grow **new media** that later become mainstream, including publishing in the eighteenth century, photography in the nineteenth, cinema in the twentieth and, more recently, building an early consumer market on the internet, and spearheading technological advances such as secure payment techniques, video-streaming, and advertising (Barss, 2010).

In general, porn has not shared a labour market with mainstream media (porn stars don't become movie stars), but some observers believe that mainstream **popular culture** is given over to a 'porn aesthetic', and that young people are prematurely sexualised by 'exposure' to 'raunch culture' (Levy, 2006). Debates on this topic often centre about avant garde or high-end photography, such that various artists have been embroiled in high-profile controversies, including Robert Mapplethorpe, Sally Mann, Bill Henson, and others; or, in the fashion domain, Terry Richardson. In other words, 'porn' is often the term used to describe innovation in representational aesthetics.

Further reading: Attwood (2009)

POSTCOLONIAL, POSTCOLONIALISM

Postcolonialism is a burgeoning field of study in its own right, drawing together strands from literary studies and critical theory, politics, and history. At its heart, postcolonialism is a critique of discourses of capitalist modernity, established in and by means of the European imperial project – in fact two such projects:

- the colonisation of the Americas (sixteenth–eighteenth centuries) by the Spanish, Portuguese, French, English and others (Greenblatt, 1993), including the subsequent African enslavement on the American continent (e.g. the work of W. E. B. Du Bois and C. L. R. James);
- the colonisation of parts of Asia, Africa and Australasia (eighteenth–nineteenth centuries) by Austria, Belgium, Britain, Denmark, France, Germany, Italy, the Knights of Malta, the Netherlands, Portugal, Russia, Spain, Sweden . . . and Japan.

After the Second World War European powers gradually withdrew from political colonisation, leaving a textual mess to clear up. Postcolonialism took its early lead from *anti*-colonial writers like Frantz Fanon, Mahatma Gandhi and Julius Nyerere. It also incorporated the literary and historical work of writers from former 'colonial literatures'.

Postcolonialism as a field of study has grown out of some of the doubts, uncertainties and controversies arising from the decolonising project in discourse. Gayatri Spivak's (1988) essay 'Can the subaltern speak?' raised the question of whether scholarship that adopts a post-colonial ('subaltern') perspective can break with colonial categories. Homi Bahbha's influential concept of hybridity sought to patrol the 'borderline negotiations of cultural difference' (Bhabha, 1996: 54).

In this mode, postcolonialism tends to focus on the relation between politics and identity (Ahluwalia, 2001), on the constitution and practice of postcolonial or 'subaltern' subjectivity (Chakrabarty, 2000), and on the clash of cultural difference through what Sara Ahmed (2000: 11) calls 'discursive appropriation'; the latter including the discursive appropriation of knowledge, prompting postcolonial critique of Eurocentrism in the practices and publications of the social sciences and humanities, as well as in their object of study.

See also: **Orientalism**, **Whiteness**

POSTMODERN, POSTMODERNISM

A social epoch, a theoretical project, and an aesthetic movement, contrasted with **modernity**. Frow (1997) argues that postmodernism is a genre of theory-writing, not a description of the world. The concept has become widely used in public as well as academic and scholarly discourse, sometimes shorn of its theoretical rationale – indeed, sometimes used as a convenient term for 'those with whom we disagree'.

It may be useful to consider the term in two ways – a condition of society (postmodernity) and as a textual practice (postmodernism), but the two are of course intertwined. Thus, the *condition* of postmodernity includes, in economics, the shift from US-based manufacturing to globalised 'post-industrial' or knowledge-based economies. The *textual practice*, in artistic and intellectual life, includes the 'cultural turn' in the sciences and social sciences, influenced by structuralism and continental philosophy, and postmodern theorising itself. In culture, the two *combined*, in the new social movements of the 1960s and their challenge to received 'meta-narratives' of progress, reason and universal truths. Postmodernism and the counter-culture alike were involved in overturning hierarchies of taste, behaviour and thought.

Whereas modernity was characterised by a belief in – or hope for – the unity of the human race in the rational pursuit of truth and enlightenment, postmodernity sees the two World Wars as ending this utopian vision. The mass genocide that characterised these events fractured the concept of a universalised 'we'. Our present epoch is now instead characterised by petit-narratives or identities characterised by, for example, **diversity**, **difference**, and fragmentation in previously unitary concepts like **nation**, **gender**, **ethnicity** and sexuality. Postmodernism is concerned with aesthetic practices that seek to articulate the 'postmodern condition'.

See also: **Modernity**

Further reading: Sim (2001)

POWER

Power is the capacity to control an entity's environment and to bring about change – causal force in human relations. It has been taken up in social and cultural theory largely in terms of various entities' power to control *other* environments – power 'over' (domination) and power 'to' (coercion).

In relation to politics, the word retains much of its resonance from ordinary language. The latter usage derives from theories of **political economy**, which understood power as emanating from the monarch – a single source of power, whose exercise was founded on threat of death, both internal (execution) and external (war). Monarchical power didn't have to be exercised by a *monarch* – the system still worked when 'abstracted' to, for example, the law (internal) and the state (external). Fundamentally this concept of power was based on *scarcity*; there wasn't enough of it to go around. If you wanted it, you had to take it from someone who had it. If you didn't have it, you were confined to your 'lack' of it by repression (ultimately, fear of death). This conceptualisation probably remains at the heart of the commonsense (ordinary language) use of the term.

More recently, power has been theorised in two competing ways by Marxism and Foucault, and both are influential on cultural and media studies.

The classic political economy approach (power as a scarce resource) was the mental map inherited by Marxism, who shifted the focus from ethno-territorial sovereignty to the social landscape of industrialisation. They saw power emanating from productive forces, i.e. capital and labour. They understood that, compared to previous epochs (feudalism, slavery), capitalism was a progressive and dynamic force in society, and also that without capital there would be no working or 'productive' class. But despite this Marxism persisted in thinking about the relations between these two forces as a zero-sum game whereby one side had power and the other side lacked it. So, for Marxism, class antagonism *as politics* took the form of one class dominating and repressing another, using the ultimate fear of death (coercion) as well as intermediate strategies of sovereignty, such as the law, divide-and-rule, patronage, **hegemony**, etc. The point was that power was still something to be taken from someone else, and exercised over them. In contemporary cultural theory, the model persists, but the place of 'class' in 'class struggle' has been taken over by self-identified oppressed or repressed groups, from women and ethnic populations to people identified by their sexual preference, age, or identity.

Foucault broke with this scenario in order to take seriously the effects of modernisation, and the changes brought about by the productive force of both capital and labour, acting on both the natural and the social world (*see* **biopower**), in an expansive cycle of growth. His own work focused on studies of *madness*, *incarceration* and *sexuality*. From these he formulated theories of *truth* (knowledge), *power* (how 'we constitute ourselves as subjects acting on others'), and *the self* (ethics) (Foucault, 1984: 351–2).

Foucault's theory of power was not based on *scarcity*, but **plenty**, and not on fear of *death* but on the 'plenitude of the possible' (1984: 267). He abandoned the idea of power as sovereignty. Instead, he introduced the idea that power was 'taking charge of life':

> Power would no longer be dealing simply with legal subjects over whom the ultimate dominion was death, but with living beings, and the mastery it would be able to exercise over them would have to be applied at the level of life itself; it was the taking charge of life, more than the threat of death, that gave power its access even to the body.
>
> (Foucault, 1984: 265)

The management of *life* required *knowledge*-power, not pain of death. This kind of power was dispersed throughout the productive forces and institutions of modernising societies; it was manifest not in gallows and armies but in knowledge, and in the organisation and administration of bodies. It was exercised in the techniques developed in institutions and discourses to govern – and so make productive – whole populations. Hence power could be seen in the minutiae of everyday transactions, in private life, and in the technologies mobilised to evaluate, measure, appraise and assign to hierarchies – and so to *produce* – 'normal' society. This was what Foucault called 'governmentality'.

Even the actions of those (including cultural critics) who sought to oppose traditional (sovereign) power had to be understood within these terms. For Foucault there was no 'outside' to power, a place from which one could take a swing at those who 'had' it. But the exercise of power in knowledge, discourse, institution, technique, administration, management, bureaucracy, and the rest was never complete; it generated its own resistances, and these needed to be understood for worthwhile political contestation to occur. Politics was conducted at the level of understanding how selves were formed and acted on others, including intellectual selves.

In communication, cultural and media studies the Marxist and Foucauldian conceptualisations of power have both been influential. Marxist-derived approaches have focused on the adversarial aspect of power: on 'struggle'. Foucauldian approaches have focused on institutionalised and administrative knowledge, truth, discourse, self, sexuality and governmentality as sites of power.

Many commentators regard power as constitutive of cultural studies, being a fundamental aspect of any study of meaning. But Mark Gibson (2007) proposes that a singular concept of power is disabling for the project; he suggests the field proceeds on the analysis of pluralised *powers*.

See also: **Biopower, Consensus, Panopticon, Plenty, Regulation**

Further reading Bennett (1992, 1998)

PRAGMATICS

The study of the interpretation of utterances, especially how the **context** of situation influences their **meaning**. Pragmatics in linguistics (Ott and Mack, 2010) is not coterminous with pragmatics in philosophy (Rorty, 1982). The aim of pragmatics is to describe these various kinds of contextual effect; but more significantly it aims to explain how language users actually make sense of each other's utterances in the face of various kinds of indeterminacy and ambiguity.

Traditionally the study of meaning in linguistics has focused upon the meaning of words or sentences as if meaning inhered within the linguistic expression itself and was ultimately determined by the linguistic system. Pragmatics, however, emphasises the role of context in determining meaning. Pragmatic issues go beyond issues of word meaning to include consideration of complicated kinds of contextual effect where the meaning of an utterance is much more than what is literally said. These kinds of inferences that go beyond the literal meaning of what is said are known as implicatures (suggested rather than explicit meanings). A further kind of contextual effect relates to the notion of speech act (where, in the words of J. L. Austin who coined the term, 'by saying something we also *do* something'). *Directives*, for instance, are a commonly occurring type of speech act designed to get someone to do something.

The contribution of pragmatics to communication studies is potentially considerable, though not always realised, since it goes to the heart of some of the most troubling issues surrounding **text** and interpretation, e.g. 'Where is meaning – in the text; or in the context?' At the same time, however, pragmatics has become closely associated with the interests of cognitive science and the study of artificial intelligence. Such links tend to produce a strong emphasis on the supposed rationality of communicators, and on the universality of the interpretative procedures that they adopt, so that much work remains to be done on the socially structured distribution and organisation of pragmatic knowledge and procedures.

See also: **Conversation analysis, Meaning, Semantics**

Further reading: Horn and Ward (2004)

PRODUCTION, PRODUCER

In the study of media, production may refer to the entire industrial apparatus (in contrast to distribution or consumption), or it may refer to the role of the producer (in contrast to directors, actors, etc.). In the movie business, producers are responsible for selecting a script and financing its production (often risking their own money, in which case they are called Executive Producers). They can hire and fire the director, although the latter manages the project and is often credited with **authorial** status. In this respect, producers are comparable to the board level of a company, while film directors are comparable to the managing director. They are assisted by 'line producers', who deal with the budgetary aspects of the production process.

In communication, cultural and media studies, although the role of the producer is certainly of significant interest, 'production' is more likely to be encountered as a term from **political economy**, following up on the presumption that production is the locus of media power, control, and thence social impact. Hence, studies of 'production' rarely investigate *producers* (the professional occupation). Rather, they follow the production *process*, from an ethnographic or sociological perspective, to determine how sense-making practices work, and how they result in the cultural forms that consumers see on page or screen.

See also: **Consumption/production**

Further reading: Deuze (2007); Ellis (2004)

PROPAGANDA

Propaganda is the Latin for propagation, and is derived from the name of an organisation set up by the Roman Catholic Church in 1622 to 'propagate the faith' in the aftermath of the Reformation and the rise of Protestantism; i.e. propagation in *adversarial* or competitive circumstances. This combative sense of propaganda was later deployed by totalitarian regimes, both communist and fascist, who took pains to make 'propagation' of state ideology a matter of policy, not chance. 'Agit-prop' – 'agitation and propaganda' – was assigned to trustworthy militants.

Meanwhile, liberal democracies, especially in Protestant countries, regarded propaganda as a 'term of reproach applied to secret associations for the spread of opinions and principles which are viewed by most governments with horror and aversion' (*OED*). But these governments did protest too much, for they too were active in propaganda, both to confound external adversaries and to promote internal discipline.

Propaganda under the guise of 'government information' is a staple of contemporary life, and its privatised form, which is PR and advertising, is a mainstay of the contemporary economy.

Propaganda is still controversial, because it infects the media of public enlightenment, especially news. It may take the banal form of PR handouts that get reproduced verbatim in the local paper, or it may take a much more expensive and sophisticated form – lobbying, political and commercial campaigns, for instance. So much so that wise readers and viewers regard everything they see and read as propaganda for something, always in someone's interest, whether in the factual or fictional media. There's a continuing need to ask of any newsworthy story: 'who says?' Scepticism about news and fictional realism is healthy, and requires some work by the reader or viewer, but simply to dismiss propaganda out of hand, or to seek to 'ban' or control it, or to purge it from the media, would be to miss the point. All communication has some sort of spin, especially communication addressed to a large, anonymous public from across demographic boundaries. So the wise reader might prefer to see propaganda as a **genre** rather than as an infestation.

The generic characteristics of propaganda, compared to realism in both fact and fiction, include these (Hartley, 1992a: 51–5):

- News and fiction draw attention *into* the text, seeking to resolve conflicts diegetically, within the story. Propaganda directs attention *beyond* the text, seeking to provoke conflict in the reader.
- News and fiction are images of the past, in which the action is completed. Propaganda aligns the reader to the future, towards actions yet to occur. News and fiction continue existing meanings. Propaganda seeks to change the future.
- News and fiction position the reader as uncommitted, even passive recipients or consumers. Propaganda calls the reader towards participation.
- News and realist fiction seek to convey the impression that they are true, unauthored, real. Propaganda seeks to produce faithfulness in a relationship between addresser and addressee.
- News and fiction employ transparency and verisimilitude to produce the effect that the techniques used in the communication aren't there. Propaganda can experiment with a much broader palette of rhetorical and visual techniques, and draw attention to its own communicative status.
- News is diegetic; propaganda dialogic.

Propaganda can still be politically controversial, especially in its clandestine form. After the events of September 11 2001, the US Defence Department set up an 'office of strategic influence', which planned to feed information, some of it false, to foreign news agencies, in an attempt to influence public opinion across the world, especially the Islamic world, in favour of the US-led 'war on terrorism'. The plan caused outrage within and beyond the USA when it was revealed in February 2002, and the 'office of strategic influence' was 'restructured'. But evidently its functions were not abandoned. Secretary of State Donald Rumsfeld explained to a press briefing in November 2002:

And then there was the Office of Strategic Influence. You may recall that. And 'oh my goodness gracious isn't that terrible, Henny Penny the sky is going to fall.' I went down that next day and said fine, if you want to savage this thing fine I'll give you the corpse. There's the name. You can have the name, but I'm gonna keep doing every single thing that needs to be done and I have.

(Quoted in Marrs, 2006: 271)

The implication of this is that propaganda is still out there, masquerading as news. It may not all be coming out of the State Department, but it's out there, all the same.

See also: **News values**

PROXEMICS

The **semiotics** of space. E. T. Hall (1973) posited that spatial arrangements may be meaningful: intimate (near), social (middling) or public (distant), for instance. People's *proximity* to one another will communicate their mutual status – lovers will 'naturally' stand closer to each other than strangers. There are reputed to be different proxemic standards in different countries, resulting in some nationalities being known for aloofness (their relaxed social space when standing is greater than an arm's-length: 'Swedes'), or touchiness (they habitually stand closer than arm's-length: 'Latins'). Adhering to proxemic standards in a given context is a good test of politeness; failing to do so can cause offence (invading personal space; being stand-offish).

Political, commercial exploitation of proxemic codes is routine. They are literally set in stone in the organisation and architecture of public space. VIPs tend to be surrounded by more space than regular folk, a truism exploited by the organisers of public spectacles from Nuremberg and the Olympics (think of the winner's podium) to Oscars night and the Presidential inauguration. Behavioural proxemic codes are made explicit and exploited in marketing, political campaigning, and reality-TV formats.

PUBLIC

Pre-dating the use of the terms **nation** and nationality, the public described the free population of a city state in Classical times. The public could literally gather in a single space within sight of each other in the Athenian Agora or Roman Forum. It was here that citizens argued, legislated and adjudicated, both in their own interest and on behalf of the majority who were not free – slaves, women, foreigners, children. With the growth of polities to many times the size of these classical antecedents, the public was 'abstracted' or virtualised – it was either an imagined community, or could only gather together by *representative* means.

The notion of the public has survived into modern times, sustaining governmental, media and academic interests, among others. The existence of the unseen public is the warrant that allows such institutions to speak and act on behalf of unknowable populations, construed as the public. They seek to *represent* public opinion, public service (broadcasting), the public interest, etc. This is the origin of the 'public sector', which comprises government-owned corporations and agencies, typically in health, education, and local-government services, but also encompassing publicly owned media corporations and cultural institutions such as museums, libraries, galleries, and archives.

The public never has included everyone. Its composition is based on strategies of inclusion and exclusion. In Western democracies, progressively over the past 250 years, most individuals – however uncomfortably – have been included; continuing outsiders may include children and youth, gays and lesbians, the disabled and migrants. Such groups have gained some recognition in newer theoretical concepts, such as **cultural citizenship**, that involve a shift from the conception of a unified public to a notion of multiple publics, or 'discourse publics' (Warner, 2002).

See also: **Cultural citizenship, Public sphere**

Further reading: Hartley (1992b)

PUBLIC SERVICE BROADCASTING

Public service broadcasting includes *all* services in those countries with a legislated public service **broadcasting** regime. For instance, in the United Kingdom, the BBC is the archetypal public broadcaster, but the commercial channels ITV and Channel 4, and the hybrid S4C, also have public-service obligations in their enabling statutes – and in their culture. In practice the term is usually restricted to taxation-funded broadcasting organisations – PSBs. In turn, PSBs are usually distinguished from other non-profit **access** or 'advocacy' broadcasters, which are known as *community media* (Rennie, 2006). PSBs commonly have a national mandate and aim for a broad **popular** audience;

community media aim for a local or sectional one. Public service broadcasting is common and prominent in Europe and its former colonies, where it is sustained by the tax dollar. It is less prominent in the USA, where PBS (Public Broadcasting Service) is sustained by donation, subscription and endowment.

At the heart of public service broadcasting is the idea that, in order to secure and conduct democratic deliberation, a nation needs a healthy **public sphere**, shielded from 'market forces', although not from all market influences: PSBs have to compete in creative and managerial labour markets; and may themselves make a lot of money by selling their own products and services. Thus, what PSBs are shielded from is direct editorial interference by owners and advertisers. In the 1990s, the growth of digital platforms meant that the 'public sphere' was no longer a scarce resource. The public-service model lost some of its political support, with commercial pressure to privatise the PSBs. The BBC under John Birt and Greg Dyke responded by updating their mission to include technological innovation (Born, 2004), especially online.

Although PSBs played a large part in the development of innovative television and radio, and more recently online services, commercial media have also played a significant role in fostering both public debate and national identity, including the acceptance of cultural difference (Hartley, 1992a). In recent years, theorists – as well as advocates for privatisation – have begun to challenge the assumption that public service broadcasting has a special claim to speak for 'the' public. And technological changes, especially the growth of the internet and the extension of choice that goes with it, have further served to undermine the rationale for 'public service' as it has been inherited from the past. However, that may not mean the end of public funding for communications media in pursuit of other policy goals. Certainly, despite hostility from commercial media (e.g. News Corporation), there is little sign of a loss of public support for 'national broadcasters' like the BBC in the United Kingdom or ABC in Australia.

See also: **Access**

Further reading: Banerjee and Seneviratne (2006)

PUBLIC SPHERE

A concept from Jurgen Habermas in *The Structural Transformation of the Public Sphere* (1962; translated into English in 1989). First published in the context of post-Second World War reconstruction and Cold War divisions in Germany, it was an attempt to think through the possibilities by means of which democracy might be realised as a communicative practice among the community, not just as an administrative apparatus. Influenced by his experience of fascism in Germany and his apprenticeship to the **Frankfurt School** as Adorno's research assistant, Habermas held out little hope of being able to identify a political philosophy that could resolve the consequences of capitalism or state control. His elaboration of the notion of the public sphere is not therefore an attempt at a prescriptive political theory, but a conception of the conditions within which healthy and just political conditions may be realised. His concept of the public sphere has been very influential in communication and media studies, although not always through detailed reference to his own account (McKee, 2005).

For Habermas, the public sphere 'cannot be conceived as an institution and certainly not as an organisation'; rather it is 'a network for communicating information and points of view' (Habermas, 1996: 360). It is the arena within which debate occurs; it involves generating ideas, sharing knowledge and constructing opinion in a way that occurs when people assemble and discuss current affairs. The ultimate model for this was the London coffeehouse culture of the Enlightenment period, which Habermas admired, although he was not initially alert to the narrow class, gender and racial basis of such a public, nor to the narrow and intolerant view of what political philosophies *could* be debated there, which would certainly not have included the republican politics of Thomas Paine, for instance, since Paine would have been arrested for sedition had he shown his face.

For Habermas, the public sphere was most constructive when not influenced by commercial interests or state control. In its original conception, the public sphere must be insulated from such powers if it is to be a *corrective* to them. Only in this way could it effectively produce democratic conditions. This proved to be a weakness in the theory, for it allowed no public-sphere function to commercial organisations and media, or to privately-owned platforms for public participation, debate, and decision-making. In fact, since the 1960s the **convergence** of political, media, and deliberative 'spheres' has accelerated, so far (despite gloomy expectations) without catastrophe for the democracies.

Habermas was interested in what people did in the public sphere; not in who they were. Fair enough, but this exposed a further weakness in the theory. Nancy Fraser (1992) among other feminists pointed out that it is unrealistic to assume that the historical exclusion of women from such forums, or the racial and property criteria needed to participate in the public sphere, can be overlooked. Rather, the likelihood is that ignoring identity differences would lead to their continued exclusion from participation. For Fraser the solution is to see not a singular public sphere but a number of public sphericules, through which groups interact and contest, and to which they can withdraw when desired.

See also: **Mediasphere, Public, Public service broadcasting**

Further reading: Hartley and McKee (2000); Poster (2000)

QUEER THEORY

An amalgam of LGBT (lesbian–gay–bisexual–transgender) studies and feminism, queer theory is an anti-essentialist 'reading' of **gender**, sexuality, and what, following Foucault, can be termed the 'sexual order'. Although it grew out of **identity politics** it involves a critique of identity. It is a burgeoning field in its own right. Leading writers include Judith Butler (e.g. *Gender Trouble*, 1990), Eve Kosofsky Sedgwick (*Epistemology of the Closet*, 1991), Sara Ahmed (*Queer Phenomenology*, 2006) and Michael Warner (*Publics and Counterpublics*, 2002). Most of these writers, and others such as Lauren Berlant, Jane Gallop, Elizabeth Grosz, Judith Halberstam, Annamarie Jagoste, Laura Kipnis and Elspeth Probyn, are familiar figures in the wider fields of communication, cultural and media studies, of which queer theory is thus an integral and influential part, sharing theoretical antecedents (especially Foucault), debates and problems that face the field as a whole.

Like **postmoderninsm**, it does what it says on the box, which is to *theorise*, in this case using a queer perspective, which has raised questions about a perceived separation from both activism and sociological or economic accounts of the material conditions facing queer communities.

Further reading: Sullivan (2003)

RACE

Race is a category of population classification based on common **ethnic** or genetic descent. However, the term is so intricately caught up in national, legal, discursive and scientific history that the *use* of it is always socially constructed. Further, racial categorisation is routinely assigned on the basis of *visible* characteristics, especially skin-colour, and so it may be only indirectly connected to biological inheritance. In other words, visible racial markers have entered the realm of the sign, where their *biological* origins do not determine the way they are used in **ideological** communication, culture, or politics. As oppressed communities all over the world will attest, assignation to one race or another on the grounds of descent is itself highly political; it may require choosing one particular ancestor and ignoring all the others.

Thus the concept of race is itself, like the concept of **nation**, *relational*. Each race is to some extent a product of its difference from others in the system; and different countries and epochs recognise different systems. Over time and across different jurisdictions, these systems change, varying such fundamental matters as the number of races that are recognised, and therefore the way that different characteristics and attributes can be distributed, distinguished and acted upon in policy and practice.

Race is therefore constantly under reconstruction. In nineteenth-century common usage the term was interchangeable with 'nation' – journalists wrote of the Czech or Belgian or Bantu 'race'. Later race was reduced to three global categories – 'Caucasian', 'Mongoloid', 'Negroid' (still used in police work, at least to describe *white* – 'Caucasian' – suspects). Later still, different jurisdictions struggled to place their populations into categories that reflected their own circumstances, rather than squeezing people into a universal standard.

The USA has developed an 'ethno-racial pentagon' for the enforcement of federal anti-discrimination and affirmative action policies. It has five categories – African, European, Indigenous, Asian and Hispanic. This pentagon seems neutral, but still replicates 'the popular colour-consciousness of the past: black, white, red, yellow and brown' (Hollinger (2000: 199–202). Two of the 'races' – Hispanics and Europeans – would be regarded as 'white' in other jurisdictions. Thus despite its desire for bureaucratic accuracy and neutrality, this categorisation remains problematic and, because of internal differences within and between each of the categories, and the difficulty of moving between them, causes major difficulties for 'mixed' families.

But the use of the 'pentagon' as an anti-discriminatory tool in US federal policy clearly moves beyond the idea of race as a universal, to recognise histories of difference in both culture and discrimination. Thus it demonstrates the category of race, for theoretical or governmental purposes, cannot be separated from historical and cultural contexts (Hall, 1997). Because it is historical and therefore culturally specific rather than universal, the 'pentagon' model would not make sense outside of the USA. In Africa, Europe, Asia or Australia, the demographic make-up of the population is different.

Australia for instance would have no significant Hispanic category. But it does make a distinction between 'Anglo-Celtic' (a union that would come as a surprise in England and Ireland) and 'multicultural' Australians – the latter being those who migrated after the Second World War, first from Southern Europe (Malta, Greece, former Yugoslavia, Italy) and later from Asia (Vietnam, Cambodia, China). So Australia has a racial 'diamond': Indigenous, Anglo-Celtic, Multicultural, Asian (Hartley and McKee, 2000).

Hence the current period is characterised by a re-proliferation of the races, an attempt to arrive at non–discriminatory descriptive categories for governmental purposes, and different racial categories in different jurisdictions.

The twentieth century was marked by anti-Semitism and the Holocaust, and this theme remains an important issue for communication scholars. However, contemporary media and cultural studies emerged in the era of civil rights and **identity politics**. As a result, critical writings on racial issues in relation to the media have tended to focus on people of colour. Concerned that people of African or Caribbean descent were *under-represented* on TV, activist writings drew attention to **stereotypes** and called for more positive images, as well as a form of semiotic proportional representation, of racially marked groups in film, TV, news and politics alike (Gray, 2000, 2004). Later, attention shifted towards Latino/Latina identity, with the same agenda. Since 9/11 the politics of race has shifted again, towards 'Middle Eastern' identities.

On the streets, there remains the working through of quite different racial policies and politics, rooted in popular prejudice and residual supremacist theories. Sometimes racial conflict involves inter-ethnic competition, such as disputes between populations where both are regarded as racial minorities, for instance rivalry between Asian and Black or Hispanic Americans.

On the other hand, Black **popular culture**, including music, dance, sport, media, and fashion, is not only one of America's most important cultural forms and a driver of **innovation**, it is also a major component of the US export economy, as African American scholar Todd Boyd has pointed out across a number of landmark publications (e.g. Boyd, 1997, 2002, 2003). Beyond the USA, Black popular culture has created the world's fastest-growing film industry,

'Nollywood', based in Lagos, Nigeria, which is an object lesson for the **creative industries** worldwide in 'the role of informal markets in creating efficient and economically sustainable media industries' (Lobato, 2010: 337).

See also: **Diaspora, Ethnicity, Identity politics, Orientalism, Representation**

Further reading: Gilroy (1987, 1993); Gray (2004); Hartley and McKee (2000)

READERSHIP, READING PUBLIC

The idea of 'the reading public' arose with the publishing industry. In modern societies, the **public** is, first and foremost, a 'reading public', and **audiences** engage in 'reading' – i.e. an active, literate encounter with **semiotic** materials – not only via traditional print forms but also in relation to audio-visual media like television and film.

Readerships are the *product* of media industries: they are populations gathered without regard to otherwise powerful distinctions of territory, demographics and wealth and constituted as the readership of books and newspapers. Once the popular press of the nineteenth century had 'invented' nationwide readerships for the first time in history, these were available to serve as a **metonym** for the nation or society as a whole. They were not just as an 'imagined community' but a real one, reading the same books and papers (and latterly watching the same shows) at the same time. These readerships could also be mobilised to act as a public, especially in times of crisis or ceremony (wars and royal weddings). These readerships (including broadcast audiences), are the largest human communities ever assembled, albeit virtually, sometimes achieving simultaneous communion in the billions. Readers and audiences are also the 'product' of media in a more commodified sense, where their aggregated purchasing power is sold to advertisers by media organisations.

REALISM

Realism is a mode of **representation** of the world, both material (the world out there) and psychological (the inner life of individuals). Historically, it describes a commitment to objectivity in the arts, sciences and in literature. Thus Shakespeare is regarded as among the first artists to 'discover' psychological realism; at the same time Francis Bacon was theorising scientific realism; and meanwhile visual artists had perfected the visual realism of perspective painting.

Realism has also sometimes been used to distinguish intellectual movements like Marxism and feminism, and textual systems like **journalism**, from others such as **structuralism**, that do not conform to realist constructions or realism as a theory of representation. The difference is that 'realist' theories seek to act on the world, while structuralist ones seek to understand how knowledge itself is constituted by and in the textual systems used to 'convey' it.

In media analysis, realism is analysed as a **convention** that works to **naturalise** the modes of production that are necessarily part of any cultural text, by drawing attention to the *verisimilitude* (truth-seemingness, or truthiness, in Stephen Colbert's word) of the characters, action, plot, etc., rather than to the apparatus of its own narration. The rhetorical imperative is to pretend that the telling isn't there, only the tale. By familiarisation and habituation to realist genres, readerships also contribute to the effect by assenting to read within the claims of the convention (this is the so-called 'willing suspension of disbelief').

The artificial conventions of **genre** can assist realism. Science fiction, for example, uses special effects to create a sense of the reality of the situations in which characters, action, plot and technology 'make sense' generically. It is therefore quite normal to have realistic portrayals of scenarios that everyone knows are 'really' impossible. Such conventions then become a sort of pact between film-makers and their audiences. For instance, even though sound cannot travel through space, it is standard practice to apply sound effects (whooshes, engine noises) to spacecraft in movies – they are by general agreement more realistic as a result.

Realism is as much **ideology** as a neutral or transparent rendering of the real into textual form. This can be demonstrated by noting that its conventions evolve over time. What was greeted as shockingly realistic in one decade looks mannerist or kitsch in the next. Realism is thus reliant on shared value judgements. And these change rapidly over time.

See also: **Aesthetics**, **Diegesis**, **Naturalism**

REALITY TV

Reality TV can be traced to the early 1990s with shows that traded on the 'reality' of the everyday tasks of emergency services, e.g. *Cops* and *999* (Roscoe, 2001: 10). *Cops* transformed the 'crime-stoppers' genre into drama. Another emergent form was docu-soap, which shares with other 'reality' formats the presentation of social issues through human-interest stories or dramatisations. One innovation arising from this development is that **ordinary** people are doing the talking – 'real' folk get to be stars. Some of the criticism aimed at this type of programming stems from regret (by experts) for the loss of the expert's role.

Reality TV makes no attempt to hide the extent to which 'reality' is in fact a product of its production values, which have increased in proportion to the genre's popularity (for example, *Big Brother, Survivor, Popstars*). Roscoe (2001: 14) argues that the audience is well aware of the artifice, and that part of the pleasure for viewers is in evaluating the performance of participants – a pleasure that is particularly rewarding during moments when their control over their performance breaks down. It is at such moments that a different kind of 'reality' pokes through. Tears, back-stabbing, injury, and facial expression in the moment of defeat are all examples of what Jane Roscoe calls 'flickers of authenticity'.

See also: **Audience, Plebiscite**

Further reading: Hill (2005); Murray and Ouellette (2009)

REARVIEWMIRRORISM

Rearviewmirrorism occurs where a new technology or medium imitates the one it is in process of supplanting. Early printed books like the Gutenberg Bible looked like medieval manuscripts. The first house in the United Kingdom made of concrete (Gregynog Hall in Wales) looks like Tudor half-timbering. The first photographs borrowed composition and genre conventions from painting and portraiture. Early television was watched in a darkened room, as if it was cinema. Digital media aspired to look like analogue; e.g. computer-generated faces and hair were celebrated for looking 'real' (i.e. like film). The implication of this concept, which was coined by Marshall McLuhan (1964), is that **new media** must establish their credentials in terms that are already familiar to producers and consumers. Only later can they be exploited for their own potential.

See also: Hartley (1992a; 1999).

REDACTION

Redaction means 'editing', but editing as a creative practice, bringing already-existing textual materials together to create new meanings. It suits a world that from 2010 could measure its information hoard in zettabytes (a zettabyte is a billion terabytes; a terabyte is a trillion bytes: Wikipedia). Faced with such **plenty**, often readily accessible through multiplatform search functions, the *creation* of new information is losing its traditional prestige (*see* **author**; **journalism**), while the effective manipulation and management of data, stories, and multimedia text becomes progressively more crucial, and the creative possibilities offered to those who can repurpose such material are only beginning to be exploited. This is redaction. In this context 'editing' doesn't just mean 'cutting down' or 'fixing' a text, which is why 'redaction' is the preferred term. It means creating something new and distinctive, using the techniques of editing, rather than authoring. Thus it includes aspects of what **copyright** enforcers regard as piracy.

A 'redactional society' is one in which editorial practices determine what is understood to be true, and what policies and beliefs should follow from this; and what is understood to be the contemporary equivalent of beautiful (e.g. innovative, artistic, entertaining, cool, original or strange), and how we should feel about that (Hartley, 2003). Redactors render chaos into coherence; and that in itself is a viable business plan for the future of the **creative industries**.

The concept was coined by Hartley (2000, 2003) to draw attention to the extent to which textual systems like journalism are shifting from a focus on originating, creating or gathering materials for publication, towards one of editing (redacting) material that already exists into new texts. This process began before internet use became widespread, but online resources have accelerated it exponentially.

REDUNDANCY

In **cybernetics**, redundancy involves securing predictability in communication by means of repetition. The term has also been used in **semiotics** and media studies. Radio presenters are trained to say things three times: 'tell 'em you're going to tell 'em; tell them; then tell 'em you told 'em'. The TV show *Tellytubbies* was built on the idea that toddlers require things to be repeated four times, which is what happens on that show, including the number of characters; and the repetition itself becomes pleasurable. Thus, despite its apparently negative connotation, people *like* redundancy.

In the famous 1945 Rosenthal photograph of the planting of the American flag at Iwo-Jima, there are six marines. This is one of the most copied images of the twentieth century (it is the model for the US War Memorial at Arlington Cemetery). But many versions make do with only four marines. Two can hardly be seen in the original, but their limbs and arms 'redundantly' repeat the stance of their more visible comrades, making an effect whose power can be measured by comparison with the pale imitations (Hartley, 1996).

Built-in redundancy is necessary for increased intelligibility. Too much information interferes with clarity. Addressee-oriented as opposed to subject-oriented communication tends towards greater redundancy. Scientific papers in specialist journals strive for low redundancy, but are very hard to read. **Mass communication**, in contrast, is highly redundant; it is sensitive to the fact that audiences don't share **codes** with communicators or with each other. Like the little white duck, it is doin' what it oughta.

REFERENT

A term used in **semiotic** analysis that describes what the **sign** stands for, whether that is an event, a condition or an object. The referent is a part of the signifying system of **language**, rather than a property of the independently existing external world of **nature**. So, for instance, there are *beaches* the world over, with various identifiable properties, but the referent of the word 'beach' will differ in different languages, depending on both the structure of the language and the historical significance of the beach in that culture.

REGULATION

The legislative framework within which all aspects of communication, culture and media operate in a given legal jurisdiction, usually justified on the grounds of *protection* (of vulnerable persons or the national interest) and *correction* (of unfair practices or the terms of trade). As regulation has consequences for the creation and distribution of wealth, not to mention routine compliance costs, it is seen by some as interference in the workings of the market. **Deregulation** is called for on the assumption that the market 'can do it better'. On the other hand, increased regulation is often called for in populist and special-interest politics, especially when it comes to calls for bans on things that people don't like. Thus legislatures must read a line between different interests. Suffice it to say that the line is never drawn at the extreme marked 'complete freedom', even in First-Amendment America, which has a full panoply of legislative regulation at both state and federal levels, as well as case-law in the courts to determine where the line should be drawn in individual cases.

It should not be forgotten that regulation extends right across the communication spectrum, including constitutional and civic rights to free speech (or lack of them); laws governing individual conduct such as defamation; general provisions of a country's education, taxation, competition, trade, industrial relations, workplace safety, intellectual property and consumer-protection regimes; measures to prevent harm to individuals such as child protection. Then there are specific rules governing the media sector, starting from the constitutional appropriation of the airwaves by the state, which then licenses out spectrum to firms, with various conditions imposed. In the day-to-day operation of media businesses, special provisions are made: e.g. to prevent the export of cultural heritage items, to protect locally produced media content (e.g. quotas), to enforce various content restrictions (e.g. certification of films), to restrict monopoly or foreign ownership of media and telecommunications organisations, and in some countries to maintain a **public service broadcasting** regime. From time to time, campaigns result in special-interest legislation, resulting in restrictions based on religious, sexual, or sectional interests that vary widely from country to country.

Regulation also has a supra-national component, especially in 'free trade' agreements, the international imposition of **intellectual property** regimes, and in diplomatic negotiations between blocs with markedly different media traditions, e.g. the USA vs European Union, or 'the West' vs China, Iran, Saudi Arabia, etc.

Foucauldian approaches to discourse offer a different perspective on regulation. Here, knowledge/power institutions regulate the discursive space for the construction of identity. Thus, at the most general levels, what it can mean to become a self, what constitutes a family, how individuals discipline their own actions, and how institutions operate to administer the lives of populations, are all regulated by 'regimes of knowledge' in a general socio-cultural process Foucault called 'governmentality'.

Using this approach, cultural policy studies has focused analytical attention on the institutional frameworks that *govern* culture, including regulatory frameworks and process. Bennett (1992: 397) maintains that cultural practices should be defined in terms of 'the specificity of the governmental tasks and programs in which those practices come to be inscribed'. As Rose (1999: 3) writes, it is 'the invention, contestation, operationalisation and transformation of more or less rationalised schemes, programmes, techniques and devices which seek to shape conduct so as to achieve certain ends'. In this sense, regulation is the practice of the self within discursive and institutional frameworks.

Regulation also has an anthropological aspect, since rules, boundaries and codes informally govern every aspect of spontaneous communication, including the rules of language (**langue**), codes of behaviour (Goffman, 1986), and the boundaries of acceptable taste or conduct.

REPRESENTATION

Three types of representation are relevant to the study of communication, culture and media:

- In language, media, and communication, representation is the means by which **signs** 'stand for' something outside of the sign-system itself: words, pictures, sounds, sequences, stories, etc. that 'stand for' ideas, emotions, facts, etc.
- In politics, representation means that a chosen few stand for the whole people as their 'representatives' in Congress or parliament.
- In media, there's a system of representation whereby **stars** and **celebrities** on the screen or page 'represent' desirable (heroes) or undesirable (villains) human characteristics, prompting **identification** among audiences.

Representations rely on learnt and shared signs and images, on the learnt reciprocity of language and various signifying or textual systems. It is through this 'stand for' function of the sign that we know and learn reality.

Representations (plural) are the concrete form (signifiers) taken by abstract concepts. Some are banal or uncontroversial – e.g. how rain is represented in the movies, since real rain is both hard to see on camera and hard to produce on cue. But some representations go to the heart of cultural and political life – **gender**, **nation**, age, **class**, etc. Since representations inevitably involve a process of selection in which certain signs are privileged over others, how such concepts are represented in news media, movies, or even in ordinary conversation, matters. In fact Dyer (1993: 1) claims how 'we are seen determines in part how we are treated; how we treat others is based on how we seen them [and] such seeing comes from representation'.

It should come as no surprise then that the way representations are **regulated** through various media, genres, and within various discourses has been given considerable attention. Typically, complaints are made about the way that such-and-such a group has been *represented* in the media, prompting accusations of left-wing or right-wing bias, sexism, racism, homophobia, and so on. This model of representation conflates the *political* meaning of the term with the **semiotic** one, calling for representations on screen to remain in proportion with the occurrence of a given topic or identity in the community, leading to calls for quotas for 'under-represented' groups. However, semiotic systems and systems of political representation don't work in the same way. 'Proportional representation' in the semiotic domain would lead to poor drama; 'more positive' representations of unfavoured people or places would not improve their socio-political conditions. Thus the politics of representation is partly **rhetorical**, a *teaching* campaign aimed at others, in order to improve the image of the group in question and so to raise its social status or reputation in the eyes of those who may have no direct contact with members of that group.

See also: **Gender, Identity politics, Image, Race**

RHETORIC

The practice of using language to persuade or influence others, and the text that results from this practice. The formal study of oratory, exposition, persuasion. Rhetoric was a formal branch of learning in medieval Europe; one of the seven liberal arts or sciences, divided into those that were studies first, the *trivium* (from which our adjective 'trivial' is descended): these were grammar, logic (dialectics) and rhetoric. Then followed the *quadrivium*: arithmetic, geometry, astronomy and music. After these, a mind was ready to tackle philosophy and theology. This curriculum fell into serious disrepute in the Renaissance and did not survive the Reformation. However, schools of Rhetoric (or 'speech communication') were established in regional universities across the USA to prepare citizens for public office in the young Republic. Rhetorical figures have also survived, along with numerous rhetorical terms (**metaphor**, for example) that have achieved the status of ordinary language. What has been lost is the *system* of rhetoric, and its practised use as an art of memory.

When **structuralism** began to disclose how much of what we know and experience is structured by the **sign** systems we inhabit and encounter, there was a noticeable revival of interest in rhetoric. There are two reasons for this. First, rhetoric as a branch of learning requires us to attend to the sign system itself (whether verbal or visual), and to concentrate on the devices and strategies that operate in texts themselves – it offers a well-established and elaborate set of terms and classifications we can use to see how sense is made, not by reference to imponderables like authorial intentions or 'truth to life' but by reference to actual discourses. Second, if rhetoric didn't already exist it would no doubt have to be invented, since so many of the various forms of cultural production we're surrounded by are themselves highly rhetorical. Publicity, advertising, newspapers, television, academic books, government statements, and so on, all exploit rhetorical figures to tempt us to see things their way. If we have available a means to unpick these strategies we can begin to take a more critical and less intimidated stance towards them.

Further reading: Ong (1982: 108–12)

SEMANTICS

The study of **meaning** from a linguistic perspective. Semantics aims to analyse and explain how meanings are expressed in language.

Enquiry is organised around three important distinctions.

(1) Sense vs reference. The meaning of a linguistic expression – a word, for instance – can be treated in terms of its connection with extra-linguistic reality. From a different perspective, however, the meaning of a word can be considered in terms of its relationship to other words in the language. A famous example of the distinction between sense and reference is the way in which objectively the same planet, Venus, can be referred to equally appropriately as 'the morning star' and 'the evening star'. Consequently, the two expressions 'the morning star' and 'the evening star' have an identical **referent**, although the *sense* of one expression exactly opposes the other. In semantics, more attention has been given to the area of *sense* relations than to that of *reference*, in line with Wittgenstein's dictum: 'the meaning of a word is its use in the language'. But ignoring either side of the contrast between sense and reference tends to lead to unbalanced theories of meaning and this can have consequences that go beyond the domains of linguistic theory. For instance, rival aesthetic theories can be divided into two camps: **realist** theories favour referential accuracy; while formalist theories stress the conventionality of artistic representation and see it as an experiment with meaning – or 'sense'.

(2) Word meaning vs sentence meaning. Other approaches to the meaning of words involve notions such as semantic features and collocation, where words co-occur regularly, such that the occurrence of one word will 'predict' another even though there is no grammatical link between them (e.g. 'unvarnished' predicts 'truth,' 'arrant' predicts

'nonsense,' 'slippery' predicts 'slope'). Whatever approach is adopted, however, it does not seem possible to account for the meaning of a sentence merely by building upwards from the individual words that make it up. Otherwise 'Man bites dog' would mean the same thing as 'Dog bites man'.

(3) Text vs context. How much of meaning is created and carried by the linguistic system and how much and in what way it is determined by crucial characteristics of the context in which any utterance is grounded. Some aspects of meaning previously considered to be semantic – i.e. part of the linguistic system itself – are now treated as part of **pragmatics.**

The history of linguistics in the twentieth century saw a continual deferral of the study of meaning. The progression during this time was from smaller units of linguistic organisation such as the phoneme to the larger, such as the *sentence* or text; it has also been a progression from substance (phonology) to significance (semantics). Meaning has now come to the centre of the stage.

See also: **Discourse, Meaning, Multi-accentuality, Pragmatics, Semiotics**

Further reading: Saeed (2009)

SEMIOSPHERE

The 'semiotic space necessary for the existence and functioning of languages', which is both the 'result and the condition for the development of culture' (Lotman, 1990: 123–5). The term was coined by Yuri Lotman, on the model of the 'biosphere'. Unlike Saussure, who sought the smallest signifying unit in language, Lotman was convinced that communication could not occur without the *system* in place first; he thought *dialogue* (between systems) was a minimum precondition for language, not the other way round. So he wrote that the 'smallest functioning mechanism' of meaning-generation is 'the whole semiotic space of the culture in question' (ibid.: 125). Hence the semiosphere is the enabling structure that allows asymmetric or mutually untranslatable messages – like the communication between mother (language of smiles) and baby (looks and burbles) – to work as communication.

See also: **Mediasphere, Public sphere**

Further reading: Hartley (1996, 2008); Hartley and McKee (2000)

SEMIOTICS, SEMIOLOGY

Semiotics is the study of **signs** and sign systems. It seeks to understand how **language** is made meaningful and how **meaning** can then be communicated in society. It is a theoretical paradigm and to some extent a methodology; not a discipline in its own right (there are few Departments of Semiotics in universities), but its influence on institutionalised ways of approaching media texts has been considerable.

Swiss linguist Ferdinand de Saussure (1974) is often considered to be the founder of semiotics, along with other figures such as the American philosopher of language C. S. Peirce, the Italian semiotic theorist Umberto Eco (1972), and the Soviet theorist of language Valentin Volosinov (1973). The most influential figure was Saussure, whose structural linguistics was very influential in the development of **structuralism** (Barthes), **deconstruction** (Derrida) and structural anthropology (Levi-Strauss) in the 1960s and 70s, with downstream influence on many fields, including film theory, media studies, **cultural studies** and philosophy.

Saussurian semiotics approaches language 'synchronically', as a phenomenon existing in the here and now, rather than 'diachronically' (as did the then ascendant discipline of philology). He was interested in its structure and the rules that allowed utterances to be generated, not in existing words. He proposed that language works as a system of **difference**, in which what any one element means (its 'value' in the system) is arbitrary, consisting precisely in being what the others are not.

This idea was taken up and applied in contexts going well beyond the realm of spoken language. Anthroplogists looked at the structure of **myths** using Saussurian concepts. Barthes used them to analyse both literary and popular cultural texts, particularly via his *Mythologies* (1973). He led the way for those working in media and cultural studies to begin to apply semiotic terms to the analysis of everything from advertising to ideology.

In fact following developments in France in the 1950s and 1960s, semiotics was knitted together with Marxism and psychoanalytical approaches in the 1970s, by intellectuals working in the Birmingham tradition of cultural studies and the *Screen* tradition of cinema studies respectively. It was this from this conjunction that the emancipationist potential of semiotics was proposed: it could help to 'demystify' dominant ideologies, and assist in the effort to understand how commonsensical representations of an apparently unarguable reality were in fact constructed, often in line with existing arrangements of power.

Semiotics, which Saussure (1974: 16) defined as the science that studies the 'life of signs in society', was yoked to the service of the 'class struggle in language'.

Media semiotics (e.g. Fiske and Hartley, 1978; Hartley, 1982) recognised that meaning was dependent on, for instance, shared cultural **codes**, which are also historical and subject to change. Thus audiences could no longer simply be thought of as passive receivers. Semiotics gave them something to do (*see* **fans**). The 'active' reader of a text was a dialogic party to the sense-making process, bringing with them cultural experiences, discourses and ideologies for the process of making sense. Semiotics was a good technique for making this largely spontaneous, untutored activity more self-reflexive and critical.

See also: **Paradigm, Sign, Signification, Syntagm**

Further reading: Barthes (1973); Chandler (2007)

SIGN

A concept from **semiotics**, a sign is anything that stands for something else in the production of **meaning**. It may include words, photographs, sounds and gestures. A sign has three characteristics. It must:

- have a physical form – you can see, hear, smell, and/or touch it;
- refer to something other than itself;
- be used and recognised as a sign; that is, it be an element in a shared cultural **code** or system, in which its **signification** will depend on its differentiation from other signs in that system.

According to Saussure's theory of semiotics, a sign is made of two equal parts:

- *Signifier.* This works at the level of **denotation**. It is objective (a material thing). Using the oft-quoted example of a red rose, the flower itself is the signifier.
- *Signified*: This works at the level of **connotation**. It is subjective (a 'mentifact' not an 'artefact'). The signified is the concept referred to by the signifier. In the instance of the red rose, what is signified may be love, passion . . . or the Labour Party.

As you can see by this example, the signified of the sign can sometimes have more than one meaning (**polysemy**), but this is often tempered by the **context** within which the sign is represented. A red rose means one thing if given to a lover on Valentine's day, another if given to a parent. In another semiotic system, a red rose means 'the Labour Party'.

Signs function not through their essential nature but through their relative position in the ordering of other signs and codes. In fact Saussure argued that there is no intrinsic value in a sign, rather its meaning arises from its **difference** from other signs within the system. So, in the above example, we know that the rose is a rose by distinguishing it from others in the paradigm of flowers – it is not a lily or a daffodil. Applying this idea to human relations, in the rules of gender, the sign 'male' only makes sense through differentiation from 'female' – there are no necessary positive contents to maleness *as a sign*.

As the above examples demonstrate, the meaning of a sign is cultural. As such the sign is an unstable entity that relies not only on contextual knowledge but also on the knowledge of other available signs within that context.

See also: **Paradigm, Semiotics, Signification, Syntagm**

SIGNIFICATION

In **semiotic** analysis, signification is the output of **signs**. Signification is the *productivity* of communication.

Roland Barthes (1973) argued that there were hierarchical orders of signification – the denotative (this is a tree), the connotative (tree connotes nature), and the mythical (nature is bountiful). Users of a semiotic system don't normally work through these three in order; they are apprehended simultaneously: an image of a tree can *signify* 'bountiful nature'.

Barthes used the example of photography to demonstrate **denotation**. The photograph denotes what was in front of the camera when the image was captured. But *how* the image is photographed, and what abstract values may be associated with the resultant picture, is a matter of **connotation**. A photograph of a face denotes that face, but what is connoted will depend on the **genre** of photography (surveillance, fashion, news, art) and on stylistic manipulations of composition, colour, etc. the same face can connote 'criminal', 'beauty', 'supermodel', etc.

The **mythical** level of signification can also be termed the **ideological**. At this level, signification is dependent on shared cultural values and beliefs. Consider the use of images of countryside in advertising. Signification here depends on the myth or ideology that opposes city and country: the country is signified as more pure and innocent than the urban lifestyle. Such myths are specific to certain cultures, and they are arguable: 'country' may connote something quite different to a confirmed city-dweller. Whilst the process of signification is universal, the **meanings** that are generated in the process will be culturally specific.

See also: **Referent, Semiotics, Sign**

STARS, STARDOM

Performers in leading roles in the Hollywood studio system, whose offscreen personalities and doings were also scripted for publicity purposes. Stars are the marketing relation between production and consumption (*see* **consumption/production**). Stars were specific to film, and thus distinguished from **celebrities** in other fields, although the distinction has become blurred, such that the term now applies indiscriminately to persons with dazzling skills, prominent billing, or disproportionate fame in any field.

Richard Dyer (2004: 1–9) argues that stars are studied for both sociological and semiotic reasons.

- *Sociologically*, stardom is studied to see how stars fit into the industry and economics of Hollywood, and how their image for **fans** and consumers sustains the business. So for instance, sociological analysis may investigate whether the phenomenon is a result of production (driven by the film-makers) or of consumption (what the **audience** demands). Such analysis tends to confirm that the function of stars is necessarily **ideological**.
- The *semiotic* approach to stars differs from the sociological as it focuses on reception rather than production: on the textual experience and meaning of stars for viewers, not on the maintenance of the system. Here stars are signs that work **intertextually** (between films) to anchor a preferred reading or meaning of the narrative. Thus, for many projects, the decisive moment is casting the lead characters, which both *predicts* and *attracts* a certain audience demographic.

Dyer's own work goes beyond both sociological and semiotic analyses by describing what can be referred to as the cultural function of stars.

He argues that stars are definers of general ideas in society. Through their **representation** of, for example, work, sexuality, ethnicity and gender, they circulate ideas about what makes an individual. For instance, Marilyn Monroe – as a star not as a person – signifies a particular type of femininity and whiteness, 'an exemplary figure of the situation of women in patriarchal capitalism' (Dyer, 1998: x). To this end stars perform a function for the audience by representing certain types of behaviour and going some way to working through the complexities of subjectivity; but as the life of Marilyn Monroe among many others eventually proved, there can be a contradiction between the public star and the private person.

See also: **Celebrity, Identification, Intertextuality, Signs**

Further reading: Dyer (1998); Fischer and Landy (2004); Redmond and Holmes (2007)

STEREOTYPE

A stereotype is literally a fixed impression. The word comes from the printing process, where rows of type are transferred (*fixed*) to a solid plate (called the stereotype) which then makes an *impression* on paper. Thence, the term also implies monotonous regularity – each impression from a stereotype is always the same.

Metaphorically, the term entered public life, via social psychology, to describe how fixed qualities or traits may be attributed to groups in the way they are represented in various media. It is usually applied to negative impressions or pernicious representational techniques. In other words, negative portrayals of people of colour may be said to be stereotyping them. But, conversely, the word stereotyping is less commonly used to describe equally fixed and equally fantastic *positive* portrayals – of, say, American heroes and buddies. Thus, stereotyping is a pejorative term – something done by opponents.

Stereotypes are not failed depictions of an external reality; they are **rhetorical** devices that play a role in the economy of narration. For instance, stereotypes can be understood as concise **conventions** for delineating character. Their use is also **intertextual**. As Dyer (1993: 15) argues, 'stereotypes always carry within their very representation an implicit narrative'. Certainly the genre of comedy has always relied on stereotypical or stock characters; therefore 'comic stereotypes' should be considered within the conventions of **genre** rather than as realistic portrayals. However, reality does enter the picture when real people perceive themselves or their identity to be stereotyped; so prompting media activism in the cause of **identity politics**.

See also: **Race**, **Representation**

STRUCTURALISM

An intellectual enterprise characterised by attention to the systems, relations and forms – the structures – that make **meaning** possible in any cultural activity or artefact. It is associated with a number of French writers who became influential in and after the 1960s.

Structuralism is not an *interpretative* approach to *real* meaning. Unlike previous kinds of literary and cultural criticism, it did not seek to reveal the hidden, essential or intrinsic meaning of a text or artefact. On the contrary, structuralists refused the very idea of essential or intrinsic meaning, together with the notion that individual texts or individual people are the source of the meanings they generate. Even when authors have specific intentions, these do not determine what texts are taken to mean. Structuralism is an analytical or *theoretical* enterprise, dedicated to the systematic elaboration of the rules and constraints that work, like the rules of a language, to make the generation of meanings possible in the first place.

Thus early structuralism was distinguished by the use of Saussurian linguistics and its terminology: especially the notions of signifier and signified (*see* **sign**); **langue** and **parole**; **synchronic** and **diachronic**; **paradigm** and **syntagm**. These and other distinctive features of a language structure were used to show how disparate and apparently un-organised phenomena were instances of the same structural patterns and relations. Further, structuralism was dedicated to showing how such structures were to be found in all kinds of cultural activity. Thus there are structuralist analyses of architecture, fashion, food, kinship networks and the unconscious, as well as of the more obvious signifying 'systems' of cinema, television and literature.

The most prominent names in structuralism are Roland Barthes (criticism) and Claude Levi-Strauss (anthropology). Other influential writers who were associated with the enterprise are Louis Althusser (Marxist theory), Jacques Lacan (psychoanalysis) and Michel Foucault (studies of sexuality, madness and incarceration in terms of theories of **power**, **discourse** and **knowledge**).

During the 1970s structuralism underwent a transformation. This was partly due to the proliferation of different positions within the enterprise, which eventually became too diverse to be understood as a unitary approach. It was also brought about by the unease which some of structuralism's original proponents began to express that it was becoming itself the very type of intellectual orthodoxy that it was originally set up to challenge. The outcome of this transformation was to produce at least three rather different fields of study:

- **Semiotics**, which had hitherto been synonymous with structuralism but which became established as a major strand within the study of media and **popular culture**.
- **Deconstruction** (Culler, 1982, 2003; Lucy, 2003), which is a mode of literary analysis, derived from the writings of Jacques Derrida. Derrida, a philosopher, showed how the philosophical assumptions that underlie writings are not by any means the guarantors of their meaning – on the contrary, the discourses in which such assumptions are presented systematically undermine the philosophy. This approach has given rise to an entire *deconstructionist* movement that has been particularly influential in literary studies in the USA. In this guise, the approach is a 'method' whose only precept is to take nothing for granted – doubt and questioning raised to the level of doctrine. Deconstruction is, then, one of structuralism's logical conclusions. Deconstruction was a procedure for showing how the very terms in which a given textual performance was couched undermined what it purported to say. Thus it was focused on the sense-making strategies rather than the referential accuracy of textual agency. The object of study (a work of literature, for instance) was given no privileged status; it was not a warrant for its own reading. On the contrary, deconstruction was dedicated to teasing out the repressed, marginalised and absent in the chosen discourse.
- *Post-structuralism* was born when *formalism* met *feminism*; and thence **identity politics**. It was more alert to psychoanalytical theories and to the role of pleasure in producing and regulating meanings than was the highly rationalist early structuralism. It was also more concerned with the *external* structures and politics – of social process, class, gender and ethnic divisions, historical changes – that make meaning possible, where early structuralism had focused on *internal* or 'immanent' textual structures. Hence post-structuralism shifted the analytic focus from the *text* to the *reader*.

Structuralism has been seen as a characteristically twentieth-century way of understanding the world. The nineteenth century was notable in many different fields for work that sought *causes and origins*

(Darwinism, Marxism, Freudianism) as the framework of explanation. Structuralism shares with other twentieth-century enterprises – in physics and astronomy especially – attention to *relations and systems* as the framework for explanation. Instead of treating the world as an aggregate of things with their own intrinsic properties, structuralism and physics respectively sought to account for the social and physical world as a complex system of relations in which the properties of a 'thing' (be it an atom, a sign or an individual) derive from its internal and external relations.

See also: **Deconstruction, Difference, Discourse, Postmodernism, Semiotics**

STYLE

The **aestheticisation** of the self and the display of difference. While style can be personal, it also refers to cultural and historical identity. Thus a period or movement can be said to display a style, as well as a person or product. Style is concerned with distinctiveness within a recognised system.

Fashion illustrates the functioning of style in contemporary culture. The trick of fashion is poised on a contradiction: you have to be seen to *emulate* the latest styles while producing an *original* style of your own. You must copy and be unique, all at once. An astute *fashionista* is one who can manipulate the highly codified rules of the fashion system (**langue**) to produce original and inspiring 'performances' (**parole**), even if the clothes chosen are vintage, grunge, or 'street'. Such a person (Kate Moss is one) 'has' style and may become 'directional' for others, thereby rolling the emulation/originality dice one more time.

Top fashion designers may push the limits of the wearable by showcasing outfits that can't be worn on the high street. Here they are acting as visionaries or **innovators** of style, not mere designers of clothes. They are the R&D arm of the consciousness industry, much like radical filmmaking styles such as surrealism or French new wave. Such avant-garde movements challenge and change what is possible in their medium.

Style serves not only to differentiate, but also to forge an identity. Identity through style is reliant on similarity; therefore copying. For a style to be *identifiable*, an outfit must belong to a **paradigm**. Individuals from various subcultures, from old-style punks to contemporary Harajuku girls, are spectacularly different from the mainstream (and can look 'all alike' to the uninitiated); but *within* the paradigm, individual choice is artfully signalled, in a kind of evolutionary arms-race of competitive differentiation. That's style.

See also: **Bricolage, Genre, Subcultures**

SUBCULTURE

An identifiable group identity, often associated with some combination of youth, music, **style**, consumption practices (e.g. choice of drugs) and mediation. As the prefix *sub* indicates, such groups form their identity in opposition to a dominant or 'parent' **culture**. Early subcultural studies argued that this opposition was carried out through style. Recent work in the area suggests that this relationship is no longer so explicit, extending the concept beyond the first-noticed 'spectacular' subcultures.

Hebdige's (1979) study of teddy boys, mods, rockers and punks is one of the founding texts of **cultural studies**. For Hebdige, the subcultural use of style and leisure activities was a form of *symbolic politics*, aimed at forming a countercultural identity and mounting a visible challenge to the **hegemony** of straight society. Thus the notion of *resistance* to the parent culture is central to Hebdige's approach. But a constant challenge to this resistance is 'ideological recuperation', where a subculture begins to lose its sense of difference as its style is incorporated into commercial culture often via the media (Hebdige, 1979: 97).

While *disapproving* stories in the press may work to create and legitimise subcultures, *approving* reports 'are the subcultural kiss of death' (Thornton, 1995: 6). Thus, punk's initial impact was reported in the media in gratifyingly outraged tones (masterfully orchestrated by punk impresario Malcolm McLaren), but before too long punk fashion-spreads in magazines and the appearance of punk iconography on London's tourism postcards signalled that the process of recuperation had begun. Teenage rebellion is fatally prey to commercial success.

Recent theorists of subculture argue that communities are being formed not so much out of resistance, but out of shared tastes and interests. Thornton (1995) uses the term 'taste cultures' to describe those who listen to dance music and go to raves and dance clubs. Taste cultures are bound together through certain commonalities, but they are less reliant on the models of resistance put forward by Hebdige. Here, music, drugs, and leisure (dance clubs and parties) rather than style, are central to meaning-making, with opposition directed towards mainstream popular music, rather than more generally towards the parent culture.

The move from subcultures to taste cultures recognises that marginal communities are not always concerned with resistance. Hebdige himself declared the death of subcultural significance along with that of the punk movement (Hebdige, 1988). But studies of the subcultural relationship between identity and leisure choices have continued (Gelder and Thornton, 1997), to the point where now there is a field called *post*-subcultural studies (Muggleton and Weinzierl, 2003)

See also: **Bricolage, Style**

SUBJECTIVITY

The social production of selfhood. During the 1970s and after, cultural studies was perhaps more interested in subjectivity than in culture itself. It became a central focus of attention during this period for political and cultural reasons, to do with the rise of **identity politics**. At the same time, **structuralism** and its aftermath suggested that subjectivity was not a natural but historical and cultural phenomenon, produced out of the resources of language and culture, rather than simply being 'given' by nature. Thus, subjectivity was implicated in new theories of **power**.

Stuart Hall (1992) argues that there have been five de-centring shifts in the concept of subjectivity since the Enlightenment that have informed our contemporary understanding of 'the subject':

*   *Marxism* demonstrated how individuals were subject to conditions not of their own making. Marxist theory undermined the notion that was a universal essence or spirit to mankind, arguing instead that individuals were products of social relations, especially those required by the expanding force of capitalism. Marxism's refusal of essential human nature suggested that ethics and morals could no longer be thought of as universal; rather they were acquired or produced by one's position in society, and indeed had a political functionality in maintaining that positionality.
*   *Freud*'s 'discovery' of the unconscious. Freud argued that an infant's being is formed in relation to others, suggesting that identity was something that was learned rather than existing as an innate essence. Theorists such as Lacan, Kristeva and more recently Žižek continued the psychoanalytic approach, arguing that **identification**

and subject-formation are an on-going process conducted in negotiation with the unconscious. Although psychoanalysis is often criticised for its irrecoverable object of study, it has been influential in
theorising subjectivity, not least because it was first to show how
reason did not rule the roost in the human imagination.

• *Saussurian* **semiotics** and structuralism marked another shift in the
way we imagine the self. Saussurian approaches to **language** led to
the structuralist contention that we cannot know ourselves outside
of language – that it *constitutes* our reality; in a sense, language speaks
us. The subject is positioned in language.

• *Foucault*'s reworking of the notions of **power**, truth, and the self.
Subjectivity was constructed and administered through **discourses**,
including those that investigated what it means to be human
(science) and what it means to be social (government). It is these
that 'discipline' subjects, making them manageable, knowable, and
restrainable.

• *Feminism* gendered the subject. What was widely assumed to be
true or universal turned out not to be true for women. Activism by
women was a major contributor to the rise of identity politics.

One would want to add that a sixth de-centring has occurred via
postcolonial and 'subaltern' studies, which have worked to decentre
the Western, universal subject, and to introduce the notion of the
hybrid, multicultural, 'subaltern' and colonised subject.

See also: **Identity politics, Postcolonial**

SYMBOL

Symbols may be simple non-verbal **signs**: something visual standing
for something other than itself, as a road sign may use a simplified
image to symbolise a bicycle, roadworks and the like. But symbols can
also be much more complex, operating at the most elaborated levels of
literary and visual culture. In communication and cultural studies, the
study of symbols is used in the following ways:

• In the theory of **semiotics** developed by C. S. Peirce, the term
'symbol' is used instead of 'sign'. Using the term symbol he argues
there is no relationship between the signifier and the signified
(Leeds-Hurwitz, 1993). What **meaning** is derived is purely reliant
on shared cultural connotations. This is most explicit in the use of
national flags where what the object itself signifies is symbolic rather

than natural. **Language** too acts symbolically, where a collection of letters come to represent an agreed-upon meaning.

- In *psychoanalysis*, in dialogue with earlier theories of symbolism in *art* and *literature*, symbolism refers to the act of representing something that has been repressed by the unconscious. For Freud, matters of sexuality, birth and maternal relationships are all aspects of the self that are repressed. Psychoanalytic theory posits the 'return of the repressed' through symbols in representation. Various branches of literary and cinema criticism have taken up this idea in the study of *symbolism*.

- The *sociological* theory of 'symbolic interactionism' argues that through symbolic communication we come to know others and ourselves around us. This was an important development within a discipline that had previously studied only observable behaviour. This theory recognised that between communication and response there is the exchange and interpretation of symbols. As a method symbolic interactionism will consider, for example, language, behaviour, and body language. Sociologically, people cue their interaction behaviour by interpreting each other's symbolic communication.

SYNCHRONIC

One of a pair of terms – the other is **diachronic** – taken from the work of Saussure (1974). They refer in this context to two different but not mutually exclusive ways of conducting **semiotic**/linguistic analysis. Synchronic analysis concentrates on the state of **language** (**langue**) at one moment. *Diachronic analysis* concentrates on the changes in a given language over time.

Saussure was strongly convinced of the need for synchronic analysis – the attempt to take language as a structured whole, within the scientific present tense, in order to investigate its internal relations. Synchronic analysis is essentially abstract, since it is empirically impossible to stop a language in its tracks to observe its present state. But abstraction was just what Saussure favoured, since his argument was that linguists had become so bogged down in the empirical fact of particular languages and their word-stores (philology) that there was no developed theory of language-in-general from which to make sense of the empirical data.

Synchronic analysis has become the norm in much semiotic work, where the emphasis has been on isolating the elements (**signs**) and their internal relationships within an abstract system (**codes**) of many different sign systems. Saussure predicted that synchronic analysis would eventually lead on to a more theoretically adequate diachronic analysis, and thence to a combination of the two, which he dubbed *panchronic*.

See also: **Diachronic, Discourse, Langue, Paradigm, Parole, Sign, Signification, Syntagm**

SYNTAGM

A syntagm is a 'chain' of **signs**, which are combined or organised in a meaningful order from a **paradigmatic** set of choices. Some examples of syntagm arrangements include a sentence, which is a syntagm of words (signs) or a melody that is a syntagm of notes (also signs). Combination is rule-governed. Choice of food from a menu involves a syntagmatic process that guides the order in which different foods are eaten (no custard *with* beef; though you may eat it *after* beef). Different cuisines have different rules of combination and sequence, so a Chinese meal (properly done) involves a syntagmatic chain of dishes that bears no resemblance to the sequence of a Western meal – which itself is a modern innovation, replacing different medieval combinations.

Analysis of syntagmatic structure is rare in contemporary media studies, although it is covered in linguistics by **semantics**. However, the study of **narrative** continues to carry on this tradition to some extent, showing how plot sequence ascribes causation as well as temporality to a story.

See also: **Narrative, Paradigm, Semiotics, Sign**

TECHNOLOGICAL DETERMINISM

Technological determinism is the doctrine that social change is determined by technological invention. For instance, Marshall McLuhan thought that modernity was caused by the invention of printing. Technological determinism is contradicted by Marxism, **political economy**, etc., which award the determining role to the economy.

Communication and media studies have a bet each way in this context, since it is clear that technological development, while driven by economic forces, nevertheless opens up possibilities not predicted by them. A simple example is the use of mobile phones for text-messaging, a 'cultural form' that was not predicted by the inventors of that technology, but which secured its commercial viability. Here the technology itself was significant (it could do things not intended). But equally, the example indicates that technology by itself is culturally inert – it has to be taken up by users. Thus, it seems that determination is multiple: economic direction by business and government, combined with the potentiality and capacity of technological inventions themselves, combined with their success or otherwise in the public arena, are all 'determining' forces.

Further reading: Arthur (2009); Edgerton (2007); Jordan (2008)

TEXT

A text traditionally refers to a sequence of writing, bounded by the medium on which it is written – page, scroll, stone. The term is inherited from Judeo-Christian traditions of textual exegesis, where scholars would take sections of holy or religious texts and explain them, either verbally (sermons) or by writing (concordances). The skill of explication of difficult passages of significant texts was secularised in the form of literary criticism, which began to take hold in the eighteenth century, when religious texts began to be supplanted by national literatures. But the *technique* of study and commentary remained the same, and so therefore did the concept of 'text'.

In the contemporary era, three developments have coincided to extend enormously what might be encompassed by the term 'text':

- *Mass education* brought a universal and not just an elite readership to texts of all kinds, and so extended both the need and the opportunity for exegesis.
- *Continental philosophy*, especially associated with Derrida and the **deconstruction** movement, contended that humans only know anything by *textualising* the world, and that there is nothing 'beyond' the text.
- *Contemporary audio-visual media* extended *verbal* textuality into visual, aural, and sequential forms – you could buy a video as easily as a book. Since the emergence of the internet, *hypertext* has both fragmented and extended the notion of text yet further.

Hence it became possible to perform 'textual exegesis' on completely non-written 'texts' such as movies, TV shows, news photos, magazines, websites, etc. Working back over the three developments noted above, texts became formidable. In a secular era of popular sovereignty the 'textual' media were held to be the bearers of significant meanings about democracy, subjectivity, identity, ideology, fantasy, etc. There seemed to be a philosophical warrant for taking textual evidence seriously not just as 'representing' the human condition but getting about as close to reality as can be got. And contemporary life is promiscuously textual. Viewing, reading, and listening suffuses everyday activities rather than being a distinct and relatively rare special event (like 'going to the theatre'). It requires a universal 'literacy', and the study of 'texts' is one means by which citizens of media can become self-reflexive in that context.

Once the pattern was set almost anything could be a text, or be subjected to textual analysis, including live events and actions. Some have objected to this exorbitant expansion of the text. But on the other hand, humans cause just about everything they touch or do to **signify** in one way or another, so to trace the process of creation, transmission and interpretation of **meaning** may well involve looking at customs, buildings, media and bodies as well as papyrus and stone.

Textual analysis is a particularist empirical analytical methodology that is central to the work of cultural and media studies. It involves examining the formal internal features and contextual location of a text to ascertain what readings or meanings can be obtained from it. It is not a tool to find the correct interpretation of a text, rather it is used to understand what interpretations are possible. Textual analysis is interested in the cultural and political implications of **representations**, not only in how meaning is constructed. Remembering that one of the aims of undertaking textual analysis is to understand the variety of meanings made possible by a text, it is essential to consider the **context** in which the text is received. This is not the social context as in **ethnography**, where the researcher aims to understand the space in which a person reads a text. Rather context in textual analysis refers to the wider world of textuality. For example, this can refer to **conventions** of **genre**, the **intertextuality** of an actor, the **narrative** of the text, as well as **discourses** that are evoked in discussions of your subject in other media texts. Textual analysis works to investigate the interplay of meanings both inside and outside the text.

See also: **Aberrant decoding, Meaning, Methodology**

Further reading: McKee (2003)

TEXTUAL SYSTEM

A textual system is a **content industry** plus a **readership** (or **audience**) and a cultural form, sustained in complex mutual relationship across a number of appropriate media **platforms**, over an extended historical time. The paradigm example of a textual system is **journalism**. Hartley (1996: 31–5) claims that as the sense-making practice of **modernity**, journalism is the most important textual system of that period. Drama is also a textual system, and its survival into modernity suggests the limits of the truth-seeking rationality of modernism. Other textual systems include science, the novel (published prose fiction), and **user-created content** (e.g. the blogosphere, the Wikipedia).

The most important *textual* feature of journalism is that it counts as true. The most important component of its *system* is the creation of readerships and **publics** that count as coterminous with the entire **nation** or society, and the connection of those readers to other systems, for instance politics, economics, social control, and the **semiosphere**. The most important *textual* feature of drama is that it is *relational* (based on conflict among persons). Drama's *system* is both pre-modern and modern (live and mediated). Also included are the technology, institutions and practices required to sustain drama – 'Hollywood', for instance.

Study of a textual system must be interdisciplinary, both *textually* (using **semiotics, content** and **genre** analysis, **ideology**, pleasure), and *socially* (using quantitative, generalising methods, **ethnography**, policy analysis, history, etc.), in order to connect the minutiae of communication with the structures, institutions, economics and history so communicated (*see* **aberrant decoding**).

USER

The 'user' is a term from computer science that describes the agent on the human side of the human–computer interface; from the expert programmer to the *end user* who runs an application. It has become a very familiar term in ordinary language and a useful concept in the study of media and communication. As a concept, 'the user' updates that of 'the **audience**' in a transformational way.

- *Active not passive*: It removes the idea, inherited from mass communication, that the audience is the end-point of a chain that leads one way only, from producer, via technology-and-text, to consumer, who is inevitably reduced to passive status with little agency beyond choosing to put their bums on *this* seat rather than *that* one and then to get what they're given. The user is a 'sit-up' agent, as well as a 'sit-back' one.

- *Dialogic not one-way*: The concept of the user reinstates a two-way model of the communication process, where users are active agents, with their own productivity, who share well as receive mediated content, participating, creating and publishing their own work (*see* **user-created content**).

- *Turns not divisions*: The concept of the user recasts the boundaries between expert and amateur, producer and consumer, cause and effect – it sees these roles as turn-taking possibilities for the same agent, rather than a fixed division of labour between them.

- *Agent not individual*: The user does not have to be a domestic consumer or even an individual. Users can be scientists, entrepreneurs, fashion designers or what you will, and they can be firms or affinity-groups as well as individuals.

- *Multiplatform and transmedia*: It applies to any computer-related activity, meaning that the same user can be imagined in relation to any media content, including broadcasting (via podcasts, for instance). Instead of different audiences (or readerships) following each platform – music, news, TV, cinema, etc. – content can follow the user.

Thus 'the user' changes mediated communication from an industrial to a social-network model, and installs what Jay Rosen dubbed the 'people formerly known as the audience' (Rosen, 2006) as the main locus of *feedback and learning* for the open, complex online system, thereby taking their place as agents for the *growth of knowledge*.

USER-CREATED CONTENT, USER-GENERATED CONTENT

Online media content created by non-professional users. The term became prevalent when the internet became both widely available to the general public and able to take video – a moment most readily marked by the launch of YouTube in 2005 (Burgess and Green, 2009). YouTube itself is a good example of the shift from media forms relying on production through an industrial-style expert pipeline (**broadcasting**) to media forms relying on user-created content (UCC), where the business model relies on high-volume *traffic* rather than high-value content. By the mid-2000s, user-created content was growing strongly across many different arenas of online activity:

- Open-source programming (e.g. Linux)
- Blogs and citizen journalism
- Crowd-sourced learning (including Wikipedia)
- Social-networking sites (MySpace; Facebook)
- DIY media (YouTube); photo-sharing (Flickr; Panoramio)
- Games (content-development by players; MMOGs (massively multiplayer online games))
- Problem-solving in online science, technology, crafts, specialist skill-sharing
- Discussion forums and communities of interest (e.g. genealogy)

Already by 2007 the Organisation for Economic Cooperation and Development reported that user-created content was an agent of **'creative destruction'** in the media ecology:

> User-created content became an important economic phenomenon despite its originally noncommercial context. The spread of UCC and the amount of attention devoted to it by users appears to be a significant disruptive force for how content is created and consumed and for traditional content suppliers. This disruption creates opportunities and challenges for established market participants and their strategies.
>
> (OECD, 2007)

User-generated content also became a familiar component of corporate websites, adding to or even taking over the previously professional task of reviewing, for example: product and book reviews on Amazon; experience reviews on tourism, hotel and travel websites; and political commentary on news sites.

Further reading: Jenkins (2006a)

VIOLENCE

Among humans, interpersonal physical attack or abuse is a form of communication; and it is one of the most commonly mediated forms. It can include domestic violence, interpersonal competitive aggression (fisticuffs), as well technologically enhanced group violence using weapons, up to and including as acts of war. What counts as violence in the media requires both **context** and cultural agreement. Sports contain forms of violent behaviour that are not so labelled, for instance in boxing, wrestling, ice hockey, and gridiron. But in another context, much less aggressive acts may 'count' as violence – in cartoons and children's TV shows, for instance.

Violence in society is often attributed to the **effects** of the media, with each new media **platform** attracting criticism for the escalation of this reputedly unwanted social behaviour. Popular fiction, comic books, film, television, video games and the internet have all endured public disquiet about their content and its supposed effects. However, the debate over violent entertainment rarely considers the *appeal* of this form of entertainment. As the social theorist Norbert Elias pointed out long ago (writing in 1939), what we call civilisation is the long history of '**affect** control', where social violence, once a pleasurable prospect for any strong young man, is progressively monopolised by the authorities, and the 'joy of killing' is confined to ritual forms (hunting) or mediated forms, where *spectating* (sports) was pretty much all that was left of the previous 'release of affect' on the battlefield (Elias, 2000: 161ff.). In other words, violence in the media is an index, not of *increased* social violence, but of its social *disappearance* compared with pre-modern eras. Except in times of social breakdown, it takes indirect, 'refined' form.

Whether or not depictions of violence provide some form of displaced affect-release for viewers is rarely considered. Instead, social-science and psychology research *assumes* 'harm' and focuses on measuring it, or looking for ways to minimise it. This is the **effects** tradition. It takes for granted that 'violence is an abstractable unit whose presence can be counted and whose influence can be studied' (Barker and Petley, 2001: 3). This model ignores 'the moral codes that different audiences bring to bear as they watch' (ibid.: 7), as well as the context in which a violent act is represented (Gauntlett, 2005).

Increased **representations** of violence do not necessarily say anything about society's *attitudes* towards these acts, let alone their social prevalence in a given country. Interpersonal violence in society, especially male/male homicide, so beloved of shoot-em-up movies and first-person games, has been steadily dropping throughout modernity; and is consistently lower in countries with long traditions of mass media (e.g. Western Europe) than it is where media entertainment – and the affluent consumer society it is based on – is relatively recent (e.g. South Africa; Mexico – countries where high levels of violence are clearly not 'effects' of media!).

It is true that international trade in action movies and first-person-shooter games is facilitated by the fact that such forms rely less on a given language than do other genres – kung-fu movies and moving targets make sense in any language. At the same time, cultural tolerance for depicted violence differs across cultures. It is well-known that Japan, which in its civil society is relatively non-violent, sustains some of the most violent media formats, such as manga, without any apparent transfer from page to street. Thus what seems raw and dangerous in one country may seem indirect, ritualised and 'refined' in another.

See also: **Content analysis, Effects, Methodology, Representation**

Further reading: Trend (2007)

VIRTUAL COMMUNITIES

A term from Howard Rheingold (2000), virtual communities are social networks interacting through mediated contact, usually online. Virtual communities are an important feature of contemporary culture, because they extend individual people's social networks from local or face-to-face contact to global dimensions, allowing 'communities of **affect**' or 'communities of interest' to arise, where minority or very specialised tastes can find a group identity, allowing otherwise isolated nodes on a long tail to clump into viable hubs.

See also: **Network theory**

VIRTUALITY

Virtuality is a **cyborg** phenomenon, experienced by the individual whose identity is extended or manipulated through her/his interaction with technology. Underlying the concept of virtuality is the presumption that technology can take us out of ourselves, allow us to create a new identity by manipulating information and allow us to wander through landscapes that are divorced from the material reality that we usually inhabit.

Virtuality has been defined by Hayles (1999: 69) as 'the cultural perception that material objects are interpenetrated by information patterns', implying an *opposition* between information and materiality. As a result of this distinction, information is *de*-materialised (wishfully), and so holds out the promise of wish-fulfilment, that one day we may be able to use information to transcend materiality. Science fiction exploits this idea, with fantasies of being able to take on a new body or to rematerialise in a different place ('beam me up Scottie'). Movies from *The Matrix* to *Inception* both rely on and promote the desire for virtuality; and see also Sconce (2000) for a comparison with out-of-body fantasies sparked by earlier technological inventions, including electricity and the cinema. Of course, virtuality is not a physical fact but a **rhetorical** accomplishment. In fact, information depends upon the material world and on technological mediation for its distribution and use. Here, the rhetorical disembodiment of virtuality takes a different form, invoking the 'weightlessness' of the **new economy**, where 'intangibles' (immaterial goods) rule the roost, suggesting that virtuality can be achieved in the information economy even if it can't be by the individual body.

See also: **Cyborg**, **Virtual communities**

VISUAL CULTURE

A contemporary form of Art History or Art Criticism, focusing on vernacular, mediated, and contemporary pop-culture visualisations, in addition to (and sometimes in opposition to) elite or 'high' arts. An early exponent was John Berger, whose landmark TV series *Ways of Seeing* was art criticism as ideology critique. Produced partly as a response to Lord Kenneth Clark's earlier BBC series *Civilisation*, Berger's series was a major influence on early cultural and media studies. It introduced the politics of culture, presenting a Marxist and social-constructivist interpretation of the Western artistic canon and treating commercial art and publicity with as much critical seriousness as the old masters. At around the same time, **structuralists** (e.g. Barthes, Eco) and film theorists (Mulvey and others associated with the journal *Screen*) began to apply **semiotics** to visual culture, to 'demystify' media 'images'. Subsequently, semiotics and linguistic models were developed for the analysis of visual communication more generally (Hodge, Kress, van Leeuwen), including some attempts at a 'semiotics of art'. In the field of built environment, Bill Mitchell and Charles Jencks pioneered the study of visual culture from an architectural and urban-planning perspective. Anthropologists of both traditional and contemporary culture incorporated analysis of visual materials as part of the study of 'material culture' (e.g. Danny Miller; Faye Ginsberg). All of this was in place before the internet era; soon, online digital media began to demand attention as part of visual culture (Bentkowska-Kafel *et al.* 2009).

Further reading: Mirzoeff (2009)

VSR

VSR = 'variation; selection; retention'; the fundamentals of Darwinian evolution by natural selection. It works for **culture** too.

See also: **Evolution**

Further Reading: Boyd (2009); Boyd and Richerson (1985); Richerson and Boyd (2005)

WHITENESS (STUDIES)

A branch of racial/ethnic studies devoted to questions of whiteness. Whether conducted by analysts of white descent or not, the study of white **ethnicity** in media, culture and communication is not generally carried forward as an attempt to recuperate an oppressed or marginal identity, but to draw attention to whiteness as an **ex-nominated** category, and to trouble or confront the too-easy presumption that racial and ethnic questions are a problem for every *other* ethnic group. Hence, the discussion of whiteness began to appear in **race** studies in the early 1990s. Some examples: In the USA, David Roediger wrote the influential *Wages of Whiteness* (2007); Cheryl Harris (1993) studied law, property and whiteness; Ruth Frankenberg (1993) studied white women; David Theo Goldberg has published extensively on race, as well as white issues. In the United Kingdom, Richard Dyer (1997) studied whiteness in cinema. In Australia, Aileen Moreton-Robinson (2004) and Ghassan Hage (1998) have both done important work, from an Aboriginal and a multicultural perspective respectively.

See also: **Ethnicity, Orientalism, Postcolonial, Race, Representation**

Further reading: Delgado and Stefancic (1997); Roediger (1999)

X, Y, Z (GENERATIONS)

Generations X (born 1960s–80s), Y (born 1981–95), and Z (born after 1995) are widely used terms in marketing, psychographic profiling and social commentary, for generational differences among consumers, citizens, media audiences and cultural style. Generation X was 'invented' by the Canadian novelist Douglas Coupland (1991). According to market-researcher Mark McCrindle (2009) the new generation of people born from 2010 will be called Generation Alpha. Their key point of difference? They will start school earlier; study longer; and be the most formally educated generation ever. The novelist who started all this agrees. Douglas Coupland has published a new novel called *Generation A*, which is promoted on his website as follows:

> Generation A mirrors the structure of 1991's Generation X as it champions the act of reading and storytelling as one of the few defenses we still have against the constant bombardment of the senses in a digital world.
>
> (www.coupland.com/2009/03/30/book-generation-a-2)

The book ends with this quotation from the late, great Kurt Vonnegut:

> Now you young twerps want a new name for your generation? Probably not, you just want jobs, right? Well, the media do us all such tremendous favors when they call you Generation X, right? Two clicks from the very end of the alphabet. I hereby declare you Generation A, as much at the beginning of a series of astonishing triumphs and failures as Adam and Eve were so long ago.
>
> (Coupland, 2009, citing Vonnegut's commencement address at Syracuse University, May 8, 1994).

Both novelists and social scientists seem to regret reaching the end of the alphabet; and both recommend starting again, from the top. Who am I to disagree?

See also: **Readership**

BIBLIOGRAPHY

Adorno, T. (2004) *Aesthetic Theory*. London: Continuum.

AFP (2010) "'Iron Lady" Rousseff wins Brazilian presidency.' Agence France Presse, 1 November. Online: www.dialogo-americas.com/en_GB/articles/rmisa/features/regional_news/201

Ahluwalia, P. (2001) *Politics and Post-Colonial Theory: African Inflections*. London: Routledge.

Ahmed, S. (2000) *Strange Encounters: Embodied Others in Post-Coloniality*. London: Routledge.

—— (2004) *The Cultural Politics of Emotion*. New York: Routledge.

—— (2006) *Queer Phenomenology: Orientations, Objects, Others*. Durham, NC: Duke University Press.

Allen, S. (ed.) 2010 *The Routledge Companion to News and Journalism*. London: Routledge.

Althusser, L. (1971) *Lenin and Philosophy and Other Essays*. Harmondsworth, Penguin.

Anderson, B. (1991) *Imagined Communities*, 2nd edn. London: Verso.

Anderson, C. (2006) *The Long Tail: Why the Future of Business Is Selling Less of More*. New York: Hyperion.

Ang, I. (1985) *Watching Dallas: Soap Opera and the Melodramatic Imagination*. London: Methuen.

—— (1996) *Living Room Wars: Rethinking Media Audiences for a Postmodern World*. New York: Routledge.

Anheier, H. and Y. Rajisar (eds) (2008) *The Cultural Economy*. London: Sage.

Anholt, S. (2007) *Competitive Identity: The New Brand Management for Nations, Cities and Regions*. Basingstoke: Palgrave Macmillan.

Ardvisson, A. (2006) *Brands: Meaning and Value in Media Culture*. New York: Routledge.

Arthur, B. (2009) *The Nature of Technology: What It Is and How It Evolves*. New York: Free Press.

Attwood, F. (ed.) (2009) *Mainstreaming Sex: The Sexualisation of Western Culture*. London: I.B. Tauris.

Bagrit, L. (1965) *The Age of Automation*. Harmondsworth: Penguin.

Banerjee, I. and K. Seneviratne (2006) *Public Service Broadcasting in the Age of Globalization*. Singapore: Asia Media and Communication Centre.

Barabási, A-L. (2003) *Linked: How Everything Is Connected to Everything Else and What It Means for Business, Science and Everyday Life*. New York: Penguin (Plume).

Barker, C. (2008) *Cultural Studies: Theory and Practice*, 3rd edn. London: Sage.

Barker, M. and J. Petley (2001) *Ill Effects: The Media/Violence Debate*. London: Routledge.

Barrell, J. (1986) *The Political Theory of Painting from Reynolds to Hazlitt: 'The Body of the Public.'* New Haven: Yale University Press.

Barss, P. (2010) *The Erotic Engine: How Pornography Has Powered Mass Communication from Gutenberg to Google*. Canada: Doubleday.

Barthes, R. (1967) *Elements of Semiology*. London: Jonathan Cape.

—— (1973) *Mythologies*. London: Paladin.

—— (1975) *The Pleasure of the Text*. New York: Hill & Wang.

—— (1985) *The Fashion System*. London: Jonathan Cape.

Beinhocker, E. (2006) *The Origin of Wealth: Evolution, Complexity, and the Radical Remaking of Economics*. Boston: Harvard Business School Press.

Bell, P. (2001) 'Content analysis of visual images.' In T. van Leeuwen and C. Jewitt (eds) *Handbook of Visual Analysis*. London: Sage Publications, 10–34.

Benkler, Y. (2006) *The Wealth of Networks: How Social Production Transforms Markets and Freedom*. Yale University Press.

Bennett, T. (1992) 'Useful culture.' *Cultural Studies*, 6: 3, 395–408.

—— (1998) *Culture: A Reformer's Science*. Sydney: Allen & Unwin.

Bennett, T.M., Emmison, M. and J. Frow (1999) *Accounting for Tastes*. Cambridge: Cambridge University Press.

Bentham, J. (1802) 'Panopticon versus New South Wales.' In J. Bowring (ed.) *The Works of Jeremy Bentham*, Vol. 4. http://oll.libertyfund.org/index.php?option =com_staticxt&staticfile=show.php%3Ftitle=1925&layout=html#chapter_ 116509

Bentkowska-Kafel, A., T. Cashen and H. Gardiner (eds) (2009) *Digital Visual Culture: Theory and Practice*. Bristol: Intellect.

Berger, J. (1972) *Ways of Seeing*. Harmondsworth: Penguin/BBC.

Bhabha, H. (1996) 'Culture's in-between.' In S. Hall and P. Du Gay (eds) *Questions of Cultural Identity*. London: Sage, 53–60.

Birdwhistell, R. (1970) *Kinesics and Context: Essays on Body Motion Communication*. Philadelphia: Pennsylvania University Press.

Boldrin, M. and D. Levine (2002) 'The case against intellectual property.' *American Economic Review: Papers and Proceedings*, 92 (2), 209–12.

—— (2005) 'The economics of ideas and intellectual property.' *Proceedings of the National Academy of Sciences*, 102: 1252–6.

—— (2008) *Against Intellectual Monopoly*. Cambridge: Cambridge University Press.

Boler, M. (ed.) (2008) *Digital Media and Democracy: Tactics in Hard Times*. Cambridge, MA: MIT Press.

Bordwell, D. and K. Thompson (2006) *Film Art*, 8th edn. New York: McGraw Hill.

Born, G. (2004) *Uncertain Vision: Birt, Dyke and the Reinvention of the BBC*. London: Secker & Warburg.

Bourdieu, P. (1984) *Distinction: A Social Critique on the Judgement of Taste*. London: Routledge.

Bourdieu, P. and J-C. Passeron (1979 [1964]) *The Inheritors: French Students and their Relations to Culture*. Chicago: Chicago University Press.

Boyd, B. (2009) *On the Evolution of Stories: Evolution, Cognition and Fiction*. Cambridge, MA: Harvard University Press.

Boyd, R. and P. Richerson (1985) *Culture and the Evolutionary Process*. Chicago: Chicago University Press.

Boyd, T. (1997) *Am I Black Enough For You? Popular Culture from the 'Hood and Beyond*. Bloomington: Indiana University Press.

—— (2002) *The New H.N.I.C.: The Death of Civil Rights and the Reign of Hip Hop*. New York: NYU Press.

—— (2003) *Young Black Rich and Famous: The Rise of the NBA, the Hip Hop Invasion, and the Transformation of American Culture*. New York: Random House.

Boyle, J. (1996) *Shamans, Software, & Spleens: Law and the Construction of the Information Society*. Cambridge, MA: Harvard University Press.

Boyle, K. (ed.) (2010) *Everyday Pornography*. London: Routledge.

Branwyn, G. (1997) *Jamming the Media: A Citizens Guide: Reclaiming the Tools of Communication*. San Francisco: Chronicle Books.

Braudy, L. (1986) *The Frenzy of Renown: Fame and Its History*, New York: Oxford University Press.

Braziel, J. and A. Mannur (eds) (2003) *Theorising Diaspora: A Reader*. Oxford: Blackwell.

Brennan, T. (2004) *The Transmission of Affect*. Ithaca, NY: Cornell University Press.

Brooker, W. (2002) *Using the Force: Creativity, Community and Stars Wars Fans*. New York: Continuum.

Bruns, A. (2005) *Gatewatching*. New York: Peter Lang.

Buck-Morss, S. (1992) 'Aesthetics and anaesthetics: Walter Benjamin's artwork essay reconsidered.' *October* 62 (Fall), 3–41.

Buckingham, D. (2000) *After the Death of Childhood*. Cambridge: Polity.

Burgess, J. (2007) *Vernacular Creativity and New Media*. QUT: PhD Thesis. http://eprints.qut.edu.au/16378

Burgess, J. and J. Green (2009) *YouTube*. Cambridge: Polity.

Butler, J. (1990) *Gender Trouble: Feminism and the Subversion of Identity*. New York: Routledge.

—— (2004) *Undoing Gender*. New York: Routledge.

Calabrese, A. and M. Borchert (1996) 'Prospects for electronic democracy in the United States: Rethinking communication and social policy.' *Media, Culture & Society*, 18: 249–68.

Caldwell, J. (1995), *Televisuality: Style, Crisis, and Authority in American Television*. New Brunswick, NJ: Rutgers University Press.

Carey, J. (1992) *The Intellectuals and the Masses*. London: Faber & Faber.

Casey, B., N. Casey, B. Calvery, L. French and J. Lewis (2002) *Television Studies: The Key Concepts*. London: Routledge.

Caso, F. and R. Collins (2008) *Censorship*. New York: Facts on File.

Cassell, J. and H. Jenkins (eds) (1998) *From Barbie to Mortal Combat: Gender and Computer Games*. Cambridge, MA: MIT Press.

Castells, M. (1996) *The Rise of the Network Society*. Oxford: Blackwell.

—— (2000) 'Materials for an Exploratory Theory of the Network Society.' In J. Hartley and R. Pearson (eds) *American Cultural Studies: A Reader*. Oxford: Oxford University Press, 414–26.

Certeau, M. de (1984) *The Practice of Everyday Life*. Berkeley: California University Press.

Chakrabarty, D. (2000) 'Subaltern Studies and Postcolonial Historiography.' *Nepantla: Views from South*, 1: 1, 9–32.

Chandler, D. (2007) *Semiotics: The Basics*, 2nd edn. London: Routledge.

Childs, P. (2008) *Modernism: The New Critical Idiom*. London: Routledge.

Chouliaraki, L. and N. Fairclough (2000) *Discourse in Late Modernity: Rethinking Critical Discourse Analysis*. Edinburgh: Edinburgh University Press.

Clifford, J. (1986) 'Introduction: Partial truths.' In J. Clifford and G. Marcus (eds) *Writing Culture: The Poetics and Politics of Ethnography*. Berkeley: California University Press, 1–26.

—— (1997) 'Diasporas.' In M. Guibernau and J. Rex (eds) *The Ethnicity Reader: Nationalism, Multiculturalism and Migration*. Cambridge: Polity.

Clover, D. (2003) 'Communication, cultural and media studies: the key concepts.' *Reference Reviews*, 17: 2, 13.

Connell, R. W. (2005) *Masculinities*, 2nd edn. Berkeley: California University Press.

Cooper-Chen, A. (2005) *Global Entertainment Media: Content, Audiences, Issues*. Mahwah, NJ: Lawrence Erlbaum.

Corrigan, T. (1998) 'Auteurs and the New Hollywood.' In J. Lewis (ed.) *The New American Cinema*. Durham, NC: Duke University Press, 38–61.

Coupland, D. (1991) *Generation X: Tales for an Accelerated Culture*. New York: St Martin's Press.

—— (2009) *Generation A*. New York: Random House. Online: www.coupland. com/2009/04/04/news-generation-a/.

Cowen, T. (2002) *Creative Destruction: How Globalistion is Changing the World's Cultures*. Princeton: Princeton University Press.

Creeber, G. and R. Martin (eds) (2009) *Digital Cultures: Understanding New Media*. Maidenhead: Open University Press.

Cubitt, S. (2005) *The Cinema Effect*, Cambridge, MA: MIT Press.

Culler, J. (1982) *On Deconstruction: Theory and Criticism after Structuralism*. New York: Cornell University Press.

—— (ed.) (2003) *Deconstruction: Critical Concepts in Literary and Cultural Studies*. London: Routledge.

Culture, Media and Sport, Department of (2001) *Creative Industries: Mapping Document 2001*. Online: www.culture.gov.uk/creative/mapping.html.

Cunningham, S. and J. Sinclair (eds) (2000) *Floating Lives: The Media and Asian Diaspora*. St Lucia: UQP.

Darley, A. (2000) *Visual Digital Culture: Surface Play and Spectacle in New Media Genre*. London: Routledge.

Davies, T. (ed.) (2008) *The Cambridge Companion to Performance Studies*. Cambridge: Cambridge University Press.

Deazley, R. (2004) *Copyright: History, Theory, Language*. Cheltenham: Edward Elgar.

Delgado, R. and J. Stefancic (eds) (1997) *Critical White Studies: Looking Behind the Mirror*. Philadelphia: Temple University Press.

Derrida, J. (1974) *Glas*, trans. J. Leavey and R. Rand. Lincoln, NB: Nebraska University Press (English translation published 1986).

Deutscher, G. (2006) *The Unfolding of Language*. London: Arrow.

Deuze, M. (2007) *Media Work*. Cambridge: Polity.

Deuze, M. and J. Banks (2009) *Co-creative Labour*. Special issue of *International Journal of Cultural Studies*, 12: 5. London: Sage.

Dicks, B., B. Mason, A. Coffey and P. Atkinson (2005) *Qualitative Research and Hypermedia: Ethnography for the Digital Age*. London: Sage.

Dijk, J. van (2006) *The Network Society: Social Aspects of New Media*, 2nd edn. Thousand Oaks, CA: Sage.

Dissanayake, E. (2000) *Art and Intimacy: How the Arts Began*. Seattle: Washington University Press.

During, S. (2005) *Cultural Studies: A Critical Introduction*. London: Routledge.

Dutton, D. (2009) *The Art Instinct*. Oxford: Oxford University Press.

Dyer, R. (1993) *The Matter of Images: Essays on Representations*. London: Routledge.

—— (1997) *White*. London: Routledge.

—— (1998) *Stars: New Edition*. London: BFI Publishing.

—— (2004) *Heavenly Bodies: Film Stars and Society*, 2nd edn. London: Routledge.

Eagleton, T. (1990) *The Ideology of the Aesthetic*, Oxford and Malden, MA: Blackwell.

—— (2000) *The Idea of Culture*. Oxford: Blackwell.

Eco, U. (1972) 'Towards a semiotic inquiry into the television message.' *WPCS*, 3: 103–21.

Edgerton, D. (2005) *Warfare State: Britain, 1920–1970*. Cambridge: Cambridge University Press.

—— (2007) *The Shock of the Old: Technology and Global History Since 1900*. Oxford: Oxford University Press.

Elias, N. (2000) *The Civilizing Process*, rev. edn; first published 1939. Malden, MA: Blackwell.

Ellis, J. (1982) *Visible Fictions: Television, Cinema, Video*. London: RKP.

—— (2004) 'Television production.' In R. Allen and A. Hill (eds) *The Television Studies Reader*. London: Routledge, 275–92.

Enzensberger, H-M. (1970) 'Constituents of a theory of the media.' *New Left Review*, 64: 13–36.

Eschle, C. and B. Maiguashca (2005) *Critical Theories, International Relations and The Anti-globalisation Movement: The Politics of Global Resistance*. London: Routledge.

Fenton, S. (2003) *Ethnicity*. Cambridge: Polity.

Feuer, J. (1983) 'The concept of live television: ontology as ideology.' In E. A. Kaplan (ed.) *Regarding Television: Critical Approaches – An Anthology*. Los Angeles: UPA/AFI.

Fischer, L. and M. Landy (eds) (2004) *Stars: The Film Reader*. London: Routledge.

Fiske, J. (1987) *Television Culture*. London: Routledge.

—— (1992) 'The cultural economy of fandom.' In L. Lewis (ed.) *The Adoring Audience: Fan Culture and Popular Media*. London: Routledge, 30–49.

Fiske, J. and J. Hartley (1978) *Reading Television*. London: Methuen. [2nd edn 2003: Routledge.]

Fitzgerald, B., J. Coates and S. Lewis (2007) *Open Content Licensing: Cultivating the Creative Commons*. Sydney: Sydney University Press.

Florida, R. (2002) *The Rise of the Creative Class*. New York: Basic Books.

Flew, T. (2008) *New Media: An Introduction*, 3rd edn. Melbourne: Oxford University Press.

Foucault, M. (1978) *The History of Sexuality, Vol. 1: The Will to Knowledge*. London: Penguin.

—— (1984) *The Foucault Reader*, ed. Paul Rabinow. New York: Pantheon.

—— (1988) *Politics, Philosophy, Culture – Interviews and Other Writings 1977–1984*. New York: Routledge.

—— (1995) *Discipline and Punish: The Birth of the Prison*. New York: Vintage.

—— (2003) *The Essential Foucault: Selections from Essential Works of Foucault, 1954–1984*, ed. P. Rabinow and N. Rose. New York: New Press.

Frankenberg, R. (1993) *White Women, Race Matters: The Social Construction of Whiteness*. Minneapolis: Minnesota University Press.

Fraser, N. (1992) 'Rethinking the public sphere: a contribution to the critique of actually existing democracy.' In C. Calhoun (ed.) *Habermas and the Public Sphere*. Cambridge, MA: MIT Press, 109–42.

Frow, J. (1995) *Cultural Studies and Cultural Value*. Oxford: Oxford University Press.

—— (1997) *Time and Commodity Culture: Essays in Cultural Theory and Postmodernism*. Oxford: Oxford University Press.

—— (2006) *Genre*. London: Routledge.

Fuller, M. and H. Jenkins (1995) 'Nintendo and new world travel writing: a dialogue.' In S. Jones (ed.) *Cybersociety: Computer-Mediated Communication and Community*. Thousand Oaks, CA: Sage, 57–72.

Gauntlett, D. (2005) *Moving Experiences: Media Effects and Beyond*, 2nd edn. London: John Libbey.

—— (2008) *Media, Gender and Identity: An Introduction*, 2nd edn. London: Routledge.

Gaut, B. (1999) 'Identification and emotion in narrative film.' In C. Plantinga and G. Smith (eds) *Passionate Views: Film Emotion and Cognition*. Baltimore: Johns Hopkins University Press, 200–16.

Gelder, K. and S. Thornton (eds) (1997) *The Subcultures Reader*. London: Routledge.

Gerstner, D. and J. Staiger (2003) *Authorship and Film*. New York: Routledge.

Gibson, M. (2007). *Culture and Power: A History of Cultural Studies*. London: Berg/ Sydney: UNSW Press.

Giddens, A. (2000) *The Third Way and Its Critics*. Cambridge: Polity.

Gillespie, M. (1995) *Television, Ethnicity and Cultural Change*. London: Routledge.

Gilroy, P. (1987) *There Ain't No Black in the Union Jack: The Cultural Politics of Race and Nation*. London: Routledge.

—— (1993) *The Black Atlantic: Modernity and Double Consciousness*. London: Verso.

Giroux, H. (1983) *Theory and Resistance in Education: A Pedagogy for the Opposition*. South Hadley, MA: Bergin & Garvey.

Gitlin, T. (1980) *The Whole World Is Watching: Mass Media in the Making and Unmaking of the New Left*. Berkeley: California University Press.

Glasgow Media Group (1982) *Really Bad News*. London: Writers and Readers Publishing Co-operative.

Goffman, E. (1986, 1st pub. 1974) *Frame Analysis: An Essay on the Organisation of Experience*. Boston: Northeastern University Press.

Gottschall, J. and D. S. Wilson (2005). *The Literary Animal: Evolution and the Nature of Narrative*. Chicago: Northwestern University Press.

Gramsci, A. (1971) *Prison Notebooks*. London: Lawrence & Wishart.

Gray, H. (2000) 'African-American political desire and the seductions of contemporary cultural politics.' In J. Hartley and R. Pearson (eds) *American Cultural Studies: A Reader*. Oxford: Oxford University Press, 242–50.

—— (2004) *Watching Race: Television and the Struggle for Blackness*, 2nd edn. Minneapolis: Minnesota University Press.

Gray, J. (2006) *Watching the Simpson: Television, Parody and Intertextuality*. New York: Routledge.

Gray, J., C. Sandvoss and C. L. Harrington (2007) *Fandom: Identities and Communities in a Mediated World*. New York: NYU Press.

Greenblatt, S. (ed.) (1993) *New World Encounters*. Berkeley: California University Press.

Gripsrud, J. (1998) 'Television, broadcasting, flow: key metaphors in TV theory.' In C. Geraghty and D. Lusted (eds) *The Television Studies Book*. London: Arnold, 17–32.

Grossberg, L. (1996) 'Identity and cultural studies – is that all there is?' In S. Hall and P. du Gay (eds) *Questions of Cultural Identity*. London: Sage, 87–107.

Habermas, J. (1989) *The Structural Transformation of the Public Sphere: An Inquiry into a Category of Bourgeois Society*. Cambridge, MA: MIT Press.

—— (1996) *Between Facts and Norms: Contributions to a Discourse Theory of Law and Democracy*. Cambridge, MA: MIT Press.

Hage, G. (1998) *White Nation: Fantasies of White Supremacy in a Multicultural Society*. Sydney: Pluto Press.

Halavais, A. (2009) *Search Engine Society*. Cambridge: Polity.

Hall, E. T. (1973) *The Silent Language*. New York: Anchor.

Hall, S. (1973) *Encoding and Decoding in the Television Discourse*. University of Birmingham: Centre for Contemporary Cultural Studies.

—— (1992) 'The question of cultural identity.' Online: www.csuchico. edu/~pkittle/101/hall.htm (via Philweb: www.phillwebb.net/regions/carib-bean/Hall/Hall.htm).

—— (1997) 'What is this "black" in black popular culture?' In V. Smith (ed.) *Representing Blackness: Issues in Film and Video*. London: Athlone Press, 123–33.

Haraway, D. (1990) 'A manifesto for cyborgs: science, technology, and socialist feminism in the 1980s.' In L. Nicholson (ed.), *Feminism/Postmodernism*. New York: Routledge.

Harris, C. (1993) 'Whiteness as property.' *Harvard Law Review*, 106: 8, 1709–1795.

Harrison, D. (2010) 'Australia world's "dumb blonde".' *The Age*, 14 October. Online: www.theage.com.au/travel/travel-news/australia-worlds-dumb-blonde-20101013-16k09.html.

Hartley, J. (1982) *Understanding News*. London: Methuen.

—— (1992a) *Tele-ology: Studies in Television*. London: Routledge.

—— (1992b) *The Politics of Pictures: The Creation of the Public in the Age of Popular Media*. London: Routledge.

—— (1996) *Popular Reality: Journalism, Modernity and Popular Culture*. London: Arnold [Bloomsbury].

—— (1999) *Uses of Television*. London: Routledge.

—— (2000) 'Communicative democracy in a redactional society: the future of journalism studies.' *Journalism: Theory, Practice and Criticism*, 1: 1, 39–48.

—— (2003) *A Short History of Cultural Studies*. London: Sage.

—— (ed.) (2005) *Creative Industries*. Malden, MA: Wiley-Blackwell.

—— (2008) *Television Truths: Forms of Knowledge in Popular Culture*. Malden, MA: Wiley-Blackwell.

—— (2009a) *The Uses of Digital Literacy*. St Lucia: UQP.

—— (2009b) 'TV stories: from representation to productivity.' In J. Hartley and K. McWilliam (eds), *Story Circle: Digital Storytelling Around the World*. Malden, MA: Wiley Blackwell, 16–36.

—— (2010) 'Silly citizenship.' *Critical Discourse Studies*, 7: 4, 233–48.

Hartley, J. and C. Lumby (2002) 'Working girls or drop dead gorgeous? Young girls in fashion and news.' In K. Mallan and S. Pearce (eds) *Youth Cultures: Texts, Images and Identities*. Westport, CT & London: Praeger, 47–67.

Hartley, J. and A. McKee (2000) *The Indigenous Public Sphere: The Reporting and Reception of Aboriginal Issues in the Australian Media*. Oxford: Oxford University Press.

Hassn, R. (2008) *The Information Society*. Cambridge: Polity.

Have, P. (2007) *Doing Conversational Analysis: A Practical Guide*, 2nd edn. London: Sage.

Hawkes, D. (2003) *Ideology*, 2nd edn. London: Routledge.

Hawkes, T. (1973) *Shakespeare's Talking Animals: Language and Drama in Society*. London: Edward Arnold.

—— (2002) *Shakespeare in the Present*. London: Routledge.

Hawkins, G. (2009) 'The politics of bottled water.' *Journal of Cultural Economy*, 1: 2, 183–95.

Hayles, N. (1999) 'The condition of virtuality.' In P. Lunenfeld (ed.) *The Digital Dialectic: New Essays on New Media*. Cambridge, MA: MIT Press, 69–94.

Hazen, D. and J. Winokur (eds) (1997) *We the Media*. New York: New Press.

Hebdige D. (1979) *Subculture: The Meaning of Style*. London: Routledge.

—— (1988) *Hiding in the Light: On Images and Things*. London: Routledge.

Hébert, L. (2006) 'The functions of language.' In L. Hébert (ed.), *Signo*. Online: www.signosemio.com.

Held, D. (1980) *Introduction to Critical Theory: Horkheimer to Habermas*. London: Hutchinson.

—— (2002) 'Is globalisation new'. *Open Democracy*, 13, update January 25. Online: www.opendemocracy.net.

Held, D. and A. McGrew (2007), *Globalization/Anti-globalization: Beyond the Great Divide*, 2nd edn. Cambridge: Polity.

Herman, E. and N. Chomsky (1988) *Manufacturing Consent: The Political Economy of the Mass Media*. New York: Pantheon.

Hill, A. (2005) *Reality TV: Audiences and Popular Factual Television*. London: Routledge.

Hills, M. (2002) *Fan Cultures*. London: Routledge.

Hirst, P. (1996) *Globalisation in Question*. University of Sheffield: PERC Occasional Paper 11.

Hodgson, G. (2007) 'Meanings of methodological individualism.' *Journal of Economic Methodology*, 14: 2, 211–26. Online: www.geoffrey-hodgson.info/user/image/meanmethind-free.pdf.

Hoggart, R. (1957) *The Uses of Literacy*. London: Chatto & Windus.

Hollinger, D. (2000) 'The ethno-racial pentagon.' In S. Steinberg (ed.) *Race and Ethnicity in the United States*. Malden, MA: Blackwell, 197–210.

Holmlund, C. and J. Wyatt (eds) (2005) *Contemporary American Independent Film: From the Margins to the Mainstream*. New York: Routledge.

Horn, L. and G. Ward (eds) (2004) *The Handbook of Pragmatics*. Oxford: Blackwell.

Howson, R. and K. Smith (2009) *Hegemony: Studies in Consensus and Coercion*. New York: Routledge.

Hutchby, I. and R. Wooffitt (2008) *Conversation Analysis*, 2nd edn. Cambridge: Polity Press.

Irwin, R. (2008) *Dangerous Knowledge: Orientalism and Its Discontents*. New York: Overlook Press.

Jacobs, J. (1984) *Cities and the Wealth of Nations*. Harmondsworth: Viking.

Jakobson, R. (1960) 'Concluding statement: linguistics and poetics.' In T. Sebeok (ed.) *Style in Language*. Cambridge, MA: MIT Press.

Jeff, L. and J. Simmons (eds) (1990) *The Dame in the Kimono: Hollywood, Censor-*

ship, and the Production Code from the 1920s to the 1960s. New York: Grove Wiedenfeld.

Jenkins, H. (1992) *Textual Poachers: Television Fans and Participatory Culture*. New York: Routledge.

—— (2000) 'Art form for the digital age.' *Technology Review*, 103: 5, 17–120.

—— (2006a) *Convergence Culture: Where Old and New Media Collide*. New York: NYU Press.

—— (2006b) *Fans, Bloggers and Exploring Participatory Culture*. New York: NYU Press.

—— (2009) 'If it doesn't spread, it's dead.' Online: www.henryjenkins.org/2009/02/if_it_doesnt_spread_its_dead_p.html.

—— (2010) 'Fandom, participatory culture, and Web 2.0: a syllabus.' Online: www.henryjenkins.org/2010/01/fandom_participatory_culture_a.html.

Jordan, T. (2008) *Hacking: Digital Media and Technological Determinism*. Cambridge: Polity.

Kagan, J. (2009) *The Three Cultures: Natural Sciences, Social Sciences, and the Humanities in the 21st Century*. Cambridge: Cambridge University Press.

Karlsson, C. (ed.) (2008) *Handbook of Research on Cluster Theory*. Cheltenham: Edward Elgar.

Kipnis, L. (1999). *Bound and Gagged: Pornography and the Politics of Fantasy in America*. Duke University Press.

Kirkup, G., L. Jones, K. Woodward and F. Hovenden (eds) (2000) *The Gendered Cyborg: A Reader*. London: Routledge.

Klein, N. (2000) *No Logo*. Toronto: Knopf.

Konner, M. (2010) *The Evolution of Childhood: Relationships, Emotion, Mind*. Cambridge, MA: Harvard University Press.

Krippendorff, K. (2004) *Content Analysis: An Introduction to Its Methodology*, 2nd edn. Thousand Oaks, CA: Sage.

Krugman, P. (1997) *Pop Internationalism*. Cambridge, MA: MIT Press.

Kuhn, A. (1990) *The Power of the Image: Essays on Representation and Sexuality*. London: Routledge.

Kuhn, T. (1962) *The Structure of Scientific Revolutions*. Chicago: Chicago University Press.

Kukathas, C. (1995) 'Are there any cultural rights?' In W. Kymlicka (ed.) *The Rights of Minority Cultures*. Oxford: Oxford University Press, 228–53.

Kymlicka, W. and W. Norman (1994) 'Return of the citizen: a survey of recent work on citizenship theory.' *Ethics*, 104: 352–81.

Laclau, E. (1977) *Politics and Ideology in Marxist Theory*. London: New Left Books.

Landry, D and G. Maclean (eds) (1996) *The Spivak Reader*. New York: Routledge.

Lanham, R. (2006) *The Economics of Attention: Style and Substance in the Age of Information*. Chicago: Chicago University Press.

Lasn, K. (2000) *Culture Jam: How to Reverse America's Suicidal Consumer Binge – and Why We Must*. New York: Harper Collins.

Leach, E. (1976) *Culture and Communication*. Cambridge: Cambridge University Press.

—— (1982) *Social Anthropology*. London: Fontana.

Leadbeater, C. (1999) *Living on Thin Air – the New Economy*. London: Penguin.

—— (2008) *We-Think: Mass Innovation, Not Mass Production*, 2nd edn. London: Profile.

Leadbeater, C. and K. Oakley (2001) *Surfing the Long Wave: Knowledge Entrepreneurship in Britain*. London: Demos.

Lee, C., W. Miller, M. Hancock and H. Rowen (2000) 'The Silicon Valley habitat.' In C. Lee *et al.* (eds) *The Silicon Valley Edge: A Habitat for Innovation and Entrepreneurship.* Stanford: Stanford University Press, 1–15.

Lee, R. E. (2003) *Life and Times of Cultural Studies: the Politics and Transformation of the Structures of Knowledge.* Durham, NC: Duke University Press.

Leeds-Hurwitz, W. (1993) *Semiotics and Communication: Signs, Codes, Cultures.* Hillsdale, NJ: Lawrence Erlbaum.

Lemert, C., A. Elliot, D. Chaffee and E. Hsu (eds) (2010) *Globalization: A Reader.* London: Routledge.

Lessig, L. (2004) *Free Culture: How Big Media Uses Technology and the Law to Lock Down Culture and Control Creativity.* New York: Penguin.

—— (2008) *Remix: Making Art and Commerce Thrive in the Hybrid Economy.* New York: Penguin. Online: http://remix.lessig.org/book.php.

Levin, T., U. Frohne and P. Weibel (eds) (2002) *Ctrl Space: The Rhetorics of Surveillance from Bentham to Big Brother.* Cambridge, MA: MIT Press.

Levy, L. (2006) *Female Chauvinist Pigs: Women and the Rise of Raunch Culture.* New York: Free Press.

Lewis, J. and T. Miller (eds) (2003) *Critical Cultural Policy Studies: A Reader.* Malden, MA: Blackwell.

Lippmann, W. (1922) *Public Opinion.* Online: www.gutenberg.org/ebooks/6456.

Lobato, R. (2010) 'Creative industries and informal economies: Lessons from Nollywood.' *International Journal of Cultural Studies*, 13: 4, 337–54.

Löffelholz, M., D. Weaver and A. Schwartz (eds) (2008) *Global Journalism Research: Theories, Methods, Findings, Future.* Malden, MA: Wiley-Blackwell.

Lotman, Y. (1990) *The Universe of the Mind: A Semiotic Theory of Culture.* Bloomington: Indiana University Press.

Lucy, N. (2003) *A Derrida Dictionary.* Malden, MA: Wiley-Blackwell.

Lumby, C. and E. Probyn (eds) (2004) *Remote Control: New Media, New Ethics.* Melbourne: Cambridge University Press.

Madianou, M. (2005) *Mediating the Nation: News, Audiences and the Politics of Identity.* London: UCL Press.

Maras, S. (2009) *Screenwriting: History, Theory and Practice.* Brighton: Wallflower Press.

Marrs, J. (2006) *The Terror Conspiracy: Deception, 9/11 and the Loss of Liberty.* New York: The Disinformation Co. Ltd.

Marshall, A. (1961) *Principles of Economics.* London: Macmillan.

Marshall, D. (ed.) (2006) *The Celebrity Culture Reader.* London: Routledge.

Marshall, T. H. (1965) *Class, Citizenship and Social Development.* New York: Anchor.

Marx, K. (1845) *The German Ideology.* Online: www.marxists.org/archive/marx/works/1845/german-ideology/ch01b.htm

McChesney, R. (2008) *The Political Economy of Media: Enduring Issues, Emerging Dilemmas.* New York: Monthly Review Press.

McCrindle, M., with E. Wolfinger (2009) *The ABC of XYZ: Understanding the Global Generations.* Sydney: UNSW Press.

McKay, G. (ed.) (1998) *DiY Culture: Party and Protest in Nineties Britain.* London: Verso.

McKee, A. (2003) *Textual Analysis: A Beginner's Guide.* London: Sage.

—— (2005) *The Public Sphere: An Introduction.* Cambridge: Cambridge University Press.

McKee, A., C. Lumby and K. Albury (2008) *The Porn Report*. Melbourne: Melbourne University Press.

McLuhan, M. (1962) *The Gutenberg Galaxy*. London: Routledge & Kegan Paul.

—— (1964) *Understanding Media: The Extensions of Man*. London: Routledge.

McQuail, D. (2005) *McQuail's Mass Communication Theory*, 5th edn. London: Sage.

Metcalfe, J. S. (1998) *Evolutionary Economics and Creative Destruction (Graz Schumpeter Lectures, 1)*. London: Routledge.

Miller, D. (2008) *The Comfort of Things*. Cambridge: Polity.

Miller, T. (2006) *Cultural Citizenship*. Philadelphia: Temple University Press.

Mills, S. (2004) *Discourse*, 2nd edn. London: Routledge.

Mirzoeff, N. (2009) *An Introduction to Visual Culture*, 2nd edn. London: Routledge.

Mitchell, W. (1998) *The Last Dinosaur Book: The Life and Times of a Cultural Icon*. Chicago: Chicago University Press.

Montgomery, L. (2011) *China's Creative Industries: Copyright, Social Network Markets and the Business of Culture in a Digital Age*. Cheltenham: Edward Elgar.

Moreton-Robinson, A. (ed.) (2004) *Whitening Race: Essays in Social and Cultural Criticism*. Canberra: Aboriginal Studies Press.

Morgan, J. (1994) 'We *aren't* the world: a farewell to multiculturalism from a sista scorned.' *Rebelle* (NY), premier issue, 32–5.

Morley, D. (1980) *The Nationwide Audience*. London: BFI.

—— (1986) *Family Television: Cultural Power and Domestic Leisure*. London: Comedia.

Morrison, D, (1998) *The Search for a Method: Focus Groups and the Development of Mass Communication Research*. Luton: Luton University Press.

Muggleton, D. and R. Weinzierl (eds) (2003) *The Post-subcultures Reader*. Oxford: Berg.

Mulgan, G. (1998) *Connexity: Responsibility, Freedom, Business and Power in the New Century*. London: Vintage.

Mulvey, L. (1990) 'Visual pleasure and narrative cinema.' In P. Erens (ed.) *Issues in Feminist Film Criticism*. Bloomington: Indiana University Press, 28–40.

Murray, S. and L. Ouellette (eds) (2009) *Reality TV: Remaking Television Culture*. New York: NYU Press.

Naficy, H. (1993) *The Making of Exile Cultures: Iranian Television in Los Angeles*. Minneapolis: Minnesota University Press.

Nayer, P. (2010) *An Introduction to New Media and Cybercultures*. Oxford: Wiley-Blackwell.

Neale, S. (1980) *Genre*. London: British Film Institute.

—— (1990) 'Genre.' *Screen*, 31: 1, 45–66.

—— (2000) *Genre and Hollywood*. London: Routledge.

Negroponte, N. (1995) *Being Digital*. New York: Knopf.

Newman, M., A-L. Barabási and D. Watts (eds) (2006) *The Structure and Dynamics of Networks*. Princeton: Princeton University Press.

Norris, P. (2001) *Digital Divide: Civic Engagement, Information Poverty and the Internet Worldwide*. Cambridge: Cambridge University Press.

OECD (2007) *Participative Web: User-Created Content*. OECD: Working Party on the Information Economy. Online: www.oecd.org/dataoecd/57/14/38393115.pdf.

O'Neill, D. and T. Harcup (2009) 'News values and selectivity.' In K. Wahl-Jorgensen and T. Hanitzsch (eds) (2009) *The Handbook of Journalism Studies*. New York: Routledge, 161–74.

Ong, W. (1982) *Orality and Literacy*. London: Methuen.

Orr, M. (2003) *Intertexuality: Debates and Contexts*. Cambridge: Polity.

O'Shaughnessy, M. and J. Stadler (2009) *Media and Society: An Introduction*, 4th edn. Oxford, Oxford University Press.

Ott, B. and R. Mack (2010) *Critical Media Studies: An Introduction*. Oxford: Wiley-Blackwell.

Parekh, B. (2000) *Rethinking Multiculturalism: Cultural Diversity and Political Theory*. London: Macmillan.

Pensky, M. (ed.) (1997) *The Actuality of Adorno: Critical Essays on Adorno and the Postmodern*. New York: SUNY Press, 1–20.

Pinker, S. (2003) *The Language Instinct*. London: Penguin.

Polan, D. (2009) 'Vagaries of a concept: the culture industry.' *The Velvet Light Trap*, 64: Fall, 94–5.

Porter, M. (1998) *The Competitive Advantage of Nations*. New York: Free Press.

—— (1999) 'Clusters and the new economics of competition.' In J. Margretta (ed.) *Managing in the New Economy*. Cambridge, MA: Harvard Business School Press, 25–48.

Poster M. (2000) 'Cyberdemocracy: the internet and the public sphere.' In J. Hartley and R. Pearson (eds) *American Cultural Studies*. Oxford: Oxford University Press, 402–13.

Potter, D. (2008) *Handbook of Independent Journalism*. US Department of State. Online: www.america.gov/media/pdf/books/journalism.pdf.

Potts, J. (2011) *Creative Industries and Economic Evolution*. Cheltenham: Edward Elgar.

Provenzo, E. (1991) *Video Kids: Making Sense of Nintendo*. Cambridge, MA: Harvard University Press.

Rabinow, P. and N. Rose (2006) 'Biopower today.' *BioSocieties*, 1: 195–217. Online: www.lse.ac.uk/collections/brainSelfSociety/pdf/Biopower-today-2006.pdf.

Redmond, S. and S. Holmes (eds) (2007) *Stardom and Celebrity: A Reader*. London: Sage.

Rennie, E. (2006) *Community Media: A Global Introduction*. Boulder, CO: Rowman & Littlefield.

Rheingold, H. (2000) *The Virtual Community: Homesteading on the Electronic Frontier*, 2nd edn. Cambridge, MA: MIT Press.

Richards, D. (2008) 'A skeptic's view of intellectual property rights.' In R. C. Bird and S. Jain (eds) (2008) *The Global Challenge of Intellectual Property Rights*. Cheltenham: Edward Elgar, 267–82.

Richardson, D. (1996) 'Heterosexuality and social theory.' In D. Richardson (ed.) *Theorising Heterosexuality*. Buckingham: Open University Press, 1–20.

Richerson, P. and R. Boyd (2005) *Not by Genes Alone: How Culture Transformed Human Evolution*. Chicago: Chicago University Press.

Riffe, D., S. Lacy and F. Fico (2005) *Analyzing Media Messages: Using Quantitative Content Analysis in Research*, 2nd edn. London: Taylor & Francis.

Robinson, K. (2010) 'Changing education paradigms.' Royal Society of Arts. Online: www.youtube.com/watch?v=zDZFcDGpL4U&feature=player_embedded.

Roediger, D. (ed.) (1999) *Black on White: Black Writers on What It Means to Be White*. New York: Schocken.

—— (2007) *The Wages of Whiteness: Race and the Making of the American Working Class*, rev. edn. London: Verso.

Rojek, C. (2007) *Cultural Studies*. Cambridge: Polity.

Rorty, R. (1982) *Consequences of Pragmatism: (Essays 1972–1980)*. Minneapolis: Minnesota University Press.

Roscoe, J. (2001) 'Real entertainment: new factual hybrid television.' *Media International Australia*, 100: 9–20.

Rose, N. (1999) *Powers of Freedom: Reframing Political Thought*. Cambridge: Cambridge University Press.

Rosen, J (2006) 'The people formerly known as the audience.' *Huffington Post*. Online: www.huffingtonpost.com/jay-rosen/the-people-formerly-known_1_b_24113.html.

Ross, A. (2009) *Nice Work If You Can Get It: Life and Labor in Precarious Times*. New York: NYU Press.

Ross, S. (2008) *Beyond the Box: Television and the Internet*. Oxford: Blackwell.

Ruskin, J. (1857) *The Political Economy of Art: being the substance (with additions) of two lectures delivered at Manchester, July 10th and 13th, 1857*. Online: http://openlibrary.org/books/OL6339583M/The_political_economy_of_art

Saeed, J. (2009) *Semantics*, 3rd edn. Malden, MA: Wiley-Blackwell.

Sahlins, M. (1976) *Cultural and Practical Reason*. Chicago: Chicago University Press.

Said, E. (1979) *Orientalism*. New York: Vintage Books.

—— (1985) 'Orientalism reconsidered.' *Cultural Critique*, 1: 89–107.

Samuel, A. (2004) *Hacktivism and the Future of Political Participation*. PhD Thesis, Harvard University. Online: www.alexandrasamuel.com/dissertation/pdfs/Samuel-Hacktivism-entire.pdf.

Saussure, F. de (1974) *Course in General Linguistics* (first published 1911). London: Fontana.

Schroeder, J. and M. Salzer-Mörling (2006) *Brand Culture*. New York: Routledge.

Schudson, M. (2001) 'The objectivity norm in American journalism.' *Journalism*, 2: 2, 149–70.

Schudson, M. and C. Anderson (2009) 'Objectivity, professionalism, and truth-seeking in journalism.' In K. Wahl-Jorgensen and T. Hanitzsch (eds) *The Handbook of Journalism Studies*. New York: Routledge, 250–64.

Schumpeter, J. (1976, 1st pub. 1942) *Capitalism, Socialism and Democracy*, 5th edn. London: Routledge.

Sconce, J. (2000) *Haunted Media: Electronic Presence from Telegraphy to Television*. Durham, NC: Duke University Press.

Sedgwick, E. K (1991) *Epistemology of the Closet*. Berkeley: California University Press.

Seiter, E. (2000), *Television and New Media Audiences*. Oxford: Oxford University Press.

Sennett, R. (1977). *The Fall of Public Man*. New York: Knopf.

Shane, P. (2004) *Democracy Online: The Prospects for Political Renewal Through the Internet*. London: Routledge.

Shattuc, J. (1997) *The Talking Cure: TV Talk Shows and Women*. New York: Routledge.

Shirky, C. (2008) *Here Comes Everybody: The Power of Organizing Without Organizations*. New York: Penguin.

Shiva, V. (2005) 'Biotechnological development and the conservation of biodiversity.' In A. Abbas and J. Erni (eds) *Internationalizing Cultural Studies: An Anthology*. Malden, MA: Wiley-Blackwell, 30–42.

Shoemaker, P. and T. Vos (2009) *Gatekeeping Theory*. New York: Routledge.

Siapera, E. (2010) *Cultural Diversity and Global Media: The Mediation of Difference.* Oxford: Wiley-Blackwell.

Sim, S. (ed.) (2001) *The Routledge Companion to Postmodernism.* London: Routledge.

Smith, M. (1995) *Engaging Characters: Fiction, Emotion and the Cinema.* Oxford: Oxford University Press.

Smith, M. and P. Kollock (eds) (1999) *Communities in Cyberspace.* London: Routledge.

Spigel. L. and J. Olsson (eds) (2004) *Television After TV: Essays on a Medium in Transition.* Durham, NC: Duke University Press.

Spivak, G. (1988) 'Can the subaltern speak?' In L. Grossberg and C. Nelson (eds) *Marxism and the Interpretation of Culture.* Urbana-Champaign: Illinois University Press, 271–316.

Stam, R., R. Burgoyne and S. Flitterman-Lewis (1992) *New Vocabularies in Film Semiotics.* London: Routledge.

Storey, J. (2003) *Inventing Popular Culture: From Folklore to Globalization.* Oxford: Wiley-Blackwell.

Strosser, N. (2000) *Defending Pornography: Free Speech, Sex and the Fight for Women's Rights.* New York: NYU Press.

Sullivan, N. (2003) *A Critical Introduction to Queer Theory.* New York: NYU Press.

Sutton, D., S. Brind and R. McKenzie (eds) (2007) *The State of the Real: Aesthetics in the Digital Age.* London: I.B. Tauris.

Tacchi, J., D. Slater and G. Hearn (2003) *Ethnographic Action Research.* New Delhi: UNESCO.

Thacker, E. (2005) *The Global Genome: Biotechnology, Politics, Culture.* Cambridge, MA: MIT Press.

Thompson, J. O. (1978) 'Screen acting and the commutation test.' *Screen*, 19: 2, 55–69.

Thornton S. (1995) *Club Cultures: Music Media and Subcultural Capital.* Cambridge: Polity.

Thussu, D. (2007) *News as Entertainment: The Rise of Global Infotainment.* London: Sage.

Traill, R. (2005–8) 'Thinking by molecule, synapse, or both?' *The General Science Journal.* Online: www.ondwelle.com/OSM02.pdf.

Trend, D. (2007) *The Myth of Media Violence: A Critical Introduction.* Oxford: Wiley-Blackwell.

Trentmann, F. (ed.) (2006) *The Making of the Consumer: Knowledge Power and Identity in the Modern World.* Oxford: Berg.

Trochim, W. (2006) *Research Methods Knowledge Base.* Online: www. socialresearchmethods.net/kb/statdesc.php.

Tunstall, J. (1986) *Communications Deregulation: The Unleashing of America's Communications Industry.* Oxford: Blackwell.

Turner, G. (2003) *British Cultural Studies: An Introduction,* 3rd edn. London: Routledge.

—— (2004) *Understanding Celebrity.* London: Sage.

—— (2010) *Ordinary People and the Media: The Demotic Turn.* London: Sage.

Turner, G. and J. Tay (eds) (2009) *Television Studies After TV: Understanding Television in the Post- Broadcast Era.* London: Routledge.

Vaidhyanathan, S. (2003) *Copyrights and Copywrongs: the Rise of Intellectual Property and How it Threatens Creativity.* New York: NYU Press.

Valerius Maximus (n.d.) *Factorum et Dictorum Memorabilium (Libri Novem)* [1st century CE]. Online: www.thelatinlibrary.com/valmax.html.

Van Schijndel, M. and J. Smiers (2005) 'Imagine a world without copyright.' *International Herald Tribune*, 8 October. Online: www.iht.com/articles/2005/10/07/opinion/edsmiers.php

Varisco, D. (2007) *Reading Orientalism: The Said and Unsaid.* Seattle: Washington University Press.

Volosinov, V. (1973) *Marxism and the Philosophy of Language.* New York: Seminar Press.

Waal, F. de (1995) 'Bonobo sex and society.' *Scientific American*, 82–8.

Wahl-Jorgensen, K. and T. Hanitzsch (eds) (2009) *The Handbook of Journalism Studies.* New York: Routledge.

Walzer, M. (1989) 'Citizenship.' In T. Ball, J. Farr and R. Hanson (eds) *Political Innovation and Conceptual Change.* Cambridge: Cambridge University Press, 211–19.

—— (1997) *On Toleration.* New Haven: Yale University Press.

Wark, M. (2004) *A Hacker Manifesto.* Cambridge, MA: Harvard University Press.

Warner, M. (2002) *Publics and Counterpublics.* Cambridge: Zone Books.

Warraq, I. (2007) *Defending the West: A Critique of Edward Said's Orientalism.* New York: Prometheus.

Warschauer, M. (2003) *Technology and Social Inclusion.* Cambridge, MA: MIT Press.

Webster, F. (ed.) (2004) *The Information Society Reader.* London: Routledge.

White, M. and J. Schwoch (eds) (2006) *Questions of Method in Cultural Studies.* Malden, MA: Wiley-Blackwell.

Williams, R. (1958a) *Culture and Society: 1780–1950.* London: Chatto & Windus.

—— (1958b) 'Culture is ordinary.' In A. Gray and J. McGuigan (eds) *Studies in Culture: An Introductory Reader.* London: Arnold, 1997, 5–14.

—— (1968) *Communications.* Harmondsworth: Penguin.

—— (1974) *Television: Technology and Cultural Form.* London: Fontana.

—— (1981) *Culture.* London: Fontana.

Wilson, S. (2002) *Information Arts: Intersections of Art, Science and Technology.* Cambridge, MA: MIT Press.

Wise, R. (ed.) (2000) *Multimedia: A Critical Introduction.* London: Routledge.

Wood, D. (2007) 'Beyond the panopticon: Foucault and surveillance studies.' In J. Crampton and S. Elden (eds) *Space, Knowledge and Power: Foucault and Geography.* Aldershot: Ashgate, 245–63.

Wright, E. O. (ed.) (2005) *Approaches to Class Analysis.* Cambridge: Cambridge University Press.

Young, I. (1990) *Justice and the Politics of Difference.* Princeton: Princeton University Press.

Zettl, H. (2010) *Sight, Sound, Motion: Applied Media Aesthetics*, 6th edn. Belmont, CA: Wadsworth.

Zittrain, J. (2008) *The Future of the Internet . . . and How to Stop It.* Cambridge, MA: Harvard University Press.

INDEX